MW00442994

The Collected Writings of James Leo Garrett Jr., 1950–2015: Volume 8

The Collected Writings of James Leo Garrett Jr., 1950–2015

Volume Eight: The Christian Life

JAMES LEO GARRETT JR.

EDITED BY
WYMAN LEWIS RICHARDSON

Foreword by Peter L. H. Tie

RESOURCE *Publications* • Eugene, Oregon

THE COLLECTED WRITINGS OF JAMES LEO GARRETT JR., 1950–2015
Volume Eight: The Christian Life

Resource Publications
An Imprint of Wipf and Stock Publishers
199 W. 8th Ave., Suite 3
Eugene, OR 97401

www.wipfandstock.com

PAPERBACK ISBN: 978-1-5326-0750-9
HARDCOVER ISBN: 978-1-5326-0752-3
EBOOK ISBN: 978-1-5326-0751-6

11/16/23

Gratefully dedicated
to the memory of
Dr. A. Joseph Armstrong
(1873–1954)
founder of the
Armstrong-Browning Library
at Baylor University
my mother's teacher
and my teacher.

The editor
(having been encouraged early in this series
by Dr. Garrett to offer his own dedication)
lovingly dedicates this series of books to
Virginia Diane Reynolds Richardson
my mother
an unparalleled teacher
of English and Latin
and a counselor to countless young people
who has shaped the lives of many
though none more so than my own.

Contents

Foreword

My Personal Stories with Garrett

My first impression of the late Dr. James Leo Garrett Jr. was his tall stature, theologically and physically. I could not reach his shoulder with my hands raised, so to speak. What did this giant and yet gentle theologian have to do with me, a small Malaysian-born Chinese?

Long story short, I moved from New Orleans Baptist Theological Seminary to Southwestern Baptist Theological Seminary to work on my PhD studies in 2005 after the devastating impact of Hurricane Katrina. Dr. Garrett was 80 years old then. I had never experienced what people called Garrett's "machine-gun" teaching style; I never had a T-shirt with the words "I survived Theo with Leo." They all sounded so wonderful. If I had been there, I would not have survived—I barely survived Hurricane Katrina.

By God's providential guidance, one day in the fall of 2007, I happened to spot Garrett far off in the distance. This was my first encounter with him in person. He ambled along on his walker because of the injury he sustained in a car accident. That semester, I was taking Dr. Yarnell's doctoral seminar on *Baptist Theologians*, and Garrett's name was on the syllabus as one of the research topics. I was writing a paper on Garrett's Baptist Distinctives and Church Unity. So, with much excitement, I went up to him and introduced myself. He couldn't run away from me because, as you remember, he was on a walker.

As we slowly approached his office, I asked Garrett whether my PhD dissertation could be about his theology. He was very modest, recommending a prominent Baptist theologian in Europe who might be more worth my time. I thought that other theologians were too far away and there was no reason to study someone's theology without knowing the theologian personally. Of course, most of the time we study theologies without knowing the original thinkers personally. "What could be better than writing someone's theology while getting to know the person personally?" I thought. With Garrett's permission and blessing, I started asking and learning from him directly, and sometimes even "bothering" him—to dialogue with him (even over meals) to understand how he viewed certain theological issues, besides what he had written.

In order to make sure he could not get rid of me, I volunteered to help him in his "congested" office, not because of the small space, but because there were just too many books and other things he was not able to organize on his own because of his injury. I learned that he was so disciplined and detailed[1] that he even printed out email threads with others, including mine, and filed them away in cabinets. I helped him do the filing and, in return, he had to let me ask him theological questions. This was, for me, the "great exchange."

As someone with a foreign background and accent, I often felt inadequate to study under a highly regarded Western theologian, like Garrett. Nevertheless, from the first moment I met him, his gentleness, humility, and respect toward me was instantly and continuously overwhelming. It made me want to learn from him all the more. He even let me critique his theological work and still, somehow, remained cool and caring.

Garrett was a "theological father" to Yarnell;[2] so, Garrett was a "theological grandfather" to me. Honestly, his academic stature was quite impossible for me to reach. Yet, I aspire to "grow up" to be like him, to teach and serve like him, manifesting the most beautiful integration of theological excellence and Christian life.

My heartfelt gratitude to the editor, Dr. Wyman Lewis Richardson, as well as the late Dr. Garrett, for giving me the honor of writing the Foreword for the final volume in this series, on *The Christian Life*, which consists of Garrett's writings in three main areas: Priesthood of All Believers; Evangelism and Missions; Worship, Prayer, and Stewardship. The latter two areas can be considered the specific functions (or "spiritual sacrifices") of the former, the Christian Priesthood. It would be a mistake to assume that these collected short pieces lack biblical-theological depth. Just the opposite. Through these brief essays, Garrett faithfully instructs people with solid biblical-theological foundations and consistently applies them to Christian and church life.

1. Garrett was known for his detailed footnotes (which were sometimes longer than the main body) and his determination to spell out authors' first, middle, and last names. Garrett's lengthy footnotes in his many academic works are his signature, demonstrating his unwavering integrity and constant labor in theological research.

2. See https://www.thegospelcoalition.org/article/james-leo-garrett-jr-gentleman-theologian/ (Accessed on 8 September 2023).

In the next section, I will offer two observations, focusing on Garrett's Christ-Christian priesthood doctrine: first is on the enduring significance of this doctrine for Garrett; and second, on Garrett's application of Christ's priesthood and his *munus triplex* (the threefold office) to the ministry of the church.

Two Observations on Garrett's Rediscovery of Christ's and Christian Priesthood Doctrine

Centrality of Garrett's Priesthood Doctrine

In 2001, Paul A. Basden put into perspective the duration and concern of Garrett's work on the priesthood of all believers: "Over the course of more than a dozen years [1975–1988], he wrote three classic articles which traced the doctrine from the New Testament through the fourth century [see below]. Convinced that this crucial teaching has suffered greatly from misunderstanding, misapplication, and neglect, Garrett sought to recover its original intent. Of particular concern to him was the Protestant tendency to transmute this concept into nothing more than radical egalitarianism or rugged individualism."[3]

- "The Biblical Doctrine of the Priesthood of the People of God" (1975);[4]
- "The Pre-Cyprianic Doctrine of the Priesthood of All Christians," (1979);[5]
- "The Priesthood of All Christians: From Cyprian to John Chrysostom" (1988).[6]

Basden gave the impression that Garrett only wrote three articles on the Christian priesthood over a period of 13 years (1975–1988); therefore, one may surmise this doctrine is not as central to his theological pilgrimage as other doctrines. Under closer scrutiny, however, this writer has learned that Garrett's interpretation of the priesthood doctrine began not in 1975, but more than ten years earlier, as demonstrated in his more pastoral-oriented

3. Basden, "James Leo Garrett Jr.," Kindle Edition, Page 303 of 415; Location 7937 of 12422.

4. Garrett, "The Biblical Doctrine of the Priesthood of the People of God," 137–49.

5. Garrett, "The Pre-Cyprianic Doctrine of the Priesthood of All Christians," 45–61.

6. Garrett, "The Priesthood of All Christians: From Cyprian to John Chrysostom," 22–33.

articles, namely, "The Priesthood of All Believers" (1964)[7] and "Recovering My Priesthood" (February 1965),[8] which was republished under "One Baptist's Quest for The Meaning of Priesthood" (June 1965).[9] His fullest form of the Christian priesthood doctrine is later found under the subtitle, "General, or Lay, Ministry: Priesthood of All Christians," within the chapter "Ministry of Churches" in the second volume of his *Systematic Theology*.[10]

Garrett stated clearly, "Yet other Southern Baptists [including Garrett himself] have reckoned the offering of spiritual sacrifices as the primary or essential function of the priesthood of all Christians and have concluded that the privilege of direct access is a corollary of the high priesthood of Jesus Christ. The present author [Garrett] began to expound this view in 1964."[11] As found in the footnote he provided,[12] he was referring to "The Priesthood of All Believers," in *Baptist Standard* (January 1964).[13] After a closer investigation, however, this writer has discovered that Garrett had actually begun the investigation at least two years earlier and already published "The Priesthood of All Believers" in *Capital Baptis*t in 1962.[14] It is beyond the scope of this paper to postulate the reason(s) for the discrepancy of the dates (1962 or 1964).[15]

So, in retrospect, over the course of more than 30 years (1962–95), Garrett rediscovered, reexamined, and reappropriated the Christian priesthood explicitly through at least six pieces of writing (both pastoral and academic). Furthermore, Garrett's passion for Christian priesthood did not seem to diminish in the final decade of his life. Recently, Yarnell mentioned in his tribute to Garrett (2020): "A particular doctrine close to his [Garrett's] heart was the priesthood of all believers, about which we were co-authoring an essay before he died."[16] *In a word, my first observation is that this priest-*

7. Garrett, "The Priesthood of All Believers," 6–7.

8. Garrett, "Recovering My Priesthood," 14–15.

9. Garrett, "One Baptist's Quest for The Meaning of Priesthood," 4, 12.

10. Garrett, *Systematic Theology*, 1st ed., 2:550–563; 2nd ed., 2:603–18.

11. Garrett, *Systematic Theology*, 2nd ed., 2:617.

12. Garrett, *Systematic Theology*, 2nd ed., 2:617, fn 72.

13. Garrett also provided information in the footnote on two other articles he wrote: "Recovering My Priesthood," in *Home Missions* (1965); "The Biblical Doctrine of the Priesthood of the People of God" (1975).

14. Garrett, "The Priesthood of All Believers," 4. I am grateful to Wyman Richardson for confirming the date of this article; this article is published in this final volume.

15. For now, the similarity of the content of these two articles may simply suggest his unintentional negligence.

16. See https://www.thegospelcoalition.org/article/james-leo-garrett-jr-gentleman-theologian/ (Accessed on 8 September 2023).

hood doctrine had always been very close to Garrett for almost six decades (1962–2020). For this reason, this writer continues to hold to the original thesis that the notion of the believers' priesthood is a theological lynchpin to his ecclesiological works and a doctrinal foundation to ecclesial ministry.[17]

The Centrality of Christ's Priesthood to Christian Priesthood

The Christian priesthood doctrine was central to Garrett's doctrine of the church and its ministry. This Christian priesthood brought about the Reformation, and since then became "one of the hallmarks of Protestant Christianity."[18] Properly used and understood, the doctrine is the key to church renewal, if not revival, today. Garrett speaks unwaveringly, "Firmly rooted in the pertinent biblical texts, emancipated from those applications which have become almost severed from the biblical foundation, and connected with contemporary needs and issues, the priesthood of all Christians is today potentially a powerful means for church renewal."[19]

One could not agree more with Garrett's statement that the Christian priesthood doctrine must be "firmly rooted in the pertinent biblical texts." Interestingly, Garrett never discusses Christians' royal priesthood (future reign with Christ as priests) as found in Rev 20:6.[20] The eschatological nature of Christian priesthood does not seem to be his central concern. Instead, he accentuates the present and active function of Christian-priests in "spiritual sacrifices" (i.e., worship, witness, stewardship, and service).[21] Since his earliest work, Garrett had already emphasized the biblical doctrine

17. See my earlier research on Garrett's Christian priesthood notion under four main themes, namely, mission, membership, ministry, and management. Tie, *Restore Unity, Recover Identity, and Refine Orthopraxy*.

18. Garrett, "The Priesthood of All Believers," 4.

19. Garrett, *Systematic Theology*, 2nd ed., 2:617–18.

20. See Garrett, "Priesthood of All Christians: From Cyprian to John Chrysostom," 22.

21. Garrett, *Systematic Theology*, 2nd ed., 2:610; Garrett, "Priesthood of All Christians: From Cyprian to John Chrysostom," 22; Basden rightly summarized, "Following a careful study of the priesthood in both testaments, he concluded that the biblical meaning of the doctrine 'is the offering of 'spiritual sacrifices' such as in worship, witness, stewardship, and service (ministry)'" (Basden, "James Leo Garrett Jr.," Kindle edition, Page 303 of 415; Location 7937 of 12422). This writer also notes, "Garrett perceives a gradual transition from the Aaronic or 'prophetic' priesthood to the 'peoplic' priesthood by emphasizing the sacrificial function; the latter became the primary assumption of the New Testament writers." Tie, *Restore Unity, Recover Identity, and Refine Orthopraxy*, Kindle edition, Page 12 of 142; Location 299 of 4351.

of the priesthood of all believers, as well as its proper practice in the present time,[22] that is, his intentional effort of translating biblical *doctrine* into present *discipleship* (or Christian life).

For Garrett, "While Christ's priesthood is not identical with the Christian priesthood in the New Testament, the former is the foundational motif and model of the latter. The overall pattern behind Jesus' ministry is his self-sacrificial service and servanthood on behalf of other people."[23] Since Christ's priesthood is the pattern of the church's priestly mission-ministry, Garrett is convinced of the primary and present priestly function of Christians, that is, "spiritual sacrifices." Furthermore, Garrett also noted that the priesthood of Christ is somehow connected to his prophetic, priestly, and kingly ministry (in the Reformed tradition, it is called *munus triplex*), and the priesthood of Christians has become the prophetic, priestly, and kingly ministry of the church.

However, one must clarify whether the church is called to fulfill the priestly function patterned after Christ's priesthood, or to fulfill the threefold (prophetic, priestly, and kingly) function patterned after Christ's *munus triplex* (i.e., the threefold office—Prophet, Priest, King), or both. This is no small matter because, in the minds of believers, it conflates the distinct roles (functions) of the Trinity and obscures the church's primary purpose in priestly mission-ministry. For the sake of clarification, I have presented my proposition elsewhere on the *munus triplex* of the Trinity in order to deal with the former aspect, namely, the Father as the proper Potentate, the Spirit as the permanent Prophet, and the Son as the perpetual Priest.[24] The next step, which I am about to take here, is to revisit the biblical narrative, to re-examine the development of the priestly ministry from the OT to the NT against the roles of prophets and kings, in order to shed light on Jesus's primary priestly pattern as the primary function of the church, instead of his prophetic and kingly ministry. The following is a proposal which does not so much challenge the traditional *munus triplex* category as it does clarify the primary and distinct role of Christ Jesus in a newly-coined concept of *munus monoplex* (the one unified role of Christ) for the sake of the church.

22. Garrett, "The Priesthood of All Believers," (1962), 4.

23. Tie, *Restore Unity, Recover Identity, and Refine Orthopraxy* Page 13–14; Location 317 of 4351. "The pattern of the Suffering Servant [e.g., 52:13—53:12] becomes the pattern of the priesthood of Christ; the pattern of the High Priest determines the pattern of the priesthood of all Christians" (Tie, *Restore Unity*, Page 13 of 142; Location 308 of 4351).

24. Tie, "*Munus Triplex* of the Trinity," 107–28.

A Proposal for the Unified Role of Christ (Munus Monoplex) and Its Implications for the Church: A Biblical Re-examination of the Threefold Office of Christ (Munus Triplex)

Christ Jesus, traditionally speaking, holds the *munus triplex*, the threefold office of prophet-priest-potentate.[25] This is a very useful and convenient theological shorthand that categorizes the major works of Jesus the God-man on earth and in heaven. Particularly in Reformed theology, the threefold classification has long become the normative standard of understanding the overall works of Christ.

Theologians of all confessions, however, recognize the limitations and drawbacks of the doctrine of the threefold office. First, some theologians challenge the *comprehensiveness* of *munus triplex*; consequently, they choose to supplement the three "offices" with other "titles," "names," or "functions" of Jesus to describe more thoroughly the overall works of Christ.[26] Second, for others, *munus triplex* merely describes three distinctly separate and isolated roles of Jesus, neglecting the *complementariness* of the three roles of Jesus. Conscientious theologians rectify the issue by emphasizing the "threefold" concept rather than the "three" roles.[27] Third, if treated uncritically, some integrate the three roles too tightly or indistinguishably and perceive Christ as performing all three roles "equally" throughout his earthly as well as heavenly ministry. Phrased otherwise, "Are the three roles of Jesus equally emphasized in Scripture in the same manner at the same time?" This is a matter of the *progressiveness* of Jesus's three functions, and it demands closer scrutiny in this chapter.

A careful re-examination from a biblical perspective offers new insights on the conventional designation of Jesus's *munus triplex*. This article proposes that the priesthood of Jesus is the unifying notion displayed throughout Scripture, while the prophetic and kingly roles of Jesus are better seen as the sub-functions of Jesus under his major priestly role. This not only provides a unified view of Jesus's role, but also eventually gives an adequate explanation of the biblical teachings concerning Christ's priesthood and Christian priesthood. Succinctly, this writer is proposing *munus*

25. Dale Moody uses "potentate" to replace "king" in order to "broaden the traditional references to Christ as king." Moody, *The Word of Truth*, 378.

26. Cullmann, for example, explores the Christological titles that refer to the earthly, future, and present works of Jesus, as well to the pre-existence of Jesus. Oscar Cullmann, *The Christology of the New Testament*. Erickson uses "three functions of Christ—revealing, ruling, and reconciling." Erickson, *Christian Theology*, 697

27. Erickson, *Christian Theology*, 697–98.

monoplex, i.e., the priesthood of Christ, as Jesus's unifying role, in reaction to the traditional classification of *munus duplex* (priest-king) or *munus triplex* (prophet-priest-king).

The paper involves three main sections. First, this writer will re-examine historically and progressively what the Old Testament (OT, hereafter) says about the roles of priests, prophets, and kings with regard to their origins, functions, and relations. Initial observations suggest that the OT regards the priesthood as the most foundational and permanent role in Israel. Second, this paper will re-examine the New Testament (NT, hereafter), specifically concerning the comprehensiveness, complementariness, and progressiveness of the threefold role of Christ. Preliminary observations indicate the emphasis on Christ's prophetic and priestly role during his incarnation; and his priestly and kingly role after his resurrection. In other words, instead of prophetic and kingly roles, Christ's priesthood is the integral and integrative notion that embraces the overall tasks of Jesus, i.e., the unified role (or *munus monoplex*) of Jesus. The third section will re-examine the priesthood of all believers in light of Christ's *munus monoplex*. It is preliminarily concluded that Christ's *munus monoplex* not only better justifies the NT teaching on the believers' priesthood, but also better explains the theological implication for the priestly task of Christ and the priestly role of Christians.

The OT Views of Priests, Prophets, and Potentates

We shall begin with a brief survey of the origins, functions, and relations of the priestly, prophetic, and kingly roles in the OT.

First and foremost, the major image of a priestly task, namely "to sacrifice," first appeared in the Garden of Eden.[28] It was God who seemingly sacrificed animals so that he could clothe Adam and Eve with "tunics of skin" (Gen 3:21).[29] Abel, however, was the very first human mentioned

28. Youngblood, "Priests," 1029. "But true priesthood began . . . in the Garden of Eden." Unfortunately, the author provides no further explanation for this general statement. Walton proposes that Adam was assigned as a priest to care for God's sacred space, the Garden of Eden: "In early interpretation, the book of *Jubilees* presents Adam as offering incense when he leaves Eden, thereby supporting both the priestly role of Adam and the identification of Eden as sacred space. In early Christian interpretation, Origen portrays Adam as high priest." Walton, *The Lost World of Adam and Eve*, 108.

29. Malone articulates well, "There is insufficient evidence for the sometimes popular claim that God taught Adam and Eve about blood sacrifice and that they in turn taught this to their sons (Gen 3:21; 4:2–5) . . . Nonetheless, apart from the fact that this is not (yet) 'a commandment spoken through Moses,' the hypothesized elements would correspond well with the kinds of teaching activity and holiness content expected of

in Scripture who offered sacrifices to God (Gen 4:4).[30] Cain also offered sacrifices, but his offering was rejected by God. Abel (Gen 4:4—first offering), Noah (8:20—first burnt and blood offering), Abraham (12:7–8; 13:4, 18; 22:2, 9, 13), Isaac (26:25), and Jacob (31:54; 35:1–7; 46:1) were acting already as "priests" offering sacrifices to God.[31] The act of offering sacrifices "was carried out by the father of a family (Job 1:5) or the head of a tribe in the days before Moses and his brother Aaron."[32] Nowhere in the OT, however, answers the question of when and how exactly the patriarchal priestly task was started. That being said, we still cannot ignore the fact that the act of sacrificing begins very early in human history, even before the existence of prophets or kings in Israel.

The OT continues to portray a picture that the earliest structure of the Israelite community did not have royal rulers, but only priestly functions and prophetic figures. Abraham (Gen 20:7), Isaac, and Jacob were indeed called "prophets" (Ps 105:15)[33] for the reason that there was "increased prominence given to the *word* of God."[34] Abraham seemed to be the first

---

God's priests." Malone, *God's Mediators*, 55. Furthermore, in light of the notion that "without the shedding of blood there is no forgiveness" (Heb 9:22), God must have "sacrificed" one animal or more to clothe the man and woman with the "tunics of skin." This act of clothing prefigured the "garments of salvation" that God would provide for his people (Isa 61:10). The cloth of salvation, ultimately, is Christ Jesus himself who was put on Christians: "For all of you who were baptized into Christ have clothed yourselves with Christ" (Gal 3:27). All scriptural references are from NASB (1995), unless indicated otherwise.

30. Abel was considered the first priest, and yet Melchizedek was the first mentioned in Genesis as the king-priest. Kang, "The Royal Components of Melchizedek in Hebrews 7," 113.

31. There is no mention whether Joseph performed any priestly tasks, besides "divination" (Gen 44:5, 15), and the latter practice was later forbidden in Israel (Lev 19:26; Num 23:23; Deut 18:10; 2 Kings 17:17; 21:6; 2 Chron 33:6). Wright asserts, "Divination is roughly the attempt to discern events that are distant in time or space, and that consequently cannot be perceived by normal means." Divination "could be used occasionally in a good sense" (e.g., 1 Sam 9:6–10), but it was usually condemned in the OT. Wright, "Divination," 279.

32. Youngblood, "Priests," 1028. Similarly, Ellingworth observes, "The implied rule appears to be that, at least until the early period of the monarchy, it was proper for the head of a family to offer sacrifice . . ." Ellingworth, "Priests," 697.

33. In context, Ps 105:15 refers to Abraham, Isaac, and Jacob (vv.9–10) as "Messiahs" (anointed ones) and "prophets." Nowhere else in Scripture calls Isaac or Jacob "prophet." Grudem notes, "While NT authors identify both Abel (Gen 4:1–8; Luke 11:50–51) and Enoch (Gen 5:18–24; Jude 14) as prophets, the first explicit mention of a 'prophet' (Heb. nābîʾ) in the OT occurs when God tells Abimelech that Abraham 'is a prophet, and he will pray for you and you shall live' (Gen 20:7, RSV)." Grudem, "Prophecy, Prophets," 701.

34. Kaiser, "Biblical Theology of the Old Testament," 340.

recognized prophet of the Lord in Israelite history. A simple look at the biblical concordance will show that the word or title "prophet" was applied to no one else until Gen 20:7 where the Lord called Abraham "a prophet." In fact, the word "prophet" was used only once, only of Abraham, in the whole book of Genesis! It is a debatable matter whether Isaac and Jacob were considered "prophets" in the book of Genesis. Nonetheless, it is worth repeating that Abraham (12:7–8), Isaac (26:25), and Jacob (35:1–7) were already carrying out the priestly task of sacrifice.

Hundreds of years later, Moses also became a prophet. Moses was considered a prophet who prophesied that God would raise up a prophet like him to speak the word of God to them (Deut 18:15–20) so that the people would know what to do and would not offer sacrifices sacrilegiously (Deut 18:9–14). Moses indeed spoke of a coming prophet (Deut 18:15–18),[35] but it was concerning the appointment of a *singular* prophet. In comparison, priestly practices or roles were much more prevalent and predominant in the OT. Moses and Aaron were legitimate priests from the tribe of Levi (Exod 6:16, 19–20, 26–28, 29b). As priests of God, they represented God and the people when they spoke to Pharaoh. Moses's role was to be "like God" in representing God, and Aaron was to be like a "prophet" to speak for God (Exod 4:14–16; 7:1–2). Although mainly Aaron was responsible to speak, both Moses and Aaron had to speak what God taught them. The specific content of the teaching is that the Lord wanted the people to come to worship him on the Mountain of God (Exod 8:20), that is, to offer sacrifices to God (Exod 8:25–27). Offering sacrifices, specifically, was not what God commanded for only Moses and Aaron; the whole people of Israel were called to participate in the priestly task.

Soon after the deliverance of Israel from Egypt, the whole priestly tribe (i.e., the Levites) was established to minister and administer sacrifices, serving in the presence of the Lord (Deut 18:1–5, 7). The images of setting up the tabernacle and the ark guarded by the chosen Levite priests in Exodus clearly communicate the crucial notions of offering sacrifices and being God's priesthood. During that time, there was still no "prophetic school"[36]

35. In general, Deut 18:15–22 was seen as the official constitution of the office of a prophet. Moses was once or twice called a "prophet" (Deut 18:15; 34:10). The New Testament writers never directly called Moses a "prophet," but made a distinction between Moses and the OT prophets (See Luke 16:29; 31; 24:37,44; John 1:45; Acts 26:22; 28:23). Two places in the NT (Acts 3:22; 7:37) quoted Deut 18:15 that God would raise up a great prophet like Moses. On the other hand, the OT also saw Moses as a priest, "Moses and Aaron were among His [God's] priests" (Ps 99:6). Moses himself was from the tribe of Levi (Exod 2:1); therefore, he was officially a priest (Deut 18:1).

36. The practice of "prophetic school" seemed to become prevalent during the time of Prophet Samuel (1 Sam 10:10–12). The practice of a prophet having a "disciple" or

or "royal family," although Miriam was also considered a prophetess (Exod 15:20). When the priesthood was officially established during Moses's time, the act of sacrificing became the major function of Israel's priesthood, that is, for Aaron and his appointed sons (Exod 28:1; Num 8:9–18). The priestly task included: mediating forgiveness (Lev 4:20, 26, 31); administering priestly services (Num 18:7); teaching God's Word (Deut 31:9–13; Lev 10:10; Mal 2:7); and judging the people (Deut 17:8–13).[37] Besides the official priests, all people were urged to participate in offering sacrifices, a crucial aspect of a priestly task.

The establishment of the Aaronic priesthood did not vitiate what God intended in the first place, that is, for the whole of Israel to offer sacrifices to God.[38] Immediately preceding the establishment of the priestly tribe, God revealed to Moses that the chosen nation of God would become a "kingdom of priests" under the condition and covenant of the people's faithful obedience to God (Exod 19:3–6). God's "kingdom of priests" or "kingly priests" (19:6) not only received "the privilege of their calling and election," but also possessed the "responsibilities to be a light to the nations and mediators of God's blessings to the world."[39] In other words, priests were mediators between God and people for the forgiveness of sins.[40]

The "royal priesthood" notion was not totally strange to God's people. Outside the nation of Israel, Genesis 14:18 mentions Melchizedek, who was called "the king of Jerusalem" and "the priest of God Most High."[41] In addition, Moses's father-in-law, Jethro, was the priest of Midian (Exod 18:1, 12), who seemed to also be the leader of his people. As a priest, he gave Moses advice on selecting capable men to be leaders and officials to judge the

"student" is illustrated in the case of Elijah and Elisha (1 Kings 19:16–21; 2 Kings 4:1).

37. "Sorting these functions into two broad categories, the priesthood serves as a bridge from God to the people through teaching, judging, mediating, and conferring the priestly blessing. It also serves as a bridge from the people to God through participation in the Temple service and wearing garments inscribed with the names of the twelve tribes." Angel, "Ezekiel: Priest-Prophet," 35–36.

38. For example, the Festival of Yahweh (Exod 10:9) involved all people (10:9–11). All Israelites were to sacrifice their firstborn animals to redeem their firstborn sons (Exod 13:15), who were to be consecrated to God (13:1–3; 12–13).

39. Kaiser, "Biblical Theology of the Old Testament," 341.

40. "In their function of offering sacrifices at the altar, the priests acted as mediators between people and God, offering sacrifices so that sin might be forgiven." Youngblood, "Priests," 1029.

41. Mathews argues, "The author of the Pentateuch, followed by other biblical authors [including the authors of Ps 110 and Hebrews], has strategically composed his material so as to portray the priest-king Melchizedek as anticipating a fulfillment of the priestly ideals that Aaron's priesthood failed to achieve from its inception." Mathews, *Melchizedek's Alternative Priestly Order*, 136; see 114–16, 139.

people's cases (Exod 18:17–26). The two non-Israelite priests (Melchizedek and Jethro) manifested their ruling position and leadership ability among their own people. These two examples suggest that priestly and kingly roles were not mutually exclusive.[42]

Kingship within Israel did not appear until the time of Samuel. Samuel, mainly as a prophet (1 Sam 3:19–20; Acts 13:20) who had ruling ("to judge") and priestly ("to sacrifice") functions (1 Sam 7:15–17; 11:14),[43] anointed Saul as the first king of Israel (10:1; 12:1, 13). King Saul, on one hand, was seemingly prohibited from acting as a priest (13:8–14),[44] but on the other hand, he joined in the prophetic utterances (10:11–12). King David also carried out the prophetic and priestly tasks (1 Chron 21:26, 28). Technically, David was to be called neither a prophet nor a priest, but a king because the prophetic and priestly positions officially belonged to Prophet Nathan and Priest Zadok at the time (1 Kings 1:32). King Solomon functioned as a priest and offered countless sacrifices with all the people (1 Kings 8:5, 62–64). In view of all the above, it is crucial to note two things relevant to this research purpose. First, that the concepts of kingdom, kingship, or kings were not consolidated until much later, after the establishment of prophetic and priestly functions.[45] Second, a king also functioned as a priest and/or prophet, but rarely three functions simultaneously or equally.

In the later part of the history of Israel, God raised up more prophets as mediatory agents to urge the apostatized kings and irresponsible priests as well as the people in general to return to their initial calling and purpose.[46] The functions of the major prophets (e.g., Jeremiah, Isaiah, Daniel, Ezekiel) and the minor prophets (e.g., Hosea, Joel, Malachi) became more

42. Mathews observes in Zechariah (esp. 3:6–8; 6:9–15) that "this text casts Joshua [the son of Jehozadak] the high priest [Hag 1:1; 3:8] as a royal figure, thus merging the offices of priest and king in an innovative and important way" (Mathews, *Melchizedek's Alternative Priestly Order*, 141, see 122–29).

43. Ackerman notes that Samuel the "priest-prophet . . . can be allowed to join the rank of Shiloh's priests, even though he does not come from the Levitical lineage that biblical tradition otherwise insists is required of priestly authority." Ackerman, "Who Is Sacrificing at Shiloh? The Priesthood of Ancient Israel's Regional Sanctuaries," 25. Furthermore, this writer observes that Hannah vowed to dedicate Samuel to become a Nazirite (1 Sam 1:11; Num 6:1–21), not a priest.

44. King Saul built his first altar to sacrifice to the Lord (1 Sam 14:35) but it was after he was rejected by God. God seemed to reject his sacrifice (14:37).

45. Some hints of the kingdom idea did appear early in Israelite history. God promised that kings would come from Abraham's seed (Gen 17:6, 16). Kaiser mentions that the forming of the kingdom was started in the Mosaic period (Exod 19:6). Kaiser, *Biblical Theology of the Old Testament*, 344.

46. Enns, *The Moody Handbook of Theology*, 34, Kindle edition, Page 37 of 739; Location 606 of 23135.

vital because of Israel's unrepentance. After the fall of Israel and Judah, the kingship was immediately interrupted and the prophetic utterances gradually subsided as the broken nation moved into the 400 years of the so-called intertestamental period where there were neither royal reigns nor prophetic promises (or revelations) among the Jews, but the priestly task seemed to remain, as witnessed in the history of prominent Jewish priestly parties, such as Hasmonaeans, Pharisees, and Sadducees.[47] The latter two became the major parties that held the priesthood in Jesus's time.[48]

Some concluding observations are in line with respect to the priesthood, prophethood, and kingship in the OT:

1) *Continuity-Discontinuity*—The priestly act began in the Garden of Eden and continued throughout OT periods, even into the NT time. The prophetic utterances, on the other hand, began much later with Abraham but only until Prophet Malachi. From there began the 400 years of silence. The royal reign began with King Saul but ended at the destruction of Israel, north and south.[49] Despite the discontinuation of the royal office (earlier) and the prophetic office (later), the people continued to carry out the priestly task, i.e., offering sacrifices. Precisely, the priestly practice precedes and is more permanent than the prophetic and kingly functions.

2) *Universality-Particularity*—The priestly functions (although conducted by the heads of the household, the appointed priestly officials, prophets, or sometimes, kings) involved the participation of all people, especially in offering sacrifices. Distinctly, prophets or kings were individuals particularly chosen to convey God's will or to rule God's people, respectively. Nonetheless, the OT does not state that all people were called to be "kings" or "prophets." On one occasion, Moses wished that all of God's people were prophets (Num 11:29). This does not mean that God's will was to make all people prophets. Prophet Joel prophesied the universal outpouring of the Holy Spirit on "all flesh" (Joel 2:28–29; cf. Acts 2:17–18), resulting in prophet-like manifestations, such as "your sons and your daughters will

47. Bruce rightly observed that "Under the Hasmonaeans, from Jonathan Maccabaeus onward, the chief priesthood and the chief civil power in Israel were combined in one person . . ." Bruce, *The Epistle to the Hebrews*, 125. See also Chapter II, "The Days of the Maccabees," in Ironside, *The Four Hundred Silent Years*, 32–66.

48. For example, Caiaphas (Matt 26:3, 57–65), Annas, John, and Alexander (Acts 4:6) were of high-priestly descent (see also Acts 5:17 about the priests of the Sadducees). See Bruce, *The Book of the Acts*, 91–92, 110; France, *The Gospel of Matthew*, 971.

49. While Messianic prophecies (that present Messiah as King) had already appeared before the Israelite monarchy (e.g., Gen 3:15 "seed of the woman"; 49:8–12 "the lion of Judah), this writer focuses on actual reigns in Israelite history in this section. See Chen, *The Messianic Vision of the Pentateuch*, 55–56, 138–44. Also see footnote 21 above in this article.

prophesy" (Joel 2:28). That the Spirit will come upon all people, however, does not mean that all will become prophets in the sense that every believer will be receiving the gift of prophecy, which was in fact given to a few, as demonstrated later in the NT (Eph 4:11; 1 Cor 12:10, 29).[50] It is not indicated elsewhere in the OT that God wanted *all* of his people to be prophets. Unlike the idea of prophethood, priesthood involved the whole group of God's people, that is, all people were called to be a "kingdom of priests" (Exod 19:3–6).[51] The priestly notion and function involving all people is much more pervasive than the prophetic or royal roles.

3) *Functionality-Identity*—The major purpose of the priests was to mediate forgiveness by offering sacrifices on behalf of the people. Prophets and kings existed because of Israel's unwillingness to trust God. Rather than listening directly to God's voice, they (out of fear of death) seemed to ask for a prophet to speak to them the word of God (Deut 18:16).[52] Rather than letting Yahweh rule as King, they demanded a human king to reign over them (1 Sam 8:4–9; Deut 17:14–20).[53] These were the indications of their disbelief and disobedience. The most distinct disobedience was their sacrifices to idols rather than to Yahweh; or they offered sacrilegious sacrifices to God (Mal 1:7–14). In the final book of the OT, Malachi warned that through the

50. Goldingay observes, "Here the 'all flesh' [Joel 2:28] to which Yahweh alludes is the entire Judahite community, but individually and universally, without limitation in terms of sex, age, or class. While prophesying might refer to something like speaking in tongues (cf. 1 Sam. 10:11; also Num. 11:25–29) . . . [t]he problem is that there is little reason to be too enthusiastic about a widespread outburst of prophecy, dreams, and visions: prophets usually say disturbing things . . ." Goldingay, *Hosea–Micah*, 235–36. If speaking in tongues is part of prophecy, and results from the outpouring of the Spirit (Acts 2:1–4, 17–18), then Paul's principle on charisma still stands, that is, the Holy Spirit distributes gifts of prophecy or *glossolalia* to a few, rather than to every believer (1 Cor 12:4–11; 28–31).

51. In Isa 66:21, God would later select people from other nations to be "priests and Levites."

52. "The LORD your God will raise up for you a prophet like me from among you, from your countrymen, you shall listen to him. This is according to all that you asked of the LORD your God in Horeb on the day of the assembly, saying, 'Let me not hear again the voice of the LORD my God, let me not see this great fire anymore, or I will die'" (Deut 18:15–16). When Israel gathered at the Mountain of God, "All the people perceived the thunder and the lightning flashes and the sound of the trumpet and the mountain smoking; and when the people saw *it*, they trembled and stood at a distance. Then they said to Moses, 'Speak to us yourself and we will listen; but let not God speak to us, or we will die'" (Exod 20:18–19).

53. "But the thing was displeasing in the sight of Samuel when they said, 'Give us a king to judge us.' And Samuel prayed to the LORD. The LORD said to Samuel, 'Listen to the voice of the people in regard to all that they say to you, because they have not rejected you, but they have rejected Me from being king over them'" (1 Sam 8:6–7).

coming of the promised priestly messenger, God would judge and purify the priests for their irresponsible teachings, which resulted in the people's unholy sacrifices (Mal 3:1–4).[54] This leads to the next section that re-examines the identity of the promised *priestly* Messiah.

Jesus as the Priest: Prophet-Priest and King-Priest

In the NT, the Jewish priestly groups remained but the appearances of Jewish prophets were rare, except Anna the Prophetess (Luke 2:36) and John the Baptist (Matt 11:9; 14:5; 21:26; Mark 11:32; Luke 1:76; 7:26; 20:6).[55] The coming of Christ, however, fulfilled the OT prophecy of Moses. Seeing it as the fulfillment of God's promise, Peter proclaimed boldly, "Moses said, 'The Lord God will raise up for you a prophet like me from your brethren; to him you shall give heed to everything He says to you. 'And it will be that every soul that does not heed that prophet shall be utterly destroyed from among the people'" (Act 3:22–23). Stephen, full of the Spirit, also declared the same thing about Christ, "This is the Moses who said to the sons of Israel, 'God will raise up for you a prophet like me from your brethren'" (Acts 7:37).

Jesus Saw Himself a Prophet

In the face of rejection, Jesus said of himself, "A prophet is not without honor except in his hometown and in his own household" (Matt 13:57; Mark 6:4; Luke 4:24; John 4:44; 6:14). Jesus, again referring to himself, said, "Nevertheless I must journey on today and tomorrow and the next day; for it cannot be that a prophet would perish outside of Jerusalem" (Luke 13:33). Jesus seemed to consider himself a prophet, even though he did not explicitly call himself a prophet.

54. Youngblood, "Priests," 1030. A "priest" was also called a "messenger" of God (in Mal 2:7, "For the lips of a priest should preserve knowledge, and men should seek instruction from his mouth; for he is the messenger of the LORD of hosts"). The coming "Messenger" (Mal 3:1) would be, therefore, the promised "priest" to purify the priesthood and make the offerings of the people pleasant to God (3:3–4, 10).

55. John the Baptist denied that he was "the Prophet" (John 1:21, 25), the one that Moses predicted (Deut 18:15, 18) and that the Jews (as well as Samaritans and Qumran community) expected to come. Köstenberger, *John*, 61.

The People Saw Jesus as a Prophet

The people who saw Jesus riding a colt into the city of Jerusalem said, "This is the prophet Jesus, from Nazareth in Galilee" (Matt 21:11). Cleopas talked of "Jesus the Nazarene, who was a prophet mighty in deed and word in the sight of God and all the people" (Luke 24:19b). Similarly, other common people considered Jesus to be a prophet (Matt 21:46; Mark 6:15: Luke 7:16; John 4:19; 9:17), despite the fact that the Pharisees tried to deny his prophetic status (Luke 7:39; John 7:52). Evidently, there was a division among the people about whether Jesus was "the Prophet" or "the Christ" (John 7:40–43), as if there was a qualitative difference between "prophet" and "Christ." Was Jesus a mere prophet?

Jesus as the Prophetic Priest

The identity of Jesus as a prophet, however, seems to be understated when Jesus asked his disciples what the people said concerning who he was. From what they heard, the disciples answered that the people saw Jesus as a prophet, in fact, a great prophet like Elijah, Jeremiah, or John the Baptist. When Jesus again asked for the disciples' own response, Peter, with the revelation from God the Father, replied, "You are the Christ" (Matt 16:16; Mark 8:29). This indicates a definite difference between "prophet" and "Christ." After Peter's confession, Jesus started to tell his disciples that he had to suffer, be killed, and rise again (Matt 16:21; Mark 8:31). The notion of the suffering Christ brings our attention to the messianic passage in the book of Isaiah, which gives prominence to the theme of sacrificial suffering or the priestly image of the promised Messiah (Isa 53:4–12).[56] The Messiah bore the sins of sinners by being killed as a *sacrificial lamb* for the forgiveness of their sins.

Grudem correctly observes that "when we look at the gospels we see that Jesus is not *primarily* viewed as a prophet or as *the* prophet like Moses . . ."; "it is significant that in the Epistles Jesus is never called a prophet or *the* prophet."[57] While being the perfect source of God's revelation—who

56. Tie, *Restore Unity, Recover Identity, and Refine Orthopraxy*, 13.

57. Grudem, *Systematic Theology*, 767–68; emphasis original. "This is especially significant in the opening chapters of Hebrews, because there was a clear opportunity to identify Jesus as a prophet if the author had wished to do so. He begins by saying, 'Long ago, at many times and in many ways, God spoke to our fathers *by the prophets*; but in these last days he has spoken to us *by his Son*' (Heb. 1:1–2). Then after discussing the greatness of the Son, in chapters 1–2, the author concludes this section not by saying, 'Therefore, consider Jesus, the greatest prophet of all,' or something like that, but rather by saying, 'Therefore, holy brothers, who share in a heavenly call, consider Jesus, *the apostle* and high priest of our confession' (Heb. 3:1)" (768; emphasis original).

alone truly and fully reveals God (John 1:1; 14:9; Heb 1:1–3)—Jesus is much greater than a prophet.[58] Rather, he is the suffering and sacrificial Christ predicted by Moses and all prophets (Luke 24:27). Simply, Jesus is the prophetic priest.

The People Saw Jesus as the King?

The magi of the East saw Jesus as the King of the Jews (Matt 2:2). Nathanael confessed that Jesus was the "King of Israel" (John 1:49). Jesus fulfilled what was prophesied when he rode a colt towards Jerusalem: "Behold your King is coming to you, gentle, and mounted on a donkey, even on a colt, the foal of a beast of burden" (Matt 21:5; cf. John 12:15). The people hailed Jesus as "the King" (Luke 19:38; John 12:13). The people, out of various motives, wanted to make Jesus King, but Jesus often refused to be called or made king (John 6:15). On one occasion, when Pilate asked Jesus whether he was the King of the Jews, Jesus did not reject the title (Matt 27:11; Mark 15:2; Luke 23:3). Jesus himself affirmed that he was truly a king, but his kingdom was the heavenly, rather than the worldly one (John 18:36).

Later, the Roman soldiers mocked Jesus, "Hail, King of the Jews" (Matt 27:11; Mark 15:18; John 19:3). Above Jesus's head was placed the written charge, "This is Jesus the King of the Jews" (Matt 27:37; Mark 15:26; Luke 23:38; John 19:19). The chief priests, scribes, and elders, as well as the thieves crucified with Jesus, mocked him, saying, "He saved others; He cannot save Himself. He is the King of Israel; let Him now come down from the cross, and we will believe in Him" (Matt 27:42, 44; cf. Mark 15:32; Luke 23:37). Jesus's royal identity was rejected and seemed to come to an end with his death.

Nevertheless, Jesus's kingship commenced at his resurrection or, more accurately, at his ascension. Because of obedience to his Father from incarnation to crucifixion, Jesus was exalted and bestowed with the lordship and kingship above all else.[59] "These will wage war against the Lamb, and the Lamb will overcome them, because He is Lord of lords and King of kings,

58. Grudem, "Prophecy, Prophets," 701.

59. "Who, although He existed in the form of God, did not regard equality with God a thing to be grasped, but emptied Himself, taking the form of a bond-servant, *and* being made in the likeness of men. Being found in appearance as a man, He humbled Himself by becoming obedient to the point of death, even death on a cross. For this reason also, God highly exalted Him, and bestowed on Him the name which is above every name, so that at the name of Jesus every knee will bow, of those who are in heaven and on earth and under the earth, and that every tongue will confess that Jesus Christ is Lord, to the glory of God the Father" (Phil 2:6–11).

and those who are with Him *are the* called and chosen and faithful" (Rev 17:14). "And on His robe and on His thigh He has a name written, King of kings, and Lord of lords" (Rev 19:16). Jesus's kingship does not begin at the second coming, but already began from his resurrection and his exaltation to the right hand of his Father (Acts 2:32–36). He is the King, but his sovereign reign will not be fully manifested until his second coming.[60]

Jesus as the Royal Priest

The NT does not have many direct references to Jesus as "a prophet" or "the prophet," except Acts 3:22–23 and 7:37, which quote Deut 18:17–20. The NT, especially the Gospels, does not see Jesus merely as a prophet, but more than a prophet. Furthermore, the NT does not provide any significant information on Jesus's prophetic role after his resurrection.[61] On the other hand, while his kingship was received as well as rejected during his early ministry, Jesus's reign was not formally inaugurated until his resurrection and his ascension to the right hand of the Father. The priestly function of Jesus began in his incarnation, was manifested in his crucifixion, and will continue to be carried out in his intercession at the right hand of the Father (Heb 7:25). "Jesus' sacrificially self-giving service (Mark 10:45; Luke 22:27); his so-called 'High-priestly Prayer' (John 17); and his perfect, precious, and permanent High-priestly role (Heb 2:17; 4:15–16; 7:23–28; 9:9—10:18)"[62] consistently highlight Jesus' continuous role as the priest.

No book is more obvious than the Book of Hebrews in teaching that Jesus is the Kingly Priest (i.e., Priest with a royal authority).[63] Rather than

60. Patterson, "The Work of Christ," 442.

61. Ortlund argues that Jesus continued his prophetic function after his resurrection; otherwise, the prophetic work he started in his earthly ministry would be incomplete. Ortlund, "Resurrected as Messiah," 761–66. Ortlund states, "But the most significant way the risen Christ executes his prophetic office is by sending the Holy Spirit throughout the church age to reveal divine truth by enlightening believers and convicting unbelievers" (763). This seems to be a sound argument if one wants to make sure that Jesus completes his prophetic task. Unfortunately, the argument overlooks the distinctively prophetic work of the Holy Spirit after Jesus' ascension. The prophetic function after Jesus' ascension was entrusted to the Holy Spirit. In other words, the prophetic task became the distinctive work of the Holy Spirit who has come to reveal, remind, enlighten, teach, etc. The prophetic task after the ascension of Jesus belongs distinctively to the Spirit. See Tie, "*Munus Triplex* of the Trinity," 122–24. More accurately, Jesus, after his ascension functions mainly as the king-priest, as this paper demonstrates.

62. Tie, *Restore Unity, Recover Identity, and Refine Orthopraxy*, 13.

63. Alexander notes that "some scholars believe he [author of Hebrews] has no place for Christ being a priest on earth prior to his ascension." Alexander, *Face to Face with God*, 4.

following the model of Aaronic or Levitical priesthood, the priesthood of Jesus is a royal priesthood patterned after the priesthood of Melchizedek who was both "king" and "priest" (Gen 14:18–20).[64] The combined concepts of "according to the order of Melchizedek" (Heb 5:5, 10; 6:20) and "sitting at the right hand of God" (Heb 1:3, 13; 8:1; 10:12; 12:2) affirm the royal function of Christ's priesthood, namely, Jesus is the Royal Priest. Jesus is the eternal High Priest (Heb 2:17; 3:1; 4:14–15; 5:10; 6:20; 7:26; 9:11–12) with a resolute royal role (Heb 5:5; 8:1; 10:12).

To put into perspective, Christ functions as a prophetic priest during his incarnation (earthly ministry) and a kingly priest during his ascension (heavenly ministry). Priesthood, in other words, is Jesus's distinctive and integrative task throughout his ministry, on earth and in heaven. Consequently, this writer proposes that Jesus's priesthood is his integral and central role, which nonetheless involves the prophetic and kingly subfunctions. To affirm the one unified role of Jesus (i.e., Christ's priesthood) is to embrace the theological conviction that Christ's priesthood is the pattern of the Christian priesthood.[65]

Christ's Priesthood and Christian Priesthood

Modern theologians are accustomed to saying something like this: "Christ's prophetic, priestly, and kingly functions/roles are the normative pattern for all Christians and churches of God."[66] This may sound like a common theological statement, but it actually lacks biblical warrant. Two major biblical-theological explanations are provided to argue that Christ's unified role of priesthood better justifies the intimate connection between Christ's priesthood and Christian priesthood.

First, prophetic gifts/tasks, as found in the NT churches, belong not to all but to a few Christians. There were *some* prophets in the Corinthian

64. Kang, "The Royal Components of Melchizedek in Hebrews 7," 96. Royal and priestly components fill the pages of Hebrews, but the prophetic element seems to be inconspicuous. At a close look, the author of Hebrews did call Jesus the "apostle" (Heb 3:1), but not once the "prophet."

65. This author acknowledges that "While Christ's priesthood is not identical with the Christian Priesthood in the New Testament, the former is the foundational motif and model of the latter. The overall pattern behind Jesus' ministry is his self-sacrificial service and servanthood on behalf of other people." Tie, *Restore Unity, Recover Identity, and Refine Orthopraxy*, 13–14.

66. As Belcher puts it, "Jesus' fulfillment of the roles of Prophet, Priest, and King, has implications for the mission of the church and for the role of individual believers," in terms of the "prophetic ministry," "priestly ministry," and "kingly ministry" of the church. Belcher, *Prophet, Priest, and King*, 159, 160, 168, 175.

church, as well as in the Ephesian (Eph 4:11) and Roman (Rom 12:6) churches, who had the charisma of prophecy (1 Cor 11:5; 12:10, 28; 14:37). If the gift of speaking in 1 Pet 4:11 included the gift of prophecy, then it could be assumed that there were also some prophets throughout Pontus, Galatia, Cappadocia, Asia, and Bithynia (1 Pet 1:1).[67] Prophethood seems to be limited to a chosen few, but priesthood is universal, that is, it belongs to all Christians. Peter quoted "royal priesthood" (1 Pet 2:9) from Exod 19:6 to identify the Christians in Asia Minor. This means that "priesthood" does not belong to Israel only, but also to all churches of God, which include both Jewish and Gentile Christians.

Unlike prophecy, which is a charisma bestowed on a few, priesthood embraces the whole people of God. As a result, to say that Christians are to pattern after the prophetic role of Christ is theologically untenable. On the contrary, to say that all Christians or churches are to model Christ's priesthood is biblically defensible. A priesthood's main task is to carry out the mediatorial works between God and people,[68] but also to "proclaim the excellencies of Him who has called you out of darkness into His marvelous light" (1 Pet 2:9). In short, Christians are "prophetic priests."

Second, we have already been resurrected or raised (proleptically) with Christ, who is now sitting at the right hand of God (Col 3:1), and yet we await the ultimate resurrection at the *parousia* when, as Scripture says, we will be the priests who reign with Christ, namely, as a royal priesthood: "Blessed and holy is the one who has a part in the first resurrection; over these the second death has no power, but they will be priests of God and of Christ and will reign with Him for a thousand years" (Rev 20:6). The book of Revelation does not identify believers as the priests who prophesy, as the kings who prophesy, or as the prophets who reign, but as the priests who reign. Christians' future function as the royal priests precisely corresponds with the exalted Christ, who is the royal priest.[69] Succinctly, Christians and Christ will reign together as God's "royal priests."

The process of the Christian royal priesthood has already begun when one trusts in God or believes in Christ: "To Him who loves us and released us from our sins by His blood—and He has made us *to be* a kingdom,

67. After Christ's resurrection and ascension, Scripture mentions "prophet" sporadically, inside or outside the church. There was in the island of Paphos a "Jewish false prophet whose name was Bar-Jesus" (Acts 13:6b) and a nameless Cretan prophet (Titus 1:12). The four virgin daughters of Philip the evangelist were prophetesses (Acts 21:9). There was a prophet named Agabus from Judea who spoke with Paul (Acts 21:10).

68. Tie, *Restore Unity, Recover Identity, and Refine Orthopraxy*, 18.

69. In Revelation, Jesus as the Lion and the Lamb gives an image of Christ's kingly-priestly identity (Rev 5:5–13).

priests to His God and Father" (Rev 1:5b–6a; cf. Rev 5:9–10; 1 Pet 2:9; Exod 19:5–6). The "royal" aspect, however, will not be fully actualized until the second coming of Christ (Rev 20:6).[70] In other words, Christ's royal priesthood is the ultimate pattern of the Christian priesthood, but the royal component of the Christian priesthood will not be fully realized until after their resurrection. This notion actually corresponds with what has been discussed earlier: Christ's kingship was inaugurated in his incarnation and consummated only after his resurrection (Phil 2:6–11). Thus, the priestly function should be the central concern of Christians. Nevertheless, they are not to neglect the royal role of the priesthood which is still awaiting consummation.

Conclusion

Christ's priesthood is the integral and integrative model for the Christian priesthood. The reasons involve: (1) Although having the task as a prophet on earth during his incarnation and receiving the role of a sovereign king in heaven at his ascension, Christ holds the continuing and permanent priesthood from his incarnation to his ascension and beyond. Christ's priesthood was already prefigured in the OT's priestly tasks, since the beginning of the history of mankind. The roles of the prophets and the kings in the OT were transient, but the priestly tasks remained in Israel. The priesthood of Christ reflects the priestly pattern of the OT, at least in terms of continuity or permanency of the priestly function; (2) Christ's priesthood is the indispensable pattern for the Christian priesthood. Some Christians are given the gift of prophecy, but all Christians participate in the mediatorial priesthood between God and sinners, just like Christ, who is the Mediator between God and people. All Christians as God's priests will possess a royal authority to rule with Christ after resurrection, but, for the present, they are to sacrifice, suffer, and serve for the sake of the Gospel and on behalf of the people. Prophetic and royal functions are significant, but "priesthood" is the central privilege and responsibility of all Christians. Their priesthood is fundamentally rooted in the priesthood of Christ, which is the integrative motif that includes both prophetic and kingly elements. Thus, I propose the

70. Whether intentionally or not, James Leo Garrett did not include Rev 20:6 in his exposition of the eschatological Christian priesthood: "Blessed and holy is the one who shares in the first resurrection! Over such the second death has no power, but they will be priests of God and of Christ, and they will reign with him for a thousand years" (ESV). In his *Systematic* Theology (vol 2, 2nd ed.), exploring the NT passages related to Christian priesthood, Garrett did not add Rev 20:6 to his three main texts, 1 Pet 2:4–6; Rev 1:5b–6; 5:9–10 (609, fn 32).

munus monoplex of Jesus (one unified role of Jesus) for your serious and further consideration.

Peter L. H. Tie
Academic Dean, Associate Professor of Theology
Christian Witness Theological Seminary
San Jose, California
October 2023

Editor's Introduction

It was with no small measure of trepidation that, eight years ago, I emailed Dr. James Leo Garrett Jr. and proposed this project. I had studied as a student under Dr. Garrett at Southwestern Baptist Theological Seminary in Fort Worth, TX, some eighteen years prior to sending that email. In the intervening years, I had maintained contact with Dr. Garrett, and my appreciation for him and his work had done nothing but increase. It was the appearance of the three-volume *Collected Works of James Wm. McClendon Jr.* from Baylor University Press that led me to propose this series. When I first noticed those volumes, I had already been collecting for some time Dr. Garrett's various articles and essays, delighting each time I "discovered" one of the more obscure pieces. The McClendon volumes led me to think that perhaps the Garrett pieces could be more than the topically arranged three-ring binders on my bookshelf that I initially envisioned. Perhaps others would benefit from seeing these works.

Dr. Garrett, to my great delight, was touched by the proposal and agreed. That led to the eight-year journey that culminates in the appearance of this final volume. I will forever cherish the many emails, phone calls, and letters that Dr. Garrett and I exchanged in mapping out this series and in the appearance of the first few volumes. I recall Dr. Garrett sharing with me that he would not live to see the final volumes appear. I challenged this idea and assured him that he would. He was, as usual, correct, and went to meet his Maker on February 5, 2020, in Nacogdoches, TX.

It is hard to say how this project has affected me. I am too close to it now and will need some time to figure that out . . . but affect me it has. As for how it has impacted my appreciation for and understanding of Dr. Garrett, I can say this with confidence: The loss of James Leo Garrett Jr. is a significant and profound loss for the church. One need only survey the online ramblings of some of our more popular self-styled theologues and then read the selections in these volumes to see the great chasm between a man like Dr. Garrett and some of our louder and more vociferous voices.

Where is the tough-minded gentleness of Leo Garrett in our day? Where is the meticulous attention to detail and the deft handling of the complexities of theological questions that one sees in Dr. Garrett's work? Where is the convictional irenicism of Leo Garrett in our day? I hasten to add that these do exist. I will not name the purveyors of these virtues here, but, thank you God, they do exist. But the great movement of theological discourse especially in Southern Baptist life seems to be trending *away* from these attributes. We desperately need Dr. Garrett's tribe to increase. Can these volumes play some small part in this needed renewal? Perhaps so. I pray so.

That the final volume in this series involves Dr. Garrett's writings on the Christian life strikes me as right and good. The arrangement of these volumes is a symbolic picture of Dr. Garrett's life: all of that study and work and research ultimately manifested itself in the high character of the man. All that came before led inevitably to this: *Christlikeness.* "Volume 8," so to speak, was always about the Christian life for Dr. Garrett. It all came down to this. It had to.

Speak to anybody who knew James Leo Garrett Jr. and they will without fail move past his astonishing scholarship to his character, to who he was. He was a Christian. So his life, much like this final volume, was a vindication of his scholarly efforts. His life revealed that his academic work was more than mere theory, more than mere words. His research was the research of daily life with Christ, no matter how arcane some of it might appear here and there.

Throughout this series, a number of people have been consistent helps and sources of encouragement: Dr. David Dockery, Dr. Malcolm Yarnell, (soon-to-be Dr.) Jill Botticelli Cabal, Dr. Matt Queen, and Dr. Madison Grace come quickly to mind. Jill Botticelli Cabal's contribution to all of these volumes simply cannot be overstated. She has helped in innumerable and significant ways. Southwestern Seminary is fortunate to have such a tremendous scholar serving as their archivist. Lisa Kelley and Audra Murray, members of Central Baptist Church in North Little Rock, have blessed their pastor and all who will read these volumes through their tireless efforts at typing, reading, proofing, and encouraging this work. Look for Lisa Kelley's award-winning fiction to be available in bookstores and online in the not-too-distant future! Thank you, ladies! I am also grateful for the assistance of Jason Corn and his careful reading of this manuscript. A number of these volumes now bear the marks of Jason's careful eye and close reading. Thank you, Jason. The following friends provided tremendous assistance, and they likewise have my thanks: Dave McClung, Chris Greer, Eric Lancaster, Bill

Newton, Condy Richardson, David Richardson, Wade Richardson, Thomas Sewell, Greg Varndell, and Terry Wright.

My mother, to whom this volume is partially dedicated, has proofed every volume and given hours upon hours of her own time to this work. She has been an amazing and wonderful help and source of encouragement! Thank you, Mom!

Roni Richardson, my wife, and Hannah, our daughter, have walked with me through every step of this journey over the last eight years. How am I to express my appreciation to them? "I love my girls," is something I say pretty frequently around the house. I am happy to say it now, here, in print, for love them I do!

Wyman Lewis Richardson
Pastor, Central Baptist Church
North Little Rock, Arkansas
October 2023

I.

The Priesthood of All Believers

1

"The Priesthood of All Believers" (1962)[1]

Since the Reformation, the priesthood of all believers has been one of the hallmarks of Protestant Christianity. It is one of the slogans most often quoted, one of the rallying cries most readily followed, one of the truths most eagerly defended, and one of the heritages most dearly cherished. Lutheran and Calvinist, Anglican and Puritan, Methodist and Baptist, Quaker and Pentecostal—all have gloried, each in his own way, in the priesthood of all believers! Yet, it is an appropriate question today whether most of us understand the biblical meaning of this great truth and are actually practicing it at the present. The Apostle Peter, the Apostle John, and the writer of the Epistle to the Hebrews afford the principal texts for an understanding of our common priesthood. See 1 Pet 2:4–10; Rev 1:5, 6; 5:9, 10; Heb 13:15–19.

Definition

Who are the priests in Christianity? The answer informally given by Protestant or Evangelical Christians has been that all true believers or all saints or all Christians are properly denominated "priests." What is the basis for such an affirmation? First, the New Testament contains no reference to any group of Christian leaders or any to whom spiritual gifts have been given who are specially called "priests." We read of "apostles," "prophets," "teachers," "elders," "bishops," "pastors," "evangelists," "deacons," "deaconesses," "widows," "miracle workers," "healers," "exhorters," "speakers in tongues," "interpreters of tongues," and the like.

1. This article first appeared in *Capital Baptist* (24 October 1962) 4.

But there is never a particular group among the body of Christians called "priests." Secondly, every New Testament reference to priests that is not a specific reference to Jewish priests or is not a reference to the high priesthood of Jesus embraces all the Christian community. Thus, the New Testament knows only two kinds of priesthood in respect to Christianity proper. One is the unique and unshared high priestly office of Jesus, magnificently delineated in the Epistle to the Hebrews. The other is the priesthood which all Christians share in common.

Relation to Others

Is the priesthood that Christians share one that is primarily or even solely exercised by Christians as individuals, or is the priesthood of all believers at least to some extent exercised in relation to fellow Christians? It is worthy of note that our texts uniformly refer either to "priesthood" or to "priests" (plural). Compare "a holy priesthood" (1 Pet 2:5); "a kingdom of priests" (plural) (1 Pet 2:9); "a kingdom, priests to his God and Father" (Rev 1:6); "a kingdom and priests to our God" (Rev 5:10). In none of these texts is the word "priest" used in the singular.

What does a careful examination of these texts do to the prevailing modern conception that every Christian is his own priest, when this priesthood is interpreted somewhat independently and individualistically? Obviously, one does not enter the "royal priesthood" in any way other than one enters the Christian life, namely, by the voluntary response and decision of faith. Yet, the apostles understood the priesthood of all believers to have some corporate significance.

A recognition of this truth may help us to see that some of our contemporary notions about the priesthood of all believers are actually corollaries or applications of the priesthood rather than its essential meaning. Some hold that the priesthood of "every believer" means that every Christian has the right to interpret the Bible for himself. Our texts contain no reference to interpreting Old Testament scriptures, and obviously the New Testament was yet in the process of being written and collected. This could not have been the primary meaning of the priesthood for the apostles. Others regard the priesthood of all believers as meaning that every member of a Baptist church has voting rights in the conduct of church business. No doubt congregational polity is one of the derivatives of the Reformation's rediscovery of the priesthood of all believers, but this could hardly be the primary meaning of the priesthood.

Yet, others regard the priesthood of all believers as being more or less synonymous with the authority of individual conscience or the obligation of every man to personal validation of his religious beliefs. This too has had some historical connection with the priesthood of all believers. Nevertheless, the apostles understood the priesthood of believers to be a truth dependent upon the high priestly work of Jesus Christ. They would hardly have recognized some modern notions of religious authority as vested in the individual conscience or reason. It is very important, therefore, that we distinguish between the primary meaning of the priesthood of all Christians as rooted in the New Testament writings and various corollaries or applications of this priesthood that have been developed during the course of Christian history.

Probably the most practical question of all is this: How are we to function as priests? The New Testament does not leave this question unanswered. Many will hastily answer that the primary function we have as priests is to go directly to the throne of grace for ourselves without human mediators or channels save only the one Mediator, Jesus Christ. This doctrine of access to the throne of God is primarily associated with the doctrine of the high priestly offices of Jesus (see Heb 4:14–16) but is not specifically mentioned in the major texts related to our common priesthood. The basic function of Christians as priests is derived from the basic function of priesthood as indicated by the functions of the Jewish priesthood. What was the main task of a priest in ancient Israel? Obviously, to offer sacrifices to God in behalf of men. Someone will object perhaps.

Did not the once-for-all sacrifice of Jesus abrogate the whole system of animal sacrifices? Why, therefore, should we be concerned with the offering of sacrifices today? In reply, it may be said that we as Christians can offer no sacrifice that can expiate, propitiate, or atone for our sins, for this only has been done by Jesus Christ the great High Priest. Yet, Peter and the writer of the Epistle to the Hebrews specifically enjoined their readers to offer up sacrifices to God. Compare "living sacrifice" in Rom 12:1. Thus the function of Christians as priests is something more than having the privilege of access to the throne of God. Rather it involves the use of this access in the continual offering of spiritual sacrifices unto God.

Specifically, what is meant by "spiritual sacrifices"? Such sacrifices include worship or the "sacrifice of praise to God, that is, the fruit of lips that acknowledge his name" (Heb 13:15). Such sacrifices include intercessory prayer (Heb 13:18, 19; see 1 Tim 2:1). Such sacrifices include acts of benevolent sharing, for Christians as priests are not to "neglect to do good and to share . . . , for such sacrifices are pleasing to God" (Heb 13:16). From Ps 51:16, 17 one may also conclude that repentance is one of those sacrifices which Christian priests are to offer to God, for "a broken and contrite heart Thou, O God, wilt not despise." The highest function of our common priesthood is not basking in our own privilege of access to divine mercy but in our bearing the burdens of our broken, oppressed, and suffering brethren.

A renewed understanding of and appreciation for the biblical doctrine of the priesthood of all believers can deepen our common ties as Christian brethren and challenge us to be much more effective in our ministry to those who are not yet participants in and partakers of this common priesthood.

2

"Recovering My Priesthood" (1965)[1]

The priesthood of "every believer" had meant for most of my life that every Christian had his own access or entrée to God's mercy-seat unencumbered by other human beings, especially by clerical or ordained priests, and aided only by Jesus Christ. As a seminary student, I had gathered a sheaf of texts from the Epistle to the Hebrews into what I then called a sermon under the title, "The Avenue to God," and preached it lustily to the members of the congregation I was then serving and repeatedly elsewhere. Then later as a theological professor, I was drawn into polemical controversy or at least into a polemical posture against the Roman Catholic Church concerning the office and functions of a special or clerical priesthood. I had not read enough of Martin Luther's writings to realize how profound and comprehensive was Luther's understanding of the priesthood which we Christians share and how little of this I myself had appropriated. In the words of Kristen E. Skydsgaard of Copenhagen, I had mistakenly identified the broken-off arrowheads of polemical controversy with the entire arrows.

Some were saying that, since every Christian is a priest before God, every Christian is his own authority in matters of belief and conduct. Others were identifying the priesthood with voting rights or privileges in a Baptist congregation. Then came the upheaval of theological controversy in denominational ranks, and the "priesthood of the believer" came to be frequently heralded as the Siamese twin of academic freedom—wherever there was one, the other was sure to follow. The priesthood was veritably a synonym for the private interpretation of Scripture. These sounded like a Babel of interpretations to my ears, and I turned once again to the New

1. This article first appeared in *Home Missions* (February 1965) 14–15.

Testament in a fresh quest for a clear answer as to what the apostles understood by the "royal priesthood" and related terms.

I read and pondered 1 Pet 2:4–10; Rev 1:5–6; and 5:9–10. There, I noted "a holy priesthood," "a kingdom of priests," (or "royal priesthood") "to offer spiritual sacrifices," "a kingdom, priests to his God and Father," and "a kingdom and priests to our God." I came to see that Heb 13:10–19, though never using the word "priest" or "priesthood," actually describes some of the functions of our common Christian priesthood.

I had little trouble finding a valid New Testament basis for the common Protestant emphasis that all saints or all believers or all Christians participate in the priesthood and are truly and fully priests. No New Testament writing applied the term "priest" to any group of Christian leaders or to any persons to whom specified spiritual gifts had been given. The priesthood, then, was as wide as the early Christian *ekklesia*. The case against the confinement of the priesthood to the ordained clergy was just as valid as it had been in Luther's day.

A second issue called for closer scrutiny. Is our priesthood something that we exercise; primarily as distinct and separate individuals, almost as if we were priests independent of each other? Is my priesthood and yours, to use a modern metaphor, essentially a pipeline to and from God's throne of grace whose master valve is turned by the great High Priest and Son of God? Or is the priesthood according to the apostles more definitely related to our common life or interrelatedness as fellow Christians? One of my ablest students investigated the extremely individualistic interpretation given to the priesthood by certain eighteenth- and nineteenth-century Baptists. Many present-day Christians understand in a very individualistic manner what for the apostles was a truth of the corporate Christian life, veritably a corollary of the doctrine of the church.

Yet, a third and more crucial issue confronted me in my quest. What, above all, should Christians as priests be doing? What should be the nature of our priestly function from an apostolic viewpoint? The central function of Jewish priests, despite all modern reassessments of the roles of prophets and priests, had been the offering of sacrifices to God in behalf of men. Moreover, Peter and the author of the Epistle to the Hebrews called upon first-century Christians to offer "spiritual sacrifices"—not propitiatory or expiatory sacrifices, for Jesus the great High Priest had done this—but "spiritual sacrifices." Hebrews 13 spelled out some types of spiritual sacrifices: worship, intercessory prayer, and beneficent sharing. Slowly but convincingly, I stood before the truth that being a Christian priest today, as in the First Century AD, is essentially to offer continually spiritual sacrifices to God and in behalf of other men. Our highest priestly function is not basking in our privilege of access to divine mercy. The access to God's mercy and assisting grace follows from our Lord's high priestly office, as may be noted in Heb 4:14–16. But offerings, not merely access, predominate in those passages that speak of our priesthood. Our highest priestly function is the bearing of the burdens of our broken, oppressed, and suffering brethren.

Then came a trip to one of our most developed Baptist mission fields, a nation in which Baptist missionaries and national leaders and many believers have been the instruments for a notable evangelical advance. On the foundation of the sacrifices of heroic pioneer missionaries has been erected a flourishing Baptist work with emphasis on evangelization and the organization of new churches, augmented by strong educational institutions and publication work. A talented and dedicated corps of leaders, missionaries, and nationals labors there.

For ten days, I was privileged to meet with missionaries from all parts of the nation. Another week was spent in one of the seminaries among teachers, students, and pastors. Every daily paper contained two words: agrarian reform. Monetary inflation had brought the nation to the brink of crisis. The atmosphere was ripe for social reform or revolution, especially on the part of three groups: farm workers, labor unionists, and university students. National Baptist pastors were reporting that their own young people were caught up in the movement for reform. Some called for Baptists to identify positively with the social reforms, though not necessarily with all reform movements, designed to alleviate stark poverty, malnutrition, and disease. Others, including both missionaries and nationals, for various reasons cautioned against any such involvement. One was a fear lest an entry be made for the "heretical social Gospel." Baptists seemed singularly unprepared for such a crisis. I pondered the question: How did such things come to be? How could Baptists who had made so many converts among the poor be so unprepared and unwilling to foster the legitimate strivings of the poor for economic opportunity and justice, for an adequate diet and reasonable health?

One fact came into focus: In this particular nation, for certain historically explicable reasons, Southern Baptists have had no ministry through medical and hospital missions comparable with what has been undertaken by them in other nations. Later, I learned that some Baptist churches in that nation do have evening medical clinics in which Baptist physicians provide, without cost, medical care for their fellow believers—a true expression of the common priesthood. But the problem remained. How were Baptists in that nation to express their benevolent concern for the total needs of their fellow countrymen? How were these men to know that Baptists truly cared for them in their total plight? Had the Baptists been so concerned to point to the priesthood as access alone as not to be enough involved in offering "spiritual sacrifices," even in "doing good"? Was what I found overseas so evident to me, and was I so oblivious to my own failures in fulfilling my own priesthood? Had I cared enough and loved sacrificially? Had I offered sacrifices of devotion and sealed my witness for my Lord with deeds of mercy and compassion?

I returned to our nation's capital as plans were being projected for the massive march for civil rights. I had tried in previous months to help to prepare one of the Baptist churches of that area for the transition toward racial justice and love translated into action. But what had I done or what was I to do that really was a priestly offering? A week at Ridgecrest with the Woman's Missionary Union afforded me the opportunity to make the most vigorous appeal for Southern Baptist involvement in a constructive healing of the racial crisis I had made. But words are more powerful when joined with priestly deeds!

Returning to Southern Seminary and to Louisville, once again I found added confirmation for my new understanding of my priestly office. My pastor preached that our Christian witness must not be merely verbal, but coupled with deeds, even as our Lord was a *doer*. This same pastor chanced to remark to me one evening that a certain member of our congregation was bearing far more than his proportionate share of the spiritual burden of our congregation. I listened carefully and quietly. He referred not to a seminary professor or a seminary student but instead to a layman, a deacon. A medical missionary cited a report that the two areas in his country with the highest percentage of baptisms and of new churches among Baptists were those areas immediately surrounding the two largest Baptist mission hospitals. Then my attention was turned to one of my colleagues of the seminary faculty who, along with his equally dedicated wife, had become involved in devoted service to the people of the "inner city" in Louisville. I recalled others who were devotedly serving in goodwill centers. The priesthood of believers was not a dead phrase, not a shibboleth of sixteenth-century controversies. It was alive, for priests were still offering living sacrifices of intercession and beneficent deeds! Such deeds were demonstrations of faith that issued in love, of love that was not limited to words, of service to "one of the least of these my brethren." I was convinced in the inner fibers of my being that herein was the true meaning of our common priesthood, and it was a ray of hope for an effectual ministry in today's world.

I prayed: God be merciful to this poor failing and faltering priest and give me the vision, the love, and the grace to fulfill that priestly calling to which we all who are Christ's have been called.

And what, my friend, of your priesthood?

3

"One Baptist's Quest for the Meaning of Priesthood" (1965)[1]

The priesthood of "every believer" had meant for most of my life that every Christian has his own access or entrée to God's mercy-seat, unencumbered by other human beings, especially by clerical or ordained priests, and aided only by Jesus Christ.

As a seminary student, I gathered a sheaf of texts from the Epistle to the Hebrews into what I then called a sermon under the title, "The Avenue to God." Later, as a theological professor, I was drawn into polemical controversy or at least into a polemical posture against the Roman Catholic Church concerning the office of functions of a special or clerical priesthood.

I had not read enough of Martin Luther's writings to realize how profound and comprehensive was Luther's understanding of the priesthood which we Christians share and how little of this I myself had appropriated. In the words of Kristen E. Skydsgaard of Copenhagen, I had mistakenly identified the broken-off arrowheads of polemical controversy with the entire arrows.

What the Scriptures Say

Some were saying that since every Christian is a priest before God, every Christian is his own authority in matters of belief and conduct. Others were identifying the priesthood with voting rights or privileges in a Baptist congregation. Others identified it with academic freedom. The priesthood was veritably a synonym for the private interpretation of Scripture. These

1. This article first appeared in *The Baptist World* (June 1965) 4, 12.

sounded like a Babel of interpretations to my ears, and I turned once again to the New Testament in a fresh quest for a clear answer as to what the apostles understood by the "royal priesthood" and related terms.

I read and pondered 1 Pet 2:4–10; Rev 1:5–6; and 5:9–10. There I noted "a holy priesthood," "a kingdom of priests" (or "royal priesthood"), "to offer spiritual sacrifices," "a kingdom, priests to his God and Father," and "a kingdom and priests to our God." I came to see that Heb 13:10–19, though never the word "priest" or "priesthood," actually describes some of the functions of our common Christian priesthood.

I had little trouble finding a valid New Testament basis for the common Protestant emphasis that all saints or all believers or all Christians participate in the priesthood and are truly and fully priests. No New Testament writing applied the term "priest" to any group of Christian leaders or to any person to whom specified spiritual gifts had been given. The priesthood, then, was as wide as the early Christian *ekklesia*. The case against the confinement of the priesthood to the ordained clergy was just as valid as it had been in Luther's day.

What Do Priests Do?

A second issue called for closer scrutiny. Is our priesthood something that we exercise primarily as distinct and separate individuals, almost as if we were priests independent of each other? Or is the priesthood according to the apostles more definitely related to our common life or interrelatedness as fellow Christians? One of my ablest students investigated the extremely individualistic interpretation given to the priesthood by certain eighteenth and nineteenth-century Baptists. Many present-day Christians understand in a very individualistic manner what for the apostles was a truth of the corporate Christian life, veritably a corollary of the doctrine of the church.

Yet, a third and more crucial issue confronted me in my quest. What, above all, should Christians as priests be doing? What should be the nature of our priestly function from an apostolic viewpoint? The central function of Jewish priests, despite all modern reassessments of roles of prophets and priests, had been the offering of sacrifices to God in behalf of men. Moreover, Peter and the author of the Epistle of the Hebrews called upon first-century Christians to offer "spiritual sacrifices"—not propitiatory or expiatory sacrifices, for Jesus the great High Priest had done this—but "spiritual sacrifices." Hebrews 13 spelled out some types of spiritual sacrifices: worship, intercessory prayer, and beneficent sharing.

Slowly but convincingly, I stood before the truth that being a Christian priest today, as in the first century AD, is essentially to offer continually spiritual sacrifices to God and in behalf of other men. Our highest priestly function is not basking in our privilege of access to divine mercy. The access to God's mercy and assisting grace follows from our Lord's high priestly office, as may be noted in Heb 4:14–16. But offerings, not merely access, predominate in those passages that speak of our priesthood. Our highest priestly function is the bearing of the burdens of our broken oppressed and suffering brethren.

Questions I Found Overseas

Then came a trip to one of our most developed Baptist mission fields, a nation in which Baptist missionaries and national leaders and many believers have been the instruments for a notable evangelical advance.

I discovered that monetary inflation had brought the nation to the brink of crisis. The atmosphere was ripe for social reform or revolution. National Baptist pastors were reporting that their own young people were caught up in the movement for reform. Some called for Baptists to identify positively with the social reforms (though not necessarily with all reform movements) designed to alleviate stark poverty, malnutrition, and disease. Others cautioned against any such involvement.

Baptists seemed singularly unprepared for such a crisis. I pondered several questions. How did such things come to be? How were Baptists in that nation to express their benevolent concern for the total needs of their fellow countrymen? How were these men to know that Baptists truly cared for them in their total plight? Had the Baptists been so concerned to point to the priesthood as access alone as not to be enough involved in offering "spiritual sacrifices," even in "doing good"?

Was what I found overseas so evident to me, and was I so oblivious to my own failures in fulfilling my own priesthood? Had I cared enough and loved sacrificially? Had I offered sacrifices of devotion and sealed my witness for my Lord with deeds of mercy and compassion?

The Priesthood a Reality

Returning home to Louisville once again, I found added confirmation for my new understanding of my priestly office. My pastor preached that our Christian witness must not be merely verbal, but coupled with deeds, even as our Lord is a *doer*. This same pastor chanced to remark to me one evening that a certain member of our congregation was bearing far more than his proportionate share of the spiritual burden of our congregation. I listened carefully and quietly. He referred to a layman, a deacon. A medical missionary cited a report that the two areas in his country with the highest percentage of baptisms and of new churches among Baptists were those areas immediately surrounding the two largest Baptist mission hospitals. Then my attention was turned to one of my colleagues of the seminary faculty who, along with his equally dedicated wife, had become involved in devoted service to the people of the "inner city" in Louisville. I recalled others who were devotedly serving in goodwill centers.

The priesthood of believers was not a dead phrase, not a shibboleth of sixteenth-century controversies. It was alive, for priests were still offering living sacrifices of intercession and beneficent deeds! Such deeds were demonstrations of faith that issued in love, of love that was not limited to words, of service to "one of the least of these my brethren." I was convinced in the inner fibers of my being that herein was the true meaning of our common priesthood, and it was a ray of hope for an effectual ministry in today's world.

I prayed: God be merciful to this poor failing and faltering priest and give me the vision, the love, and the grace to fulfill that priestly calling to which we all who are Christ's have been called.

What, my friend, of your priesthood?

4

"The Biblical Doctrine of the Priesthood of the People of God" (1975)[1]

The doctrine of the priesthood of all Christians has been misunderstood, misapplied, and neglected as much as, if not more than, it has been opposed or denied during Christian history. Protestants have stressed as a key segment of their Reformation heritage "the priesthood of all believers" so as to clarify the open access for all to the grace of God and to support and expand the role of lay persons in the church, but the egalitarian and the individualistic conclusions sometimes drawn, if they are not antithetical to, have been severed from the New Testament rootage of the concept. Roman Catholics, overcoming their longstanding reluctance to embrace the concept as true, have in recent years been encouraged by the documents of Vatican Council II, especially "The Dogmatic Constitution on the Church," to affirm "the priesthood of the faithful" without denying the peculiar clerical priesthood via the sacrament of orders.

All Christians who take seriously the priesthood of all Christians and find it actually or potentially significant and applicable to the twentieth-century scene are obliged to seek out and find the meaning of the priesthood of the people of God within the Old and New Testaments.

1. This article first appeared in *New Testament Studies: Essays in Honor of Ray Summers in His Sixty-Fifth Year*, edited by Huber L. Drumwright Jr. and Curtis Vaughan, 137–49. Waco, TX: Markham Press Fund of Baylor University Press, 1975.

The Priesthood of Israel

Unquestionably, the New Testament concept of Christians as "a kingdom of priests" has its roots in the Old Testament. This may be seen by a comparison of 1 Pet 2:9 RSV ("a chosen race, a royal priesthood, a holy nation, God's own people") with Exod 19:4–6a, in which text the Lord says to Israel through Moses: "You have seen what I did to the Egyptians, and how I bore you on eagles' wings and brought you to myself. Now, therefore, if you will obey my voice and keep my covenant, you shall be my own possession among all peoples; for all the earth is mine, and you shall be to me a kingdom of priests and a holy nation." Four aspects of this important Old Testament text should be noted. First, its preamble refers to God's mighty act of the Exodus (v. 4). Secondly, it prescribes a basic condition: "if you will obey my voice and keep my covenant." Thirdly, it contains a basic trilogy of identifications of Israel: "my own possession among all peoples," "a kingdom of priests," and "a holy nation." Finally, the future tenses ("you shall be," vv. 5, 6) suggest a later fulfillment or realization of what is being affirmed about Israel.[2]

This principal Old Testament text about Israel's priesthood must be understood in the larger context of Israel's self-understanding. As Cyril Eastwood has emphasized, Israel came to be "the People of God" by revelation, by election, and by covenant. "And I will walk among you, and will be your God, and you shall be my people" (Lev 26:12, RSV). Israel's unique role as the people of Yahweh was due to God's election of Israel. The election was explained by Moses according to the Deuteronomic account (7:6–8) as due not to Israel's population but to God's electing-love.[3] The covenant of Yahweh with Israel is not to be seen after the analogy of diplomats negotiating with one another at the United Nations. Rather, the covenant with Israel involved divine initiative. God graciously called Israel to the covenant, and Israel was necessarily required to respond freely in covenant-faithfulness. Exodus 19:5–6 identifies Israel as "a holy nation" as well as the people of Yahweh's possession. John D. W. Watts has observed: "Before Israel became a nation, it was a people—the people of Jahweh. This fact is basic and determinative for the study of the Old Testament conception of the people of God."[4] It may well be that the word "nation" in Exodus 19:6 has much

2. On the significance of the tenses, see Manson, *Ministry and Priesthood*, 51–52, and Eastwood, *The Royal Priesthood of the Faithful*, 25. Cf. the use of the present tense in 1 Pet 2:9 and of the aorist tense in Rev 1:6.

3. On the difference between electing-love (*ahavah*) and covenant-love or loyalty-love (*chesed*), see Smith, *The Distinctive Ideas of the Old Testament*, 118–82.

4. Watts, "The People of God: A Study of the Doctrine in the Pentateuch," 233.

less political or national connotation than the term "nations" in the Israelite demand for a king (1 Sam 8:5).

What was the meaning of the term "a kingdom of priests" (Exod 19:6)?

> There was a time at the beginning of Hebrew history when no priestly class existed. In those early days, the head of the Hebrew household was the equivalent of a priest. Although he had certain priestly duties, he was in no sense an official priest.[5]

The term "a kingdom of priests" seems, however, to have meant more than an aggregation of individual Israelite fathers who exercised priestly functions.[6] Indeed, it likely meant as well the priestly character and function of Israel under Yahweh's kingship, especially in relation to non-Israelite peoples.[7] But what were the priestly duties in ancient Israel? Recent Old Testament scholarship has greatly modified the sharp distinction, common in earlier decades, between the role of the priest and the role of the prophet in Israel.[8] Consequently, priests are understood to have had in the early phases of the distinct Aaronic priesthood a prophetic or didactic role. For example, "And the Lord said to Moses, 'See, I make you as God to Pharoah, and Aaron your brother shall be your prophet . . .'" (Exod 7:1). "Its [i.e., Jerusalem's] heads give judgment for a bribe, its priests teach for hire, its prophets divine for money" (Mic 3:11). T. F. Torrance identifies the "double character" of the priesthood of the Old Testament as "mediation of God's Word" and "priestly witness to God's revealed Will." He sees Moses as "the unique mediator" of the Word of God and Aaron "in secondary status . . . as the liturgical priest who carries out in continual cultic witness the actual mediation that came through Moses." Moreover, the making independent of the cultic priesthood from the mediation of the Word, according to Torrance, was the occasion for God sending the prophets, "most of them out of the priesthood itself."[9] But Eastwood finds other reasons for the "transition from the teaching

5. Eastwood, *Royal Priesthood of the Faithful*, 18.

6. Examples of such priestly actions include Abraham's preparation to offer Isaac (Gen 22, esp. v.12); Abraham's erection of an altar at Beersheba (Gen 26:25); Gideon's erection of an altar to Yahweh on the site of a destroyed altar of Baal and his offering a burnt offering (Judg 6:25–27); and Manoah's offering of a cereal offering (Judg 13:19).

7. Manson, *Ministry and Priesthood*, 52, interprets "a kingdom of priests" as a community ruled over by a king-God in person or his anointed viceregent which all the subjects are priests" and then declares that this "plain meaning was automatically excluded when an exclusive priestly caste was established in fact and confirmed in its rights and privileges by the legislation of the Priestly Code."

8. See Mowinckel, *Psalmestudien, III*, 4–23; Johnson, *The Cultic Prophet in Ancient Israel*; Haldar, *Associations of Cult Prophets among the Ancient Semites*.

9. Torrance, *Royal Priesthood*, 3–5.

ministry to the sacerdotal ministry": (1) the settled existence in Canaan with the building of temples and the influence of rival religions; (2) the rise of the written, as distinct from the oral, tradition and correspondingly the rise of Levites and scribes; (3) the heightened sense of the holiness of Yahweh, man's awareness of sin, and the necessary repetition of sacrifices; (4) the increasingly hereditary nature of the priesthood; (5) the centralization of worship at Jerusalem; and (6) the assumption of greater power by priests during the postexilic period in the absence of a king.[10] Torrance calls the postexilic period "the era of liturgised law and legalised liturgy" with "no room for the prophet."[11] Indeed, "the functions of the priest had undergone a complete change. Instead of being the interpreter of the Word and the Law and the Will of God, he became the indispensable intermediary between men and God, and Judaism became a theocracy ruled by a hierarchy."[12]

But neither the role of ancient Israelite fathers as priests within their families nor the developing Aaronic-Levitical priesthood nor both together can provide all the clues needed for the meaning of "the kingdom of priests" in Exod 19:6. The Septuagint reading of these words is *βασίλειον ἱεράτευμα*. The exegetical tradition that derives from the Masoretic text understands "kingdom of priests" and "holy nation" to be "*mutually dependent*" and hence tends to understand "a holy kingdom of priests." Such is to be found in Aquila's Greek, the Bohairic, the Old Latin, and the Vulgate versions. The Targums refer to "kings (and) priests and a holy nation" and the Book of Jubilees to "a kingdom and priests and holy nation" and to "a priestly and royal nation." Another exegetical possibility, espoused by John Hall Elliott in his recent monograph on 1 Pet 2:4–10, regards *βασίλειον* as a substantive rather than as an adjective; hence one may translate it "kingdom" or "royal residence." The term *ἱεράτευμα* connotes "activity, person-relatedness, and collectivity "and may be rendered "body of (functioning) priests." Elliott sees "behind this LXX formulation" in its Alexandrian setting "a missionary consciousness and the concern for witness to the Umwelt." [13]

Two conclusions may be drawn as to the meaning of the term "a kingdom of priests." It must be understood in a setting wider than the Aaronic or special priesthood of the Old Testament. Such a setting has already been identified as "peoplic." Furthermore, the term must be understood in terms of the shift in the basic duties of the special priesthood from the prophetic to the sacrificial. Moreover, since during the New Testament era the sacrificial

10. Eastwood, *Royal Priesthood of the Faith*, 22–23.

11. Torrance, *Royal Priesthood*, 7.

12. Eastwood, *Royal Priesthood of the Faithful*, 23.

13. Elliott, *The Elect and the Holy*, 90–101, 120–21, 63–85.

function appeared to be primary, it should not be surprising to find this assumption accepted by the New Testament writers.

The Suffering Servant of the Lord songs or poems in Deutero-Isaiah[14] uniquely embody the "kingdom of priests" motif and afford a transition to the New Testament doctrines of the high priesthood of Jesus and of the priesthood of all Christians. Although the interpretations of the Servant vary and include principally the individual,[15] the idealized,[16] and the collective.[17] Eastwood is probably correct in stating that "it is impossible to keep the thoughts expressed in these interpretations permanently apart; they overlap at several points."[18] A passage closely related to the Servant-poems specifically refers to Israelites as "the priests of the Lord" and "the ministers of our God" (Isa 61:6).

As with the prophets, the Spirit of the Lord is put upon the Servant (Isa 42:1). The Servant is "chosen" (42:1) and "called from the womb" (49:1). The Servant's mouth is likened to "a sharp sword" (49:2). Unlike those prophets who receive divine revelation through dreams or ecstatic visions, the Servant obediently receives the divine word in a fully conscious state (50:4–5).

Not only the prophetic but the royal element is ascribed to the Servant. Isaiah 61:1 refers to an anointing. "Kings" and "princes" are said to "prostrate themselves" before "the servant of the rulers" because of Yahweh who has chosen the Servant (49:7). The Servant "shall be exalted and lifted up" so as to "startle many nations" and so that "kings shall shut their mouths because of him" (52:13, 15).

Yet, it is the sacrificial role of the Servant rather than the prophetic or the royal which predominates in the Servant poems. The suffering of the Servant is due to his being rejected by men (53:3; cf. 50:6), is in behalf of the sins of others (53:4–6), is voluntary and without protest (53:7), includes death (53:8–9), and constitutes an offering for the sin of many transgressors (53:10–12)."

The Servant's role involves a mission that transcends Israel/Judah. "It is too light a thing that you should be my servant to raise up the tribes of Jacob and to restore the preserved of Israel; I will give you as a light to the nations that my salvation may reach to the end of the earth" (49:6, RSV).

14. Isa 42:1–4; 49:1–7; 50:4–9; 52:13–53:12.

15. I.e., Deutero-Isaiah. Jeremiah, Zedekiah, or Jehoiachim.

16. I.e., personified or idealized Israel, or the remnant of Israel.

17. I.e., the incorporation of all Israelites in the Servant (as an expression of the Hebrew concept of corporate personality).

18. Eastwood, *Royal Priesthood of the Faithful*, 10.

Thus, in the Servant of the Lord, "we see that Israel is called and chosen to fulfill a corporate, priestly function, which not only prefigures the coming King. Priest and Servant, of the New Testament, but also the kingdom, priesthood and servanthood which He initiates."[19] Similarly, Torrance concludes:

> The conception of the Suffering Servant is the great characteristic of the Church's ministry, and it is that which above all determines the nature of priesthood in the Church. That applies to the Church's threefold participation in Christ's Prophetic, Priestly, and Kingly Ministry, for the Church is engaged in all these as a servant bearing the cross like the man of Cyrene (Matt 27:32). It is indeed in terms of the suffering servant-ministry that we are to see the basic unity in the church's prophetic, priestly, and kingly functions. [20]

The Priesthood of Christians

In the light of the prominence of the concept of priesthood in the Old Testament and in certain New Testament books, one may be surprised to discover its absence from the self-identifications in the teaching of Jesus.

When we turn to the gospels, we find that Jesus makes no use of the ideas of priesthood. He lays no claim to the title of priest for himself nor does he confer it on his disciples. In his parables, the imagery is not taken from the Temple and its ritual, but from ordinary life. Those who came into contact with him might think of him as prophet, or rabbi, or even Messiah. They did not think of him in terms of priesthood. In first-century Palestine, this was perfectly natural. Jesus was regarded as the son of Joseph; and, as Joseph was not a priest, neither was his son. [21]

Manson has pointed out three considerations that help to explain the absence of Jesus' self-identification as a priest and yet the prominent role of priesthood in the interpretation of Jesus' ministry by certain New Testament writers. First, Jesus "did think of the Temple as the natural place for men to go and worship God, as is shown by the parable of the Pharisee and the Publican; and he did take active steps, in the Cleansing of the Temple, to ensure that the Court of the Gentiles should be, in fact as well as in theory,

19. Ibid., 14.
20. Torrance, *Royal Priesthood*, 87.
21. Manson, *Ministry and Priesthood*, 45.

a place of prayer for all nations."[22] Secondly, although Jesus "did not belong to the official hierarchy" and thus "was not in a position to pose as a rival to Annas or Caiaphas," it is possible "that his ministry was priestly in a way of which the Temple dignitaries had no inkling." Thirdly, early Christians actually described the death of Jesus "in the terminology of the sacrificial cultus"[23] and as a self-sacrifice, "an offering made to God in which priest and victim are identical."[24]

The absence of specific references in the Gospels to Jesus as a priest is also somewhat compensated by the priestly implications in Jesus' affirmed and enacted servanthood in the Gospels. Matthew specifically connects the ministry of Jesus with the Servant of the Lord (12:17–21; Isa 2:1–4; cf. Matt 11:4, 5). In the teaching of Jesus, self-giving service is central to his own mission (Mark 10:45; Luke 22:27).[25] His visit to the synagogue in Nazareth (Luke 4:16–22) "shows clearly the difference between Jesus and John the Baptist. John was the prophet of doom, Jesus was the Priest of Good Tidings who stood before them offering God's gifts because He offered Himself."[26] Jesus' cleansing of the temple in Jerusalem (Matt 21:12–13), which had become a place of profit for the Jewish priesthood rather than "a house of prayer for all nations," is "indicative of the universal nature of priesthood which His appearing had inaugurated." In his reply to the request of the Greeks (John 12:20–26), Jesus pointedly refers to the servanthood and "fellowship" of his disciples. Jesus' washing of the feet of his disciples (John 13:1–17) is "a symbol of inward cleansing" and therefore a priestly act in which the disciples "are instituted into a royal priesthood in the New Covenant." In the celebration of the Passover meal with his disciples (Mark 14:17–26), Jesus associates them with his own sacrifice and hence with his priesthood. In these sayings and in these dramatic actions, the followers of Jesus "emerge as members of a Kingdom and sharers of a Servanthood and Priesthood which are theirs as well as His forever."[27]

The high priesthood of Jesus is implied in John 17—what Protestants since David Chytraeus in the sixteenth century have called his "High-priestly Prayer"[28]—and is specifically and carefully delineated in the Epistle to the Hebrews. According to John 17, Jesus dedicates or offers himself for the sake

22. Ibid., 46.

23. Cf. 1 Cor 5:7; Eph 5:2; Rev 5:6; Mark 14:24.

24. Manson, *Ministry and Priesthood*, 46–48.

25. Eastwood, *Royal Priesthood of the Faithful*, 38–39.

26. Ibid., 40–41.

27. Ibid., 39, 41–43.

28. Hoskyns, *The Fourth Gospel*, 494.

of his disciples (v. 19) and intercedes with the Father in behalf of his present (vv. 9–17) and future (vv. 20–23) disciples. In Hebrews, Jesus is called "the apostle and high priest of our confession" (3:1) who "when he had made purification for sins, . . . sat down at the right hand of the Majesty on high" (1:3b; cf. 4:14). He partook of our humanity "so that he might become a merciful and faithful high priest in the service of God, to make expiation for the sins of the people" (2:17b). The fact that he can "sympathize with our weaknesses" and "in every respect has been tempted as we are, yet without sinning," should encourage Christians "with confidence [to] draw near to the throne of grace" to "receive mercy and find grace to help in time of need" (4:15, 16). The very role of the Jewish high priest was "to offer gifts and sacrifices for sins" for men and to God, and this included "sacrifice for his own sins as well as for those of the people" (5:1, 2). He was called by God to the successional or Aaronic priesthood; likewise, Jesus was chosen by the Father, but for a unique or Melchizedekan priesthood (5:5, 6, 10; 6:20; 7:3, 17). The superiority of the Melchizedekan priesthood is seen in that Abraham, the ancestor of the Levites, paid tithes to Melchizedek (7:4–10). Furthermore, Jesus was descended from a nonpriestly tribe, Judah, and entered upon his priesthood "by the power of an indestructible life" and with the Father's oath (7:11–22). The high priesthood of Jesus continues permanently so that "He is able for all time to save those who draw near to God through him, since he always lives to make intercession for them" (7:23–25). As the sinless One, he does not need to offer sacrifices for his own sins, and the once-for-all offering of himself made unnecessary daily sacrifices for the sins "of the people" (7:26–28). The priestly ministry of Jesus is "more excellent" than that of Aaronic priests because he mediates a new and better covenant (8:6–13) because he serves in a heavenly rather than an earthly sanctuary (8:1–5; 9:1–9a), and because he has offered in his death a once-for-all effective sacrifice for sin (9:9b-10:18). In view of the high priestly work and office of Jesus, Christians ought to "hold fast the confession" of their hope (10:23) rather than to spurn Jesus and "fall into the hands of the living God" (10:29–31).

The high priesthood of Jesus as interpreted in the Epistle to the Hebrews is basic to, though not identical with, the New Testament concept of Christians as a "royal priesthood." Eastwood has aptly observed:

> Priesthood in the New Testament is founded upon the Person and Work of Christ. All the same, there is a difference between His Priesthood and ours: we are servants sharing that Servanthood which He as the Servant *par excellence* creates. Divine love constitutes ours. He is Priest by nature; we are priests by

> faith-union with His sacrifice. His Priesthood consists in offering His life for the sins of the world, ours in sharing the inestimable benefits of His offering. While His Priesthood is incommunicable, it is nevertheless the pattern of that general servanthood and universal priesthood of those who by faith and obedience have chosen to become lowly servants of the divine will.[29]

Where, one may ask, does the New Testament specifically and unambiguously teach that all Christians are priests? The principal texts are three: 1 Pet 2:4–10; Rev 1:5b, 6; and Rev 5:9, 10. Peter admonishes his Christian readers to be "built into a spiritual house, to be a holy priesthood, to offer spiritual sacrifices acceptable to God through Jesus Christ" (v. 5). Then, borrowing three terms used in Exodus 19:5, 6,[30] he declares them to be "a chosen race, a royal priesthood, a holy nation, God's own people" (v. 9a). John affirms that Jesus Christ "made us a kingdom, priests to his God and Father" (Rev 1:6a) and declares of the redeemed multitude from all nations that God "hast made them a kingdom and priests to our God, and they shall reign on earth" (5:10).[31] It is significant that in none of these passages does the word "priest" appear in the singular; the term is either "priesthood" or "priests." Furthermore, an examination of the lists of "spiritual gifts" (charismata) given by Paul (Rom 12:4–8, 1 Cor 12:4–11, 27–31; Eph 4:7–14) and of the lists of qualifications for church leaders in the Pastoral Epistles (1 Tim 3:1–13; 5:3–22; Titus 1:5–9) leads to the conclusion that nowhere in the New Testament is the term "priest" used to refer to a charismatic gift or a role of leadership that belongs to certain Christians but not to all Christians. In addition to those primary New Testament texts on the priesthood of Christians identified above, there are several passages that allude to the functions, especially the sacrificial functions, of the royal priesthood: Rom 12:1; 15:16; Phil 2:17; 4:17, 18; and Heb 13:15, 16. It may be asserted, therefore, on adequate exegetical grounds, that to all Christians Peter, John, Paul, and the author of the Epistle to the Hebrews ascribe a common royal priesthood with sacrificial functions. The argument for a special or clerical priesthood within Christianity must rest on some basis other than the New Testament.

29. Eastwood, *Royal Priesthood of the Faithful*, 45–46.

30. It is significant that the Old Testament source of three of the terms used in 1 Pet 2:9 is the *locus classicus* pertaining to the peoplic priesthood of Israel, not a passage pertaining to the Aaronic priesthood.

31. According to Rev 20:6 RSV, those who share "in the first resurrection" "shall be priests of God and of Christ, and they shall reign with him a thousand years."

Protestants have tended to be more interested in the scope of the priesthood in New Testament Christianity than in the function of that priesthood. Consequently, the question of function must be carefully examined. Some interpreters have, on the basis of Heb 4:14–16, concluded that the principal function of Christians as priests is to take advantage themselves of the access that Jesus Christ has opened to the Father's "throne of grace" so as to "receive mercy and find grace to help in time of need." In view of the context, however, it should be noted that the access is a corollary of the doctrine of the high priesthood of Jesus being set forth in the Epistle to the Hebrews, and it may be legitimately argued that such a passage does not attempt to identify the function or functions of Christians in their own derived priestly office. First Peter 2:5 ("to offer spiritual sacrifices acceptable to God through Jesus Christ") does supply a primary clue to the function of Christians as priests. Accepting the late Old Testament emphasis on the sacrificial function of the Jewish priesthood, Peter asserts that the royal priesthood of the Christian calls for "sacrifices," specifically "spiritual sacrifices." Such a term seems to differentiate these from the Temple sacrifices. The acceptability of these sacrifices depends on Jesus Christ.[32] Here is no contravention of his unique, once-for-all high priestly sacrifice. Here is no possibility of a propitiatory or expiatory sacrifice for sin by Christians. Rather, 1 Pet 2:5 affirms that priesthood involves the offering of sacrifices and so also with the Christian priesthood. The central function of the royal priesthood of Christians accordingly is the offering of "spiritual sacrifices."

The New Testament writers are specific in identifying what they mean by such "spiritual sacrifices." The pertinent passages suggest at least four basic meanings or types of sacrifices: worship, witness, stewardship, and service.[33] The Epistle to the Hebrews declares: "Through him [Christ] then let us continually offer up a sacrifice of praise to God, that is, the fruit of lips that acknowledge his name" (13:15). Paul's admonition to the Christians at Rome to present their bodies "as a living sacrifice, holy and acceptable to God" identifies such a sacrifice as "spiritual worship" (12:1).[34] Similarly, in Heb 9:14, "the blood of Christ" who offered himself to God is said to "purify"

32. Rev 1:5b, 6 and Rev 5:9, 10 make the priesthood of Christians to depend on the sacrificial death of Jesus.

33. Eastwood, *Royal Priesthood of the Faithful*. 4:55, "the marks of the royal priesthood" in the New Testament as Baptism, Sacrifice. Worship, and Mission." Yet, in no New Testament text is an explicit connection made between baptism and priesthood. Sacrifice seems rather to be the more basic category of which the other marks are examples.

34. "Spiritual worship" is λογικὴν λατρείαν.

the "conscience from dead works to serve the living God."[35] Witness, as well as worship, is specifically related to the priesthood of Christians. Those who are "a royal priesthood" are "to declare the wonderful deeds of him who called" them "out of darkness into his marvelous light" (1 Pet 2:10).[36] Paul interprets his entire missionary career as that of one who by divine grace is "a minister of Jesus Christ to the Gentiles in the priestly service of the gospel of God, so that the offering of the Gentiles may be acceptable, sanctified by the Holy Spirit" (Rom 15:15, 16). Even his imminent death in Rome can be described "as a libation upon the sacrificial offering" of the faith of the Philippian Christians (Phil 2:17). Gifts given by the Philippian Christians through Epaphroditus for Paul in his proclamation of the gospel to the Gentiles are "a fragrant offering, a sacrifice acceptable and pleasing to God" (4:18). The sacrifices of Christians as priests are also to be in the nature of ministering service (*diakonia*). The author of the Epistle to the Hebrews admonishes his readers: "Do not neglect to do good and to share what you have, for such sacrifices are pleasing to God" (13:16).[37]

In conclusion, the New Testament clearly teaches the priesthood of all Christians, a concept rooted in but not identical with the unique high priesthood of Jesus. Its basic function is the offering of "spiritual sacrifices" such as in worship, witness, stewardship, and service (ministry).

35. The word "serve" is λατρεύειν. Eastwood, *Royal Priesthood of the Faithful*, 49–51, is probably right in noting that the New Testament writers deliberately use λατρεύειν to refer to worship rather than the more levitically oriented term λειτουργεῖν.

36. Eastwood's (*Royal Priesthood of the Faithful*, 51) eucharistic interpretation of this text seems to the present writer to be very doubtful.

37. The Greek term translated "to do good" is εὐποιΐας; and the term translated "to share what you have" is κοινωνίας.

5

"The Pre-Cyprianic Doctrine of the Priesthood of All Christians" (1979)[1]

The doctrine[2] of the priesthood of all Christians as taught during the patristic era has been the subject of detailed research by neither patristic scholars[3] nor historians of this particular doctrine.[4] The more surprising is this fact when one discovers that, whereas the universal Christian priesthood did not constitute a major theme for controversy during the age of the Church Fathers, there are numerous passages in extant patristic literature pertaining to this doctrine.

To understand the development of the doctrine of the priesthood of all Christians during the age of the Fathers, one should perceive as clearly as possible the Old Testament background to and the New Testament meaning of the doctrine. Rooted in the concept of the entire People of Israel as

1. This article first appeared in *Continuity and Discontinuity in Church History: Essays Presented to George Huntston Williams on the Occasion of His 65 Birthday*, edited by F. Forrester Church and Timothy George, 45–61. Studies in the History of Christian Thought 19. Leiden: E. J. Brill, 1979.

2. The term "doctrine" is utilized in preference to "dogma," which would wrongly imply ecclesiastical or conciliar definition, and to "idea" or "concept," which would tend to suggest only the personal beliefs of certain individual Christians during the patristic age.

3. No extensive monograph concerning the patristic doctrine of the priesthood of all Christians has been produced in the modern age, to the knowledge of the author.

4. Eastwood, *The Royal Priesthood of the Faithful*, 56–101, has interpreted the doctrine according to Clement of Rome, the *Didache*, Polycarp, Justin Martyr, Irenaeus, the *Epistle to Diognetus*, Clement of Alexandria, Tertullian, Origen, Cyprian, John Chrysostom, Augustine, and Narsai. Eastwood's responsible interpretation of the doctrine during the patristic age is not, however, based upon an extensive location and examination of all pertinent passages in extant patristic literature.

"a kingdom of priests" (Exod 19:6) and related to, but in no sense identical with, the doctrine of the high priesthood of Jesus as set forth in the Epistle to the Hebrews, the royal priesthood was ascribed to all Christians by New Testament writers (1 Pet 2:9; Rev 1:5b, 6; 5:9, 10). Its chief function was identified as the offering of "spiritual sacrifices" (1 Pet 2:5), such as in worship, witness, gifts to an apostle, and diakonic ministry.[5]

The first epoch or era in the post-biblical development of the priesthood of all Christians extended from the Apostolic Fathers and the so-called Apocryphal New Testament to the writings of the third-century bishop of Carthage, Cyprian, whose emphasis on the clerical priesthood marked the advent of a new era in the development of the doctrine under investigation. The priesthood of all Christians does not figure prominently in the theology of the Apostolic Fathers; yet there are a few passages pertinent to this priesthood. The *Didache* refers to true Christian prophets and teachers as "high priests"[6] and admonishes:

> On the Lord's own day, assemble in common to break bread and offer thanks; but first confess your sins, so that your sacrifice may be pure.[7]

The "sacrifice" seems to be worship, of which breaking of bread and offering of thanks are integral parts, and is to be preceded by confession of sin. The most detailed passage[8] in the *Didache* concerning thanksgiving and the breaking of bread contains no reference to priesthood or sacrifice but is characterized by a servant Christology. Clement of Rome refers to Jesus Christ as "the High Priest and Ruler of our souls"[9] and as "the High Priest who offers out gifts, the patron and helper in our weakness."[10] Clement likens the proper conduct of Christian worship to the divine prescriptions for the sacrifices in ancient Israel's worship.

5. See the author's "The Biblical Doctrine of the Priesthood of the People of God," 137–49.

6. 13.1–3.

7. 14.1, Kleist, *The Didache Epistle of Barnabas, The Epistles and Martyrdom of St. Polycarp, The Fragments of Papias* [and] *The Epistle to Diognetus*. This "sacrifice" is connected with Mal 1:11, 14.

8. 9.1–10.6.

9. *Epistle to the Corinthians* 61.3; 64, Kleist, *The Epistles of St. Clement of Rome and St. lgnatius of Antioch.*

10. Ibid., 36.1. The word "gifts" may also be translated "offerings." Clarke *(The First Epistle of Clement to the Corinthians*, 40) concludes that "The 'offerings' (ποσφορών) are the prayers of the worshipping congregation. . . . To the early Church, which used the same technical term for prayers and for the Eucharist gifts, the two things must have seemed closely connected."

> For the high priest has been given his own special services, and the priests have been assigned their own places and Levites have their particular duties. The layman (λαϊκός) is bound by the rules for laymen.[11]

Clement extends this analogy to apply to a single place of worship, i.e., "Jerusalem only."[12] He also quotes the Psalms relative to the sacrifice of confession of sin and the "sacrifice of praise."[13] All these texts should be understood in the context of the epistle's major concern, namely, schism in the Corinthian congregation. Ignatius of Antioch applies the language of sacrifice to the martyrdom of Christians[14] and asserts the superiority of Jesus as high priest to the Jewish priests, "for he is himself the door to the Father, through which Abraham and Isaac and Jacob and the prophets and the apostles and the church enter."[15] Polycarp refers to Jesus as "the eternal high priest himself" and "the eternal heavenly high priest"[16] and to Christian widows as "God's altar"[17] and is reported to have prayed that his own forthcoming martyrdom might be accepted before God "as a rich and acceptable sacrifice."[18] *The Epistle of Barnabas* contains no reference to Christians as "priests." This omission was perhaps due to the author's regarding such a term as belonging to the Jewish dispensation and, unlike the epistle's major motifs—new people, new covenant, second creation, new and circumcised heart, new temple, etc., not reflective of the uniquely Christian in an anti-Judaic interpretation of Christianity. Similarly, the *Shepherd* of Hermas, with the possible exception of one passage,[19] is silent on the royal priesthood, and the so-called *Second Letter of Clement of Rome* and the fragments from Papias are likewise silent. Among the Apostolic Fathers only the *Didache*, Clement, Ignatius, and Polycarp specifically refer to the offering of

11. 40.5, Goodspeed, *The Apostolic Fathers.*

12. 41.2.

13. 52.1–4.

14. *Romans,* 2.2; 4.2.

15. *Philadelphians,* 9.1.

16. *Philippians,* 12.2 and *The Martyrdom of Polycarp,* 14.3. The latter passage is part of a prayer ascribed to Polycarp and said to have been offered just prior to his martyrdom.

17. *Philippians* 4.3. The context suggests that the conduct of the widows is always seen by God.

18. *The Martyrdom of Polycarp,* 14.2.

19. Bk. 3, similitude 2, contrasts the poor man who is rich in intercession and confession and who prays for the rich man with the rich man who out of his wealth supplies the necessities of the poor man but then concludes that both are partners and accomplish their work in a manner acceptable to God.

spiritual sacrifices by Christians; for the *Didache* and Clement there are the sacrifices of worship or praise, whereas Ignatius and Polycarp allude to the sacrifice of martyrdom.

The writings that comprise the Apocryphal New Testament do not set forth the theme of a common priesthood of Christians except possibly in the statement in the Gnostic *Gospel of Philip* that "some" who "are in the tribe of the priesthood . . . will be able to go within the veil with the high priest."[20] The absence of mention of Christians—or of Gnostics—as priests prevails throughout the extant Gnostic literature. One notable exception is to be found in Ptolemy's threefold classification of the laws, i.e., those pure laws which the Saviour fulfilled, those laws "bound up with lower things and wrongdoing" which He abrogated, and those "typical and symbolical" laws which He "transformed from the sensible and phenomenal into the spiritual and invisible." Under the last Ptolemy declares:

> For the Saviour commanded us to offer sacrifices, but not of irrational animals or incense but of spiritual praises and gloryings and thanksgiving, and through fellowship and beneficence toward neighbours.[21]

In the *Odes of Solomon*, sometimes regarded as Gnostic, sometimes as Essene, appears the text:

> I am a priest of the Lord, and to Him I do priestly service: and to Him I offer the sacrifice of His thought. For his thought is not like the thought of the world nor the thought of the flesh, nor like them that serve carnally. The sacrifice of the Lord is righteousness, and purity of heart and lips.[22]

The second-century apologists had little place for the priesthood of all Christians in their writings, chiefly, it seems, because sacrifices tended to be identified exclusively by the apologists with the system of pagan sacrifices which they were seeking to refute. The earliest of the extant writings, the *Apology of Aristides*, declares that the true God "requires not sacrifice and libation nor any one of the things that appear to sense"[23] but does acknowledge that Christians "are ready to sacrifice their lives for the sake of Christ."[24] Justin Martyr mentions in his *First Apology* in the context of pagan worship that sacrifices are offered to idols or images, to demons, and to

20. 133.1–5, Wilson, *The Gospel of Philip*.

21. *Letter of Ptolemaeus to Flora*, 3, Grant, *Second Century Christianity*.

22. 20.1–3, as translated by Harris and Bernard, *The Odes of Solomon*.

23. From the Gk., ch. 1, Kay, *The Anti-Nicene Fathers*, 10:264.

24. Ch. 15.

pagan deities of all kinds.[25] He insists that "God does not need the material offerings which men can give, seeing indeed, that He Himself is the provider of all things."[26] Moreover, God

> has no need of bloody sacrifices, libations, and incense. But we praise Him to the best of our power by prayer and thanksgiving for all our nourishment . . . [Indeed,] the only worship worthy of Him is not to consume by fire those things that He created for our sustenance, but to employ them for the good of ourselves and the needy, and, with thankful voices, to offer Him solemn prayers and hymns . . .[27]

Justin does not specifically connect the royal priesthood and the Eucharist, although in reference to the latter he speaks of "prayers and thanksgiving."[28] In his *Dialogue with Trypho*, he is more explicit concerning the royal priesthood. Christians refuse to offer sacrifices to pagan deities that they formerly worshipped, even when it means their own death.[29] God did not need, according to Justin, sacrifices from the Israelites but ordained and received them on account of the sins of the Israelites, principally idolatry.[30] Jesus Christ is the Melchizedekan high priest,[31] indeed an eternal priest[32] whose priesthood is conjoined with kingship.[33] A Gentile, e.g., "a Scythian or a Persian," and his offerings can now through the Son of God be acceptable to God.[34] In another context, Justin affirms:

> Having been set on fire by the word of His calling, we are now of the true priestly family[35] of God, as He Himself testifies when He says that in every place among the Gentiles pure and pleasing sacrifices are offered up to Him. But God receives sacrifices from no one, except through His priests.[36]

25. Chs. 9, 12, 62, and 24.
26. Ch. 10.
27. Ch. 13, Falls, *Saint Justin Martyr*.
28. Chs. 65–67.
29. Ch. 46.
30. Chs. 22, 67.
31. Chs. 32, 33, 63, 83, and 118.
32. Chs. 33, 36, 42, 96, and 118.
33. Chs. 36, 86, 96, and 118.
34. Ch. 28.
35. The Greek word is γένος. *ANF* translates γένος as "race." It is possible that Eastwood (*The Royal Priesthood of the Faithful*, 61–66) has overdrawn the relation in Justin between the priesthood of all Christians and Christians as a third race.
36. Ch. 116.

Justin refuses to accept the Jewish interpretation of Mal 1:10–12, which applies the passage to "the prayers of the Jews who were then in the Dispersion" but instead gives it a Christian eucharistic interpretation.[37] Pressing his polemic against Trypho, Justin insists that

> there is not one single race of men—whether barbarians, or Greeks, or persons called by any other name, nomads, or vagabonds, or herdsmen dwelling in tents—among whom prayers and thanksgivings are not offered to the Father and Creator of the universe in the name of the Crucified Jesus.[38]

Even at the parousia of Jesus, according to Justin, the sacrifices to be offered will not be "of blood" but "only of true and spiritual praises and thanksgiving."[39] Athenagoras makes no direct reference to Christians as priests but reiterates Justin's point that God has no need of sacrifices.[40] Sextus declares: "The only sacrifice acceptable to God is through God to do good to one's fellow men."[41] Coupled with the apologists' polemic against pagan sacrifices, therefore, one finds in Justin that Christians are regarded as a priestly people among whom Gentiles can offer to God acceptable sacrifices and among whom prayers and thanksgivings are universally offered.

Melito of Sardis interprets the priesthood of Christians in language obviously drawn partly from 1 Pet 2:9:

> This is he who rescued us from slavery to freedom, from darkness to light, from death to life, from oppression to an eternal kingdom, and made us a new priesthood and a chosen people forever.[42]

In the writings of Irenaeus of Lyons, priestly sacrifices continue to be identified with the Eucharist. He reiterates the emphasis made by the apologists that God did not need the sacrifices made by the Israelites but ordained them as an antidote to idolatry,[43] although now God rejects these

37. Chs. 117, 41.

38. Ch. 117.

39. Ch. 118.

40. *A Plea for the Christians,* 13.

41. Line 47. The Greek text and the Latin translation by Rufinus of Aquileia are given by Chadwick, *The Sentences of Sextus.* Chadwick (16, 17, 106) interprets διά θεόν and *pro deo* as meaning "with God's help."

42. Sect. 68, Bonner, *The Homily on the Passion by Melito, Bishop of Sardis, with Some Fragments of the Apocryphal Ezekiel.*

43. *Against Heresies,* 4.14.3.

in view of the true sacrifice of Christ.[44] Irenaeus concludes that "God did not seek sacrifices and holocausts from them, but faith, and obedience, and righteousness, because of their salvation."[45] Jesus fulfills the high priestly role[46] and is akin to Melchizedek[47] and to the about-to-be-offered Isaac.[48] Even his second advent may be described as "sacerdotal."[49]

The reader of *Against Heresies* can find passages in which Irenaeus could easily have become more explicit about the royal priesthood of Christians.[50] For example, mention of the Old Testament "sacerdotal and liturgical service" could have led to a comparable mention of the sacerdotal functions under the New Covenant, but instead Irenaeus refers to the giving of the Holy Spirit.[51] Likewise, the prayers of the church "to the Lord, who made all things, in a pure, sincere, and straightforward spirit, and calling upon the name of our Lord Jesus Christ" are not described as a priestly sacrifice but as the opposite of "angelic invocations" and "incantations."[52] Cyril Eastwood has attempted to connect the royal priesthood with the doctrine of recapitulation in Irenaeus,[53] but the two are never mentioned by Irenaeus in the same context. Irenaeus, when referring to the Old Testament incident in which David ate the shewbread reserved for priests, calls "all the apostles of the Lord" and "the disciples of the Lord" "priests."[54]

44. Ibid., 4.17.2. Irenaeus quotes, as if from Scripture, the following: "The sacrifice to God is an afflicted heart: a sweet savour to God is a heart glorifying Him who formed it."

45. *Against Heresies*, 4.17.4.

46. Ibid., 4.8.2.

47. *Proof of the Apostolic Preaching*, 48, Smith, ACW, 79.

48. *Against Heresies*, 4.5.4.

49. Ibid., 4.20.11.

50. Lawson, *The Biblical Theology of Saint Irenaeus*, 254–55, says concerning *Against Heresies*, 4.17.5, that "Irenaeus gives a hint that he held a doctrine of the universal priesthood of all believers" and that logically this "does not . . . preclude the conception of a special priesthood in addition, representatively exercising the function which in principle belongs to the whole priestly community." Paul Beuzart *(Essai sur la théologie d'Irenée*, 158–60), while stating that Irenaeus holds to the universal priesthood, observes that he "assimilates the disciples to the Levites of the old law" and admits and develops the distinction between clergy and laity.

51. *Against Heresies*, 3.11.8.

52. Ibid., 2.32.5. Eastwood *(The Priesthood of the Faithful*, 69) quotes this passage presumably as evidence that Irenaeus teaches the royal priesthood.

53. Eastwood, *The Royal Priesthood of the Faithful*, 68.

54. *Against Heresies*, 4.8.3. This passage contains the difficult text which *ANF* translates: "For the righteous possess the sacerdotal rank." However, from Antonius Melissa and John of Damascus has been derived an alternate reading which *ANF*, 1:471.6, translates: "Every righteous king possesses a priestly order."

According to Irenaeus, the church's "oblation" is "reckoned a pure sacrifice with God."[55] The New Covenant has not dispensed with sacrifice; rather "the species alone has been changed, inasmuch as the offering is now made, not by slaves, but by freemen."[56] Such sacrifices are not to be offered "merely to outward appearance," as the history or sacrifice from the age of Cain and Abel shows. They "do not sanctify a man, . . . but it is the conscience of the offerer that sanctifies the sacrifice when it is pure, and thus moves God to accept (the offering) as from a friend."[57] That Irenaeus regards the Eucharist as an offering or oblation of the church is clear; whether he reckons it *the* oblation may be debated. The Eucharist as thanksgiving constitutes "first-fruits of His own things," is offered with altar and temple in heaven, and glorifies God's name among the Gentiles.[58]

Irenaeus, who could have been more explicit about the priesthood of all Christians, nevertheless does acknowledge the same, together with the true sacrifices that Christians are to offer. For Irenaeus, the chief oblation is the Eucharist.

Clement of Alexandria tends to interpret the royal priesthood in the light of his Christian gnosis. Frequently he refers to the high priestly office of Jesus Christ. Melchizedek is "a synonym for righteousness and peace,"[59] and Jesus is the antitype of Isaac, who "was the son of Abraham, as Christ the Son of God, and a sacrifice as the Lord, but he was not immolated as the Lord."[60] As high priest, Jesus is identified with "the first Administrator of the universe,"[61] "prays for and exhorts men,"[62] alone knows "the worship of God,"[63] and reveals the good and the right.[64] Through adoption, he "has deigned to call us brethren and fellow-heirs."[65]

55. Ibid., 4.18.4; cf. 4.18.1.

56. Ibid., 4.18.2.

57. Ibid., 4.18.3.

58. Ibid., 4.18.4; 4.18.6; 4.17.5. Recent interpreters of Irenaeus have tended to agree that according to Irenaeus it is not Christ but gifts from the created order that are offered in the Eucharist. Cf. Wingren, *Man and the Incarnation*, 165–66; Ochagavía, *Visibile Patris Filius*, 137–38.

59. *The Stromata*, 4.25 *(ANF,* 2).

60. *The Instructor,* 1.5 *(ANF,* 2).

61. *The Stromata,* 7.2.

62. *Exhortation to the Heathen,* 12 *(ANF,* 2).

63. *The Stromata,* 2.5.

64. Ibid., 2.9.

65. Ibid., 2.22. Charles Bigg's *(The Christian Platonist of Alexandria,* 106) statement, "Clement speaks of Jesus as our High Priest, but only in the Philonic sense, as our Representative and Intercessor," seems dubious if it means that the High Priest,

Only in *The Stromata* does Clement specifically set forth the royal priesthood in its application to Christians. Here he exhibits the most distinctive aspect of his teaching on the priesthood, namely, that the high priesthood is to be identified with the gnostic or spiritual Christians. Of the gnostic Clement declares: "He is . . . the truly kingly man; he is the sacred high priest of God."[66] He elaborates on this gnostic priesthood:

> This is the function of the Gnostic, who has been perfected, to have converse with God through the great High Priest, being made like the Lord, up to the measure of his capacity, in the whole service of God, which tends to the salvation of men, through care of the beneficence which has us for its object; and on the other side through worship, through teaching and through beneficence in deeds.[67]

The gnostic's virtues of moderation such as "mildness, . . . philanthropy, and eminent piety" "are a sacrifice acceptable in the sight of God;"[68] and "'the humble heart with right knowledge is the holocaust of God.'"[69] The gnostics' progress will continue until "they come to the Good itself, to the Father's vestibule, so to speak, close to the great High Priest."[70] Clement gives to certain Old Testament passages pertaining to the Jewish priesthood and the tabernacle an allegorical interpretation leading to Christian gnosticism. The ark of the covenant is either "the eighth region and the world of thought, or God," the high priest's robe is "the symbol of the world of sense" and points to the Saviour's "ministry in the flesh," and "the broad gold mitre indicates the regal power of the Lord."[71] The gnostic high priest, having put off the created world, having been washed, "not in water" but "by the gnostic Word in his whole heart," and having risen "above other priests," enters into "face to face" "contemplation" and "hearing" of "the Word Himself."[72]

By emphasizing that God does not need that sacrifices be offered to Him, Clement stands with the apologists, of whom he is one. Indeed, "neither by sacrifices nor offerings, nor on the other hand by glory and honour,

according to Clement, is not fully and essentially the Son of God. Tollinton, *Clement of Alexandria*, 2:227, sees Clement's doctrine as a blending of the Epistle to the Hebrews with Egyptian ritual.

66. *The Stromata*, 7.7.
67. Ibid., 7.3.
68. Cf. Phil 4:18.
69. *The Stromata*, 7.3; cf. Ps 51:17, 19.
70. *The Stromata*, 7.7.
71. Ibid., 5.6.
72. Ibid.

is the Deity won over." Instead "we glorify Him who gave himself in sacrifice for us, we also sacrificing ourselves,"[73] and "the sacrifice which is acceptable to God is unswerving abstraction from the body and its passions."[74] Clement also identifies prayer as "the best and holiest" expression of Christian sacrifice and the "common voice" of the church at prayer as the "breathing together" (σύμπνοια) of the church. God does not desire "costly" material sacrifices but is pleased with "that compounded incense . . . which consists of many tongues and voices in prayer . . . and [is] brought together in praises."[75] Indeed, the gnostic's whole life is a holy festival. His sacrifices are prayers, praises, readings in the Scriptures before meals, psalms and hymns during meals and before bed, and prayers also again during night. By these he unites himself to the divine choir, from continual recollection, engaged in contemplation which has everlasting remembrance.[76]

Clement does not explicitly connect the priesthood of Christians with his concepts of Christians as a "third form" beyond Greeks and Jews[77] and of martyrdom as sacrifice.[78] He is quite specific in applying the priestly office and role to the gnostic Christian. Eastwood is correct in noting the importance of Clement's statement:

> Those . . . who have exercised themselves in the Lord's commandments, and lived perfectly and gnostically according to the Gospel, may be enrolled in the chosen body or the apostles. Such an one is in reality a presbyter of the Church, and a true minister (deacon) of the will of God, if he do and teach what is the Lord's; not as being ordained by men, nor regarded righteous because a presbyter, but enrolled in the presbyterate because righteous.[79]

Ascribing to Clement a concept of "hierarchical clericalism," Eastwood finds that Clement "does not hesitate to place the true spiritual gnostic on the same level as the cleric" and that the Christian gnostic's "spiritual qualifications" give to him "clerical honour, if not all the clerical functions."[80]

73. Ibid., 7.3.

74. Ibid., 5.11.

75. Ibid., 7.6. Völker *(Der wahre Gnostikerr nach Clemens Alexandrinus*, 549), says concerning Clement: "Er halt sich hier völlig in der neuteslamentlichen Linie: die Gebete sind das eigentliche Opfer der Christen, sie sind der Weihrauch, der vom Altar des Herzens aufsteigt."

76. *The Stromata*, 7.7.

77. Ibid., 6.5; 6.17.

78. Ibid., 4. esp. 13, 16, and 18.

79. Ibid., 6.13.

80. *The Royal Priesthood of the Faithful*, 72.

Taking Clement's thought in its entirety, however, one may more aptly ask to what extent Clement has narrowed or constricted gnostically rather than clerically the apostolic doctrine of the priesthood of all Christians.

In view of his relation to Clement of Alexandria and of his work as a biblical exegete, Origen would be expected to have formulated a more precise concept of the royal priesthood than Clement or to have made it an integral part of his thought. Such, however, is not the case, for seemingly only in his biblical homilies and scholia does he unambiguously teach the general priesthood. In *On First Principles* he mentions only the Jewish priesthood.[81]

Most of Origen's other extant writings contain passages in which the high priesthood of Jesus is mentioned. He is the high priest "through" whom but not "to" whom men are to pray,[82] for he is

> praying for those who pray and pleading with those who plead. He will not pray for us as His friends if we do not pray constantly through His intercession. Nor will He be an advocate with God for His followers if we do not obey His teaching; that we ought always to pray and not to faint.[83]

As high priest, Jesus "offered Himself in sacrifice;"[84] he is "the high priest of all angels;"[85] he who is asked to "bear our prayers and sacrifices and intercessions to the supreme God" is to be worshipped.[86] Both "the more intelligent people" and "the common folk" pray to the Creator "by the mediation of a high priest who has shown to men the pure way to worship God."[87] Hence men ought not to pray to demons.[88] Jesus is "the absolute Word holding converse with the Father"[89] and "restores all things to His Father's kingdom, and arranges that whatever defects exist in each part of creation shall be filled up so as to be full of the glory of the Father."[90]

In ascribing priesthood to men within Christianity, Origen makes a place for a limited or special priesthood, although not that of the Christian gnostic. This special priesthood is variously identified by Origen. In

81. 4.1.3.
82. *Prayer,* 15.4; O'Meara, *Origen,* 12.
83. Ibid., 10.2.
84. *Exhortation to Martyrdom,* 30.
85. *Against Celsus,* 5.4; Chadwick, *Origen.*
86. Ibid., 8.13.
87. Ibid., 7.46.
88. Ibid., 8.26.
89. *Commentary on the Gospel of Matthew,* 12.39 *(ANF,* 10).
90. *Commentary on the Gospel of John,* 1.40 *(ANF,* 10).

a context pertaining to the limitations on the apostolic granting of remission of certain sins,[91] he seems to ascribe priesthood to the apostles, who "know from their instruction by the Spirit for what sins, when, and how they must offer sacrifice" and "also the sins for which they must not do so."[92] Origen then decries those who "have taken to themselves powers beyond the priestly dignity, perhaps because they are unversed in the craft of the priesthood, and boast that they can forgive idolatries, and remit fornications and adulteries."[93] Furthermore, in introducing his *Commentary on the Gospel of John* he draws an analogy between the people of God under the Old Covenant who offered "tithes and first fruits" to God "through Levites and priests" who had "no possessions but tithes and first fruits" and "the whole people of Christ" who ought to provide support for Christian scholars "who devote themselves to the divine word and have no other employment but the service of God." According to Origen, "those who fulfill a more distinguished office than their kinsmen will perhaps be high-priests, according to the order of Aaron."[94] In yet a third context Origen identifies martyrs as "priests" who "offer themselves in sacrifice" both as priests "without blemish" and as victims "without blemish." Such martyrs "do not assist in vain at the altar of heaven, but procure for them that pray the remission of sins."[95] Origen even speaks of "heavenly elders" and "diviner high-priests who are ordained under the one High-Priest."[96] In summary, Origen's con-

91. I.e., idolatry, murder, and adultery. *Prayer,* 28.9–10.

92. Ibid., 28.9.

93. Ibid., 28.10, Jay, *Origen's Treatise on Prayer*. William Fairweather (*Origin and Greek Patristic Theology*, 198), comments: "According to Origen every Christian is a priest in virtue of the spiritual sacrifice which he offers. Through almsgiving, charity, self-mortification, martyrdom, we share in the sacrifice of Christ, and so in His priesthood. But it is only in this moral and figurative sense that any layman can be called a priest. Origen did not allow the treatment meted out to himself to lead him to belittle the office of the ministry. He magnifies it more than Clement does and shows a distinct leaning towards a restricted use of the priestly name. Those who bear it, however, must have a character in keeping with it." Cadiou, *Origen: His Life at Alexandria*, 311ff., defends Origen's high regard for ministerial ordination even by citing his criticisms of the conduct of the ordained, in an anti-Protestant context. Daniélou, *Origen*, 44–51, sees in the era of Origen (1) the existence of "two distinct types of authority," that of the Scripture-oriented *didaskaloi,* of whom *Origen* was a leading example, and that of the worship-oriented priests and (2) the incorporation of the former into the latter. Although acknowledging (pp. 44–45) in Origen "a certain depreciation of the whole clerical hierarchy," Daniélou (50) insists that "he does not at all deny that ordination to the priesthood confers special powers on the visible hierarchy."

94. 1.3.

95. *Exhortation to Martyrdom,* 30.

96. *Commentary on the Gospel of Matthew,* 12.20.

cept of the special priesthood is, variously identified with the apostles, the scholars, and the martyrs.

Only in a few passages does Origen specifically mention the priesthood of all Christians. These involve the quoting or paraphrasing of 1 Pet 2:5, 9 in contexts in which Origen is expounding other biblical texts.[97] While commenting on John 2:21, he clearly says: "The body is the Church, and we learn from Peter [1 Pet 2: 5] that it is a house of God, built of living stones, a spiritual house for a holy priesthood."[98] Similarly, when expounding Leviticus, he writes:

> He has given instructions so that we may know how we may approach God's altar. For it is an altar upon which we offer our prayers to God. That we may know, then, how we ought to offer them, He bids us put aside our soiled garments—the uncleanness of the flesh, the faults of character, the defilements of lust. Or do you not recognize that the priesthood has been given to you also, that is to the whole Church of God and the nation of believers? Hear how Peter says concerning believers: "chosen race," says he, "royal priesthood, holy nation, a people in possession" [1 Pet 2:9]. You have therefore a priesthood being a priestly nation. Therefore, you ought to offer God a sacrifice of praise, of prayers, of pity, or purity, of righteousness, of holiness.[99]. . . You have heard of the two sanctuaries; one as it were visible and open to the priests; the other invisible, to which the High Priest alone had access, while the rest remained outside. . . . And pray do not marvel that the sanctuary is open to priests only. For all who have been anointed with the unction of the sacred chrism have been made priests, just as Peter says to the whole church, "But you are a chosen race, a royal priesthood, a holy nation" [1 Pet 2:9]. You are, therefore, "a priestly race," and thus you draw near to the holy places.[100]

Origen, in distinction from his identification of apostles, of scholars, and of martyrs as special priests, mentions the priesthood of all Christians

97. When 1 Pet 2:5 or 2:9 is quoted by Origen, the emphasis does not always rest upon priesthood. In *Exhortation to Martyrdom,* 5, 1 Pet 2:9 is quoted, but the comments pertain to "the chosen generation." In *Against Celsus,* 5.10, Origen applies this text to the Hebrew people only. He quotes 1 Pet 2:5 in his argument that Christians do not build "lifeless and dead temples to the author of all life" but stress the temple of the body and its future resurrection *(Against Celsus,* 8.19).

98. *Commentary on the Gospel of John,* 10.23.

99. *Homilia in Levitieum,* 9.1, quoted by Eastwood, *The Royal Priesthood of the Faithful,* 79, and revised by the present author.

100. Ibid., 9.9.

only when commenting on or expounding Holy Scripture. Tertullian, on the other hand, alludes to it in his ethical and apologetic writings.

Priesthood for Tertullian, however, does not always mean the priesthood of all Christians. Frequently the North African alludes to pagan and to Jewish priests. Christians refuse "to offer sacrifice for the well-being of the emperor," although they customarily pray for him and other rulers.[101] In a Montanist treatise, he identifies the wearing of the soldier's crown with idolatry, for "crowns adorn the very doors, victims, and altars of idols; their ministers and priests wear them, also."[102] Tertullian chides non-fasting Christians in a pungent contrast with the pagans:

> Hence *you are* more irreligious, in proportion as a heathen is more conformable. He, in short, sacrifices his appetite to an idol-god; *you* to (the true) God will not. For to you your belly is god, and your lungs a temple, and your paunch a sacrificial altar, and your cook the priest, and your fragrant smell the Holy Spirit, and your condiments spiritual gifts, and your belching prophecy.[103]

In *On Idolatry*, Tertullian frequently refers to pagan priests and sacrifices.[104] Yet, he allows Christian attendance of "private" pagan marriage ceremonies provided that the ceremony be not entitled "assisting in the sacrifice" and that one is not "invited to act as priest and perform a sacrifice."[105] In reply to Jews, Tertullian interprets the history of sacrifices under the Old Covenant as being characterized by both "earthly sacrifices" which foreshadowed Israel and "spiritual sacrifices" which foreshadowed Christianity. "Thus, accordingly, the spiritual 'sacrifices of praise' are pointed to, and 'an heart contribulate' is demonstrated an acceptable sacrifice to God."[106] Tertullian frequently refers to Jesus Christ in priestly terms. He is "the Priest of God the Father unto eternity,"[107] "the universal high priest of the Father,"[108] "the high priest of salvation,"[109] and "the successful Suppliant of the Father"

101. *Apology*, 27–33, esp. 28.2; Daly, *Tertullian*.

102. *The Chaplet*, 10.9; Quain, *Tertullian*, 255.

103. *On Fasting*, 16 (*ANF*, 4).

104. Chs. 2, 5, 12, 13.

105. Ibid., 16; Greenslade, *Early Latin Theology*, 102.

106. *An Answer to the Jews*, 5, (*ANF*, 3). Tertullian quotes Gen 4:2–14; Mal 1:10–11; Ps 51:17; 50:14; and Isa 1:11–14.

107. Ibid., 14.

108. *Against Marcion*, 4.9; Evans, *Tertullian*. Cf. *Monogamy*, 7.

109. *On the Flesh of Christ*, 5; Evans, *Tertullian's Treatise on the Incarnation*, 21.

for remissible sins.[110] Priesthood is also a term that Tertullian applies to the clergy, especially in contexts in which he is arguing against digamy, or second marriages for Christians who are widows or widowers. He argues:

> The pagans have a priesthood of widows and celibates—though, of course, this is part of Satan's malevolence; and the ruler of this world, their *Pontifex Maximus*, is not permitted to marry a second time. How great purity must please God, since even the Enemy affects it![111]

Tertullian even claims to have found in Leviticus a text which reads "My priests shall not pluralize marriages," but modern scholars have been unable to locate such a text. Arguing as to a higher standard in Christianity, he asserts that

> with us the law which requires that none but monogamists are to be chosen for the order of the priesthood, is more comprehensive in its scope and exacting in details. So true is this that . . . there have been men deposed from office for digamy.[112]

Rejecting the view of his opponents that only ordained clerics are forbidden to remarry, the Montanists ask:

> Whence do we take our bishops and clergy? It is not from among all of us? And if not all are obliged to monogamy, whence will we have monogamists for the clergy? Are we to institute some special order of monogamists so that we may choose the clergy from its ranks?[113]

The question expects a negative answer, for Tertullian continues:

> Indeed, whenever we are minded to exalt ourselves with swelling pride at the expense of the clergy, then "we are all one" [cf. John 17:21; Gal 3:28], then we are all priests, for "He hath made us priests to God and His Father" [cf. Rev 1:6; 5:10]! But when we are called upon to be the peers of priests in discipline, we lay aside our fillets—and pair off![114]

Both in the latter passage in *Monogamy* and in a similar one in *An Exhortation to Chastity* one may see how Tertullian, accepting both the general

110. *On Modesty*, 19 (*ANF*, 4).

111. *To His Wife*, 1.7; LeSaint, *Tertullian*, 20.

112. *All Exhortation to Chastity*, 7.

113. *Monogamy*, 12.

114. Ibid.

priesthood of Christians and the special clerical priesthood, argues from one to the other. In the former he, assuming that clerical priests can marry only once, argues from the priesthood of all Christians in behalf of singular marriages for all Christians. In the latter he, assuming that clerics are in a special sense priests, argues from the general priesthood and the occasional clerical functions of laymen to singular marriages for all Christians. There must be no double standard! He says:

> It would be folly to imagine that lay people may do what priests may not. For are not we lay people also priests? It is written: "lie hath made us also a kingdom, and priests to God and His father" [Rev 1:61].[115]

Moreover, since lay people in cases of necessity do baptize and offer the Eucharist, "How much more serious a crime is it for a lay digamist to perform sacerdotal functions, when a priest who becomes a digamist is removed from his priestly office!"[116]

In a context utterly distinct from the issue of digamy, Tertullian expounds the priesthood of all Christians in terms of prayer:

> For this is the spiritual oblation which has wiped out the ancient sacrifices. . . . We are the true worshippers and the true priests, who, praying in the Spirit, in the Spirit offer a sacrifice of prayer as an oblation which is God's own and is well pleasing (to him), that in fact which he has sought after, which he has provided for himself.[117]

Tertullian is, therefore, both a witness to the general priesthood of all Christians as taught in the New Testament and by Christian writers of the second and early third centuries and a pioneer in applying to the ordained clergy in a very special sense the category and language of priesthood. James Morgan has interpreted this dual usage as follows:

> Tertullian is the first, who expressly advances sacerdotal claims on behalf of the Christian ministry and calls it "sacerdotium,"

115. *An Exhortation to Chastity*, 7.

116. Ibid.

117. *On the Prayer*, 28; Evans, *Tertullian's Tract on the Prayer*, 37. Roberts, *The Theology of Tertullian*, 188–89, is hardly justified in stating that this "passage may be understood in a figurative sense, so as not to oppose the view . . . of the office of the bishop as a priest" and concluding that Tertullian's question, "Are not we lay people also priests?" involves "the notion of the layman as a literal priest."

although he also emphatically affirms the universal priesthood of all believers.[118]

The extant writings of Hippolytus afford no evidence of his teaching the priesthood of all Christians. In the fragments from his *Commentary On Daniel* Jesus is called "the perfect King and Priest," "the Priest of priests," and "the heavenly Priest."[119] In *The Apostolic Tradition,* bishops are referred to three times as God's "high priests," presbyters offering to God "the bread and the cup" are identified as "priests," the deacon is said to be "not ordained for a priesthood," and the Holy Spirit is called "the high priestly Spirit."[120]

Four of the Apostolic Fathers recognize that Christians offer to God "spiritual sacrifices." Although the apologists characteristically refute any necessity for offering sacrifices, Justin Martyr identifies Christians as "the true priestly family of God" and Gentile prayers as acceptable to God. Melito of Sardis points to the *locus classicus,* 1 Pet 2:9. Obliquely acknowledging the general priesthood, Irenaeus regards the Eucharist as the chief sacrifice offered by Christians. Clement of Alexandria limits the general priesthood to the gnostics or pneumatics. Origen at various times identifies apostles, scholars, and martyrs as "priests" but in his exegetical works clearly teaches the priesthood of all Christians when quoting 1 Pet 2:5, 9. Tertullian applies the sacerdotal category and language both to all Christians and to clerics, and by the latter usage, in which he is joined by Hippolytus, he prepares the way for Cyprian's exclusive application or the term "priests" to the clergy, especially the bishops.

118. Morgan, *The Importance of Tertullian in the Development of Christian Dogma,* 122. Quoting Hatch, *The Organization of the Early Christian Churches,* 142, Morgan concludes that the general acceptance of the clerical priesthood and the expression of its corollaries came about a century and a half after Tertullian's time. Adolf Harnack (*A History of Dogma,* 2:129) associates Tertullian's concept of priesthood more closely with that of Irenaeus than with that of Cyprian.

119. *Fragments from the Commentary on Daniel,* 2.14, 15, 17 (*ANF,* 5).

120. 3.4; 9.11; 30; 4.11; 9.2; 3.5, Dix *The Treatise on the Apostolic Tradition of St Hippolytus of Rome.*

6

"The Priesthood of All Christians: From Cyprian to John Chrysostom" (1988)[1]

The present study, which attempts to trace the Christian doctrine of the priesthood of all Christians from Cyprian in the mid-third century AD to John Chrysostom at the end of the fourth century, builds upon two previously published studies by the same author.

In "The Biblical Doctrine of the Priesthood of the People of God,"[2] the author interpreted the corporate priesthood of Israel in the Old Testament, with special reference to Ex 19:4–6a, and, after summarizing the application of sacerdotal language to Jesus, identified those New Testament texts (1 Pet 2:4–10; Rev 1:5b–6; 5:9–10) which specifically teach that all Christians are priests, and interpreted the central function of the priesthood of all Christians as being the offering of "spiritual sacrifices" to God, such as in worship, witness, stewardship, and service (cf. Rom 12:1;15:16; Phil 2:17; 4:17–18; Heb 13:15–16).

In "The Pre-Cyprianic Doctrine of the Priesthood of All Christians"[3] the author concluded:

> Four of the Apostolic Fathers [*Didache,* Clement of Rome, Ignatius, Polycarp] recognize that Christians offer to God "spiritual sacrifices." Although the apologists characteristically refute any necessity for offering sacrifices, Justin Martyr identifies

1. This article first appeared in *Southwestern Journal of Theology* 30 (1988) 22–33.
2. Garrett, "The Biblical Doctrine of the Priesthood of the People of God," 137–49.
3. Garrett, "The Pre-Cyprianic Doctrine of the Priesthood of All Christians," 45–61.

> Christians as "the true priestly family of God" and Gentile prayers as acceptable to God. Melito of Sardis points to the *locus classicus,* 1 Peter 2:9. Obliquely acknowledging the general priesthood, Irenaeus regards the Eucharist as the chief sacrifice offered by Christians. Clement of Alexandria limits the general priesthood to the Gnostics or pneumatics. Origen at various times identifies apostles, scholars, and martyrs as "priests" but in his exegetical works clearly teaches the priesthood of all Christians when quoting 1 Peter 2:5, 9. Tertullian applies the sacerdotal category and language both to all Christians and to clerics, and by the latter usage, in which he is joined by Hippolytus, he prepares the way for Cyprian's exclusive application of the term "priests" to the clergy, especially the bishops[4]

The writings of Cyprian, the bishop of Carthage in the middle of the third century, constitute a major turning point in the history of the concept of the priesthood of all Christians. Prior to Cyprian, the concept had a place in patristic thought despite and alongside the emergence of the concept of the clerical priesthood. After Cyprian's delineation of a doctrine of the clerical priesthood, the latter attained to dominance in patristic usage even though the general priesthood continued to appear in patristic literature.[5]

The present study investigates the concept of the priesthood of all Christians and its corollary, the offering of spiritual sacrifices, in Cyprian and in the Christian writers between Cyprian and the era of John Chrysostom, Jerome, and Augustine of Hippo Regius that began at the end of the fourth century and the outset of the fifth. The other writers of the third century will be treated briefly, and then the fourth-century authors will be arranged in linguistic-geographical fashion: Greek writers in Egypt, Greek writers in Asia Minor, Greek writers in Syria-Palestine, one Syrian writer, and the Latin writers of northern Africa, Gaul, Sicily-Italy, and Spain.

4. Ibid., 61.

5. Lightfoot, *St. Paul's Epistle to the Philippians*, 256, observed that the application of *sacerdos* to the clergy, a step completed in Cyprian, made the "transition from the universal sacerdotalism of the New Testament to the particular sacerdotalism of a later age." More specifically, although Tertullian had been able to use priestly language both in reference to all Christians and to the clergy, Cyprian abandoned the former and developed the latter.

Cyprian

Cyprian alludes to the contemporary sacrifices to idols,[6] especially those imperial sacrifices enjoined under Decius and refused by the Christian confessors.[7] Likewise, at times Cyprian refers to the priesthood of Christ. In his *Testimonies against the Jews,* one of his earliest writings, he contends for a new sacrifice and a new priesthood, manifestly that of Christ, but does not develop the christological implications.[8] Elsewhere Christ is called "a priest of the Most High God"[9] and "the advocate for our sins before the Father."[10]

Cyprian's prevailing usage of *sacerdos* and *sacerdotium* is in reference to the clergy, especially the bishops Maurice Bévenot in his earlier translation of *The Lapsed* translates *sacerdos* as "bishop" rather as "priest."[11] E. W. Watson had previously concluded that *sacerdos* is one of four[12] terms used by Cyprian for "bishops," that in his writings "there is no passage where *sacerdos* must . . . be equivalent to presbyter," and there are five passages in Cyprian where *sacerdos* may mean "presbyter."[13] Cyprian, for example, writes that Cornelius, bishop of Rome, "ascended to the sublime summit of the priesthood [i.e., the episcopate] through all of the steps of religious service" and "suffered whatever he could suffer and conquered first by his priesthood the tyrant afterwards overcome by arms and war."[14] He refers to "the faith and religion of the sacerdotal office which we exercise."[15] In defending himself as a bishop against his critic Florentinus, Cyprian declares that, unless he be absolved from the charges, "for six years already the

6. *The Dress of Virgins,* 11.

7. *The Lapsed,* 8.

8. Bk. 1, propositions 16, 17; cf. bk. 2.

9. *Letters,* 63:4 (Fathers of the Church [FC hereafter], 41:204). The enumeration of Cyrpian's Letters will here follow the scheme of Pearson, Fell, Hartel, Lacey, and Deferrari rather than the scheme of Rigault, Baluze, Migne, and Wallis.

10. *The Lord's Prayer,* 3 (FC, 36:128).

11. *St. Cyrian: The Lapsed; The Unity of the Catholic Church* (Ancient Christian Writers, 25). According to Bévenot, *sacerdos* "expresses the bishop's sacrificial and mediatorial functions; *episcopios,* his hierarchical position" (92, fn. 132). In his later translation, *De Lapsis and De Mcclesiae Catbolicae Unitate,* Bévenot made similar renderings of *sacersos* (35, fn. 3; 39, m.3).

12. The other three are *episcopus, autistes,* and *praepositus.*

13. Watson, "The Style and Language of St. Cyprian," 4:257–60. Yet, Sister Rose Bernard Donna (FC, 51) customarily rendered *sacerdos* as "priest."

14. *Letters,* 55:9 (FC, 51:139).

15. Ibid., 74:8 (FC, 51:291); cf. 73:26 (FC, 51:285).

brotherhood have not had a bishop, and the people a leader, nor the flock a shepherd, nor the Church a ruler, nor Christ a bishop, nor God a priest!"[16]

Cyprian associates "priests" and "a priesthood" variously with the martyrs, the confessors, the virgins, the lapsed, and the schismatics. God's priest, that is, the bishop, is to heed the legitimate requests of confessors and those awaiting martyrdom for the remission of sins of others.[17] Confessors are not to speak ill "against the brethren and priests of God."[18] The clergy are to offer oblations and sacrifices for the commemoration of the martyrs and for the confessors.[19] Virgins who have forsaken their virginity are rebuked for disobeying "the priests of God."[20] The priestly authority of the bishop is undermined by the clamor for immediate restoration of the lapsed.[21] Even some presbyters, "not reserving for the bishop the honor of his priesthood and of his see, have already begun to be in communion with lapsed and to offer for them the Holy Sacrifice and to give them the Eucharist. . . ."[22] Felicissimus and his associates formerly sought "to arm a portion of the broken brotherhood against the priesthood of God," and "have now turned with their poisoned deceit to the destruction of the lapsed."[23] Similarly,

> . . . Basilides and Martial, contaminated by the certificates of idolatry and bound by the consciousness of heinous deeds, ought not to govern the bishopric and administer the priesthood of God.[24]

Revolt against priestly authority is, according to Cyprian, wrong.

> Another altar cannot be set up nor a new priesthood be made contrary to the one altar and the one priesthood. Whoever has gathered elsewhere scatters.[25]

But "salutary remedies" for the lapsed are available from the priest-bishop.[26] The schismatics in the baptismal controversy are identified as those

16. Ibid., 66:5 (FC, 51:226).
17. *The Lapsed,* 18; 36.
18. *The Unity of the Church,* 21 (FC, 36:117).
19. *Letters,* 12:2; 39:3.
20. Ibid., 4:5 (FC, 51:14).
21. *The Lapsed,* 22.
22. *Letters,* 17:2 (FC, 51:50).
23. Ibid., 43:2 (FC, 51:107).
24. Ibid., 67:1 (FC, 51:232).
25. Ibid., 43:5 (FC, 51:109).
26. *The Lapsed,* 14 (FC, 36:69).

"who erect false altars and unlawful priesthoods and sacrilegious sacrifices and false names."[27]

> Hence the bond of the Lord's peace is broken; hence fraternal charity is violated; hence truth is adulterated, unity is broken, there is a plunging into heresies and schisms, when priests are disparaged, when bishops are envied. . . .[28]

Concerning the schismatic, Cyprian asks:

> Does he seem to himself to be with Christ, who acts contrary to the priests [i.e., bishops] of Christ, who separates himself from association with His clergy and His people? . . . An enemy of the altar, a rebel against the sacrifice of Christ, . . . despising the bishops and abandoning the priests of God, he dares to set up another altar, . . . to profane the truth of the Lord's offering by false sacrifices. . . .[29]

How does the Carthaginian bishop understand the role of the qualifications of the priest-bishop? G. S. M. Walker has noted that Cyprian "followed Clement of Rome in equating bishops with Old Testament priests, but made presbyters and not deacons the equivalent of Levites."[30] Repeatedly, Cyprian cites the revolt of Korah, Dathan, and Abiram against Moses and Aaron and their destruction (Numbers 16) as precedent for and warning against rejection of priestly authority.[31] In writing to Cornelius of Rome, Cyprian expresses his certitude that Christ "both appoints and protects [His] priests" and refers to "the Chair of Peter and the principal Church whence sacerdotal unity has sprung."[32] The significance of the priest-bishop in Cyprian's writings is due partly to Cyprian's tendency to constrict the scope of the Church's oblations to the eucharist and to interpret the eucharist as a sacrifice of Christ's passion.[33] Cyprian rebuked the covetousness of

27. *Letters,* 69:1 (FC, 51:245).

28. *Jealousy and Envy,* 6 (FC, 36:298).

29. *The Unity of the Church,* 17 (FC, 38:113).

30. Walker, *The Churchmanship of St. Cyprian,* 36.

31. *Letters,* 3:1; 69:8; 75:16.

32. Ibid., 59:6, 14 (FC, 51.178, 186).

33. Ibid., 37:1; 63:1, 4, 14; 76:3. The word "tendency" is used because in *The Lord's Prayer* Cyprian does retain the idea of prayer as sacrifice. Harnack, *History of Dogma,* 2:136, noted that Cyprian was both "the first to associate the specific offering, i.e., the Lord's Supper, with the specific priesthood" and "the first to designate the *passio domini*s, nay the *sanguis Christi* and the *dominica hostia,* as the object of the eucharistic offering." Bernard, "The Cyprianic Doctrine of the Ministry," 228, stated that there is no doubt "that Cyprian's doctrine of priesthood meant, primarily, a doctrine of *sacrifice*"

priest-bishops[34] and emphasized a conciliar decision that those "honored by the divine priesthood and consecrated for the clerical ministry" should not be named in wills as administrators of property.[35] Humility is a requisite for priests,[36] and only those should be ordained priest-bishops who "may be able to be heard in the prayers which they offer for the safety of the people of the Lord."[37] Priestly ordinations "ought not to be performed except with the knowledge of the people present."[38] Even in his own troubled era, Cyprian was confident, there remained "a portion of priests which has not at all succumbed to the ruin of affairs and the shipwrecks of faith."[39] Amid imperial persecution and schismatic conflict and their effects, Cyprian, a functioning bishop, elaborated a concept of the particular priesthood of bishops that was to influence later Christian thought, especially in the Latin West.[40]

Cyprian does not specifically teach that the priesthood belongs to and is exercised by the whole people of God.[41] Rarely does he quote those New

---

and concluded that the "office of a bishop is primarily a sacrificial office, as was that of the Jewish priests."

34. *The Lapsed,* 6.

35. *Letters,* 1:1–2 (FC, 51:3–5).

36. Ibid., 66:3.

37. Ibid., 67:2 (FC, 51:233); cf. 70:2.

38. Ibid., 67:4 (FC, 51:234).

39. Ibid., 67:8 (FC, 51:237).

40. Eastwood, *The Royal Priesthood of the Faithful,* identified Cyprian's contribution as follows:

> [H]e conceived that the bishops were a *special priesthood* and had a *special sacrifice to offer.* So the High Priestly Race gave place to a High Priestly Class, and the spiritual sacrifices gave place to an actual sacrifice offered to God in the Eucharist. That the latter was conceived of as something other than a purely spiritual sacrifice is beyond dispute. This transition cannot be regarded as a slight deviation in the Church's teaching on priesthood, it is rather the antithesis of the interpretation which was prevalent in the first two centuries (80–81).

Eastwood concluded that "Cyprian's interpretation of the Eucharist effectively obscured this idea of the universal priesthood" by positing a bishop-priest "with independent, exclusive and dominical powers" to be exercised "in the service of the Eucharist" (84). Furthermore, Cyprian's concept of the clerical priesthood prepared the "soil" that "enabled the plant of sacerdotalism to thrive for a thousand years," and the universal priesthood, according to Eastwood, would not "be revived by the Church until the appearance of Martin Luther in the sixteenth century" (87). Some Catholic patristic scholars, e.g., David Balas, O.C., reject Eastwood's conclusion as the loss of the doctrine of universal priesthood.

41. Certain writers on Cyprian's thought have sought to defend or explain his silence on the priesthood of all Christians. Benson, *Cyprian,* 38–39, asserted that "there is no sufficient reason to question his belief in it." More dubious is Benson's denial that the "universal Lay-priesthood" is "a specially Christian doctrine" on the basis that "it

Testament texts most central to the royal priesthood and its sacrificial functions.[42] When referring to Christians as "the elect people of God," Cyprian does not allude to "the kingdom of priests."[43] Specific terms are used for the non-ordained members of the church; *populus* is most often used, while *plebs* and *laici* are to be found.[44]

Cyprian, however, clearly retains two essential aspects of the pre-Cyprianic doctrine of the priesthood of all Christians, namely, prayer and Christian deeds of mercy as sacrifices to God. In expounding the petition for forgiveness of sins in the Lord's Prayer, he says:

> For God has ordered us to be peace-makers and of one heart and of one mind in His house. . . . Thus, neither does God receive the sacrifice of the dissident, and He orders him to turn back from the altar and first be reconciled with his brother, so that by pacifying prayers God can also be pacified. The greater sacrifice to God is our peace and fraternal concord and a people united in the unity of the Father and of the Son and of the Holy Spirit.[45]

Cyprian emphasizes that "Our Father" rather than "My Father" appears in the Lord's Prayer.

> Our prayer is public and common, and when we pray, we pray not for one but for the whole people, because we, the whole people, are one. God, the Teacher of prayer and concord, who taught unity, thus wished one to pray for all, just as He Himself bore all in one.[46]

Regarding the acceptance of sacrifices, Cyprian observes:

---

is coeval with the religious instinct of mankind." Bernard, "The Cyprianic Doctrine of the Ministry," 238, wrote in the context of the administration of sacraments concerning Cyprian:

> Neither he nor any Catholic would have challenged, or found difficulty in, the New Testament doctrine of the priesthood of the whole Christian people, clergy and laity. The Church is a priestly body. But it does not follow that the lay part of the Church has a priestly prerogative, when distinguished and treated as separate from the clerical part.

42. Cyprian does not quote 1 Pet 2:9–10; Rev 1:6; Heb 13:15–16; Rom 15:16; and Phil 2:17. He does quote Phil 4:18 in *The Lord's Prayer,* 20; Rev 5:6–10 in *Testimonies against the Jews,* 2:15; and Rom 12:1–2 in *An Exhortation to Martyrdom,* 8, and in *Letters* 76:3. Cf. "A Table of the Texts of Scripture Cited by St. Cyprian . . ," in Marshall, *The Genuine Works of St. Cyprian,* 2:192.

43. *Letters,* 63:8.

44. Cf. Watson, "The Style and Language of St. Cyprian," 257.

45. *The Lord's Prayer,* 23 (FC, 36:147–48).

46. Ibid., 8 (FC, 36:132).

> For even in the sacrifices which Abel and Cain first offered God did not look upon their gifts but upon their hearts, so that he who pleased Him in his heart pleased Him in his gift.[47]

Likewise, he comments:

> Your debts will be forgiven you, when you yourself shall forgive; your sacrifices will be accepted, when you shall come to God as a peacemaker.[48]

In a comment on Phil 4:18, Cyprian declares that the Apostle Paul teaches that acts of mercy in behalf of the poor are "sacrifices to God."[49]

It will not be feasible hereafter to trace in detail the concept of the clerical priesthood in the writings of those Christian authors who lived after the time of Cyprian, but only to take note of concepts of the clerical priesthood when these particularly affected the concept of the priesthood of all Christians.

Lactantius, Victorinus, and Methodius

Between Cyprian and the outbreak of the Arian controversy, there were only three Christian writers whose extant works display an awareness of the priesthood of all Christians—Lactantius the apologist, Victorinus the commentator on the Apocalypse, and Methodius of Olympus and Tyre, who in a homily alluded to the royal priesthood. Lactantius, in addition to his identification of Jesus as the "great Priest,"[50] indicates the nature of spiritual sacrifices:

> There are two things which ought to be offered, the gift and the sacrifice; the gift as a perpetual offering, the sacrifice for a time. But with those who by no means understand the nature of the Divine Being, a gift is anything which is wrought of gold or silver; likewise anything which is woven of purple and silk: a sacrifice is a victim, and as many things as are burnt upon the altar. But God does not make use either of the one or the other, because He is free from corruption, and that is altogether corruptible. Therefore, in each case, that which is incorporeal must

47. Ibid., 24 (FC, 36:148).

48. *Jealousy and Envy,* 17 (FC, 36:308).

49. *The Lord's Prayer,* 33 (FC, 36:156). Cf. Pontius, *Life of Cyprian,* 7–10, for an account of Cyprian's encouragement and organization of Christians in Carthage to help pagans as well as Christians during a plague.

50. *The Divine Institutes,* 4:14 (ANF, 7:114).

> be offered to God, for He accepts this. His offering is innocency of soul; His sacrifice praise and a hymn . . . For we ought to sacrifice to God in word; inasmuch as God is the Word, as He Himself confessed. Therefore, the chief ceremonial in the worship of God is praise from the mouth of a just man directed towards God.[51]

Victorinus of Petau interprets Rev 1:6 as referring to "a church of all believers; as also the Apostle Peter says: A holy nation, a royal priesthood' (1 Pet 2:9)."[52] Concerning Rev 5:8–9, he says:

> The proclamation of the Old Testament associated with the New, points out the Christian people singing a new song, that is, bearing their confession publicly. It is a new thing that the Son of God should become man. It is a new thing to ascend into the heavens with a body. It is a new thing to give remission of sins to men. It is a new thing for men to be sealed with the Holy Spirit. It is a new thing to receive the priesthood of sacred observance, and to look for a kingdom of unbounded promise. The harp, and the chord stretched on its wooden frame, signifies the flesh of Christ linked with the wood of the passion. The phial signifies the Confession, and the race of the new Priesthood. But it is the praise of many angels, yea, of all, the salvation of all, and the testimony of the universal creation, bringing to our Lord thanksgiving for the deliverance of men from the destruction of death.[53]

Methodius, in *The Banquet, or a Treatise on Chastity,* interprets symbolically the golden altar in the Holy of Holies of the Old Testament tabernacle as a type of later virginity,[54] but, elsewhere, in the ninth of nine encomiums to Jerusalem as a city and as the Church of God he declares in a paraphrase of 1 Pet 2:9:

> Hail, thou people of the Lord, thou chosen generation, thou royal priesthood, thou holy nation, thou peculiar people—show forth His praises who hath called you out of darkness into His marvelous light; and for His mercies glorify Him.[55]

51. Ibid., 6:25 (ANF, 7:192–93).
52. *Commentary on the Apocalypse of the Blessed John* (ANF, 7:344).
53. Ibid., (ANF, 7:350).
54. 5:8 (ACW, 27:89).
55. *Oration concerning Simeon and Anna,* 13 (ANF, 6:393).

The Christian writers who alluded to the royal priesthood between the outbreak of the Arian controversy and the advent of writers such as John Chrysostom, Jerome, and Augustine of Hippo Regius may now be studied in respect to their linguistic and geographical identity.

Greek Christian Authors in Egypt

Certain of the Greek writers of Egypt provide evidence that the royal priesthood of all Christians was not an extinct concept during the fourth century. In view of the large number of his extant writings, the references of Athanasius to the theme under investigation may be said to be proportionally few. In addition to frequent references to the clerical priesthood and to the concentrated attention given to the high priestly office of Jesus,[56] Athanasius does twice mention common prayer, spiritual sacrifices, and the royal priesthood *per se*. Concerning the Eucharistic sacrifice at Easter, he writes:

> And the sacrifice is not offered in one place, but "in every nation, incense and a pure sacrifice is offered unto God." So when in like manner from all in every place, praise and prayer shall ascend to the gracious and good Father, when the whole Catholic Church which is in every place, with gladness and rejoicing, celebrates together the same worship to God, when all men in common send up a song of praise and say, Amen; how blessed will it not be, my brethren! Who will not, at that time, be engaged, praying rightly?[57]

Athanasius concludes a discussion of the problem of the relation of the Mosaic or Pentateuchal commandment of sacrifice and the prophetic criticism of sacrifices by asserting that sacrifices were ordained in Israel after the defection to Baal and declaring:

> Thus then, being before instructed and taught, they learned not to do service to anyone but the Lord. They attained to know what time the shadow would last, and not to forget the time that was at hand, in which no longer should the bullock of the herd be a sacrifice to God, nor the ram of the flock, nor the he-goat, but all these things should be fulfilled in a purely spiritual manner, and by constant prayer and upright conversation, with godly words. . ..[58]

56. *Discourses against the Arians*, 2.14:7–10.

57. *Festal Letter* 11:11 (Nicene and Post-Nicene Fathers, 2d series, 4:537).

58. *Festal Letter* 19:4 (NPNF, 2d ser., 4:546).

Spiritual sacrifices include or are properly accompanied by "distribution to the poor."[59] When commenting on Ps 73:2 [i.e., 74:2] Athanasius connects the redeemed "'inheritance' prepared for the kingdom" with the "royal priesthood" of 1 Pet 2:9,[60] and in commenting on Ps 67:30 [i.e., 68:29] he declares:

> His "temple" means the Church, and the "kings" are indeed those who have believed in Christ, following that which has been spoken of them: "But you are a royal priesthood" [1 Pet 2:9]. It therefore refers to those who through faith have been called from the earthly temple, which is the Church, to the Jerusalem above, that they themselves may offer gifts, to be sure spiritual gifts.[61]

The *Prayer Book* attributed to Serapion of Thmuis refers to the eucharistic sacrifice as "this living sacrifice"—language probably drawn from Rom 12:1.[62]

Didymus the Blind in his comments on Ps 49 [i.e., 50]:23 identifies the divinely revealed "way" as being "not through the sacrifices of corporeal victims but through the divine 'sacrifice of praise.'"[63] On Ps 50:21 [i.e., 51:19] he declares:

> This verse discloses that righteousness which through faith in Jesus Christ calls together all the believers. Yet, that very righteousness is a spiritual offering and a spiritual sacrifice; having the same meaning is that verse, "Offer the sacrifice of righteousness"[Ps 4:6; i.e., 4:5]; then also "they place above the altar" spiritual "bulls," not occupying the earth and pulling ploughs but souls which are none other than the souls of the martyrs, seen above the altar and there offered after the fashion of bulls. For in Revelation [6:9] there are seen beneath the heavenly altar the souls of those slain on account of the name of Jesus and his testimony.[64]

In commenting on 1 Pet 2:4, Didymus connects "spiritual offering" with Ps 69:14 [i.e., 69:13?] and with Ps 4:6 [i.e., 4:5] and identifies Jesus as "the High

59. *Festal Letter* 45 (NPNF, 2d ser., 4:553).

60. *Expositiones in Psalmos*, in Migne, *Patrologia Graeca*, 27:334. An Egyptian liturgical fragment of undetermined date uses the term "reasonable sacrifice" in a similar Eucharistic prayer. Cf. Palmer, "Papyrus Fragment of the Araphora of S. Mark," 2:67.

61. *Expositions in Psalmos*, in Migne, *PG*, 27:302.

62. 1, 1; *Bishop Sarapion's Prayer-Book*, Wordsworth, 62.

63. *Expositio in Psalmos*, in Migne, *PG*, 39:1394.

64. Ibid., 39:1399.

Priest" "who after the order of Melchizedek abides in eternity."[65] The same Egyptian writer commented on 1 Pet 2:9 as follows:

> According to the old arrangement of the law there was a kingship and there was a priestly class; the priestly descended from Levi, and the royal class descended from Judah. The one reigned among the Hebrews, and the other possessed the priesthood. To that order, therefore, the Gospel succeeded, establishing one and the same priest and king. For Christ is both. Concerning Him it was said: "You are a priest forever" [Ps 109:4; i.e., 110:4]; and again, "I have raised him to be a king with justice." But also He said of himself: "But I have been appointed king by Him" [Ps 2:6], that is, "by God." Since these things were thus arranged, it was necessarily determined by Him who is at the same time King and Priest that there would be a chosen people, at the same time both royal and priestly.[66]

Thus Didymus, evidently unaware, as were other patristic writers, that 1 Pet 2:9 was derived from Exod 19:5–6, sees the concept of the royal priesthood as a derived conflation of the royal and priestly offices of Christ.

The only Greek writer from Egyptian monasticism, whether anchorite or coenobitic, whose extant works clearly allude to the royal priesthood is Macarius the Elder, author *of Fifty Spiritual Homilies.* Antony refers to the offering by Christians of themselves to God as a sacrifice,[67] but seemingly does not allude to Christians as priests. *The Sayings of the Fathers* and later the works of Isidore of Pelusium afford evidence of the completely clerical usage of the language and concept of priesthood.[68]

Macarius expounds the high priestly office of Jesus not only in the traditional context of the offering of himself as sacrifice and the cleansing of men's consciences from the "leprosy of sin" but also in relation to the Christian's death to sinful passions.[69] Similar to the royal priesthood, though not identical, is the concept of "the royal pearl" in Macarius:

> The great, costly, royal pearl, which serves for a king's crown, is suitable only for a king, and only a king can wear it. Another

65. *In Epistolam S. Petri Primant Enarratio,* in Migne, *PG,* 39:1762.

66. Ibid., 39:1763.

67. *Epistola* 2, *Ad Arsinoitas,* 8, in Migne, *PG,* 40:985; *Epistola* 3, 6, in Migne, *PG,* 40:991; *Epistola* 5, 1, in Migne, *PG,* 40:994; *Epistola* 7, in Migne, *PG,* 40:1018–19. Both *hostiam* and *sacrificium* are used in the parallel Latin translation.

68. *Epistolarum Libri Quinqué de Interpretation Divinae Scripturae, passim,* in Migne, *PG,* 78:177–1646.

69. Macarius, *Fifty Spiritual Homilies of St. Macarius the Egyptian,* 32:5; 44:4; 1:6.

> man is not allowed to wear such a pearl. So unless a man is begotten by the royal Spirit of God, and is made to be of the royal family of heaven and a child of God, according as it is written, "But as many as received Him, to them gave He power to become children of God" [John 1:12], he cannot wear the costly pearl of heaven, the image of the inexpressible light, which is the Lord, being no king's son. For those who possess and wear the purple, live and reign with Christ forever.[70]

Macarius alludes directly to the royal priesthood at least four times; the eschatological nature of the royal priesthood appears thrice.

> Christianity, then, is no ordinary thing. . . . Recognize therefore thy nobility, that thou art called to kingly dignity, "a chosen generation, a royal priesthood, and a holy nation" [1 Pet 2:9]. The mystery of Christianity is foreign to this world. The visible glory of the emperor and his wealth are earthly, and perishable, and passing away; but that kingdom and wealth are divine things, heavenly and glorious, never to pass away or be dissolved. For they reign together with the heavenly King, in the heavenly church. . . .[71]

Again, Macarius says:

> In the Old Testament, Moses and Aaron, when they held the priesthood, had much to suffer. . .. Peter was the successor of Moses, entrusted with Christ's new church and with the true priesthood; for we have now a baptism of fire and the Spirit, and a circumcision in the heart.[72]

Macarius is even more specific:

> To sum it all up, we are not yet "a chosen generation, a royal priesthood, a holy nation, a peculiar people" [1 Pet 2:9], forasmuch as we are still "serpents, a generation of vipers" [Matt 23:33].[73]

First Peter 2:9 is also quoted by Macarius in a passage in which he has referred to the writing of the law on the hearts (Jer 31:33).[74]

70. Ibid., 4:23.
71. Ibid., 27:4.
72. Ibid., 26:23.
73. Ibid., 25:5.
74. *Epistola* 2, in Migne, *PG*, 34:415.

Evagrius of Pontus in his *Centuries* identifies Christ as being high priest after his humanity; the author of the accompanying commentary, Rabban mar Babhai, says:

> "He implores God for all rational creatures," as it stands written, "He sits on the right hand of God and prays for us" [Rom 8:34], which means He advances all rational creatures, moves them to the summit, in which He separates them from evil and brings them from evil and brings them to foreknowledge through His preaching and the commands which He has given to the Church, of which He is Head.[75]

The more rational and mystical approach of Evagrius is evident in his references to the priesthood ascribed to Christians. The three altars are explained by the commentator in reference to the offering of silent prayer by those "who have taken upon themselves that inexpressible light," the worship that includes psalm singing, study of Scripture, and verbal praying, and the deeds of mercy and love to the needy.[76] In the headdress of the Aaronic priesthood is to be seen the fearless espousal of the truth by the Christian priest,[77] and the shoulder gown of Jewish priests suggests "that excellent state of the soul which shows itself in conduct" and which is a mark of the "true priest of God."[78]

Both Athanasius and Didymus have a residue of emphasis on spiritual sacrifices. Both Athanasius and Macarius interpret eschatologically the royal priesthood. For Evagrius the mystical way to God involves silent prayer, worship, and diakonal service.

Cappadocian Fathers

Among the extant Greek Christian writings of the fourth century from Asia Minor, only those by the three Cappadocian Fathers seem to contain references to the priesthood of all Christians, and even here such references are far less numerous than the usages of the language of priesthood to indicate the clergy.

Basil of Caesarea frequently alludes to ministers or the clergy as "priests," as, for example, when he writes:

75. *Centuries*, 5:46, in Frankenberg, *Evagrius Ponticus*, 337.

76. Ibid., 2:57, in Frankenberg, *Euagrius Ponticus*, 171.

77. Ibid., 4:48, in Frankenberg, *Evagrius Ponticus*, 293.

78. Ibid., 4:50, in Frankenberg, *Evagrius Ponticus*, 297.

> Let not the clerical rank make thee proud, but rather let it humble thee. . . . Humble thyself in exact proportion to the stage of thy advancement to the higher position of priestly dignity, fearing the example of the sons of Aaron.[79]

Basil's somewhat predominant emphasis upon the clerical priesthood may be a bit surprising in view of the lay character of the monastic movement in its beginnings.[80] More Platonic than the idea of prayer as spiritual sacrifice, which occurs in the writings of earlier Fathers, is Basil's understanding of prayer.

> And that prayer is good which imprints a clear idea of God in the soul; and the having God established in self by means of memory is God's indwelling. Thus, we become God's temple. . ..[81]

Yet, Basil, commenting on Isa 1:11, related Ps 51:17 and Rom 12:1 both to the Old Testament sacrificial system and to the death of Christ.

> For not by the blood of animals, nor by sacrifices placed on the altar, but by a contrite heart God is reconciled, since "the sacrifice to God is a broken spirit" [Ps 50:19; i.e., 51:17] . . . And even a multitude was rejected; indeed He demands one sacrifice. Let every one offer himself to God, presenting himself a living sacrifice, acceptable to God, through reasonable worship offering a sacrifice of praise to God [Rom 12:1]. After, however, a multitude of sacrificial victims according to the law was rejected as fruitless, there has been approved and offered in the last times one sacrifice for the destruction of sin. Truly the Lamb of God has carried the sin of the world [John 1:29], offering himself an oblation and sacrifice in an odor of sweetness [Eph 5:2].[82]

Unambiguous references in Basil to the priesthood of all Christians are few. In his *Liturgy*, he indicates that Christ,

> brought us to the knowledge of thee, the true God and Father, having acquired us to himself for a peculiar people, a royal priesthood, a holy nation . . .[83]

79. "Concerning Renunciation of the World and Spiritual Perfection," 211B, C, in Clarke, *The Ascetic Works of Saint Basil*, 71.

80. Even in his "Shorter Rules," however, as Clarke has pointed out, Basil only refers to ordained priests in his coenobia three times *(64*, 231, and 265), *The Ascetic Works*, 39.

81. *Letter* 2, 4 (NPNF, 2d ser., 8:111).

82. *Enarratio en Propbetam Isaiam*, 1:24, in Migne, *PG*, 30:165, 166.

83. "The Divine Liturgy of Our Father among the Saints Basil the Great" in Robertson,

Elsewhere, he writes:

> . . . for Christ as truly the rock *(petra)* is unshaken; to be sure Peter *(Petrus)* is unshaken on account of the rock *(petram)*. For Jesus bestows his honors and does not withdraw them; but what he assigns, he retains. He is light. "You are the light of the world" [Matt 5:14]. He is Priest; he makes priests. He is Sheep. "Behold, I send you as sheep in the midst of wolves" [Matt 10:16].[84]

Basil in his *Liturgy* even addresses God the Father as "Royal Priesthood":

> O Royal Priesthood, Pure Father, intercede with Christ the God, that our souls may be saved.[85]

Gregory of Nazianzus frequently alludes to the priesthood in the sense of the pastoral office in his *Orations*, and such is the characteristic usage of priesthood in his *Letters* and *Poems*. Especially when he seeks to explain his own flight from the pastoral duties of a bishop or to extol his own father, Athanasius, or Basil of Caesarea does he identify priests with the pastoral function of bishops[86] Gregory also teaches the high priesthood of Christ.[87] Rom 12:1 is quoted in the context of self-purification[88] and in reference to complete dedication of all parts of the body and hence of the whole person to God;[89] but the same text also serves as specific qualification for clerical priesthood.[90] The sacrifice of self and the sacrifice of praise were joined by Gregory in an Easter oration:

> Let us sacrifice not young calves, nor lambs that put forth horns and hoofs [Ps 64:32; i.e., 69:31(?)], in which many parts are destitute of life and feeling; but let us sacrifice to God the sacrifice of praise upon the heavenly Altar, with the heavenly dances; let us hold aside the first veil; let us approach the second, and look into the Holy of Holies [Heb 13:15; 10:20]. Shall I say that which is a greater thing yet? Let us sacrifice *ourselves* to God; or

---

The Divine Liturgies of Our Fathers among the Saints John Chrysostom and Basil the Great, with That of the Presanctified, Preceded by the Hesperinos and the Orthos, 359.

84. *Homilía de Poenitentia*, 4, in Migne, *PG*, 31:1483.

85. "The Divine Liturgy of Our Father among the Saints Basil the Great," in Robertson, *The Divine Liturgies*, 385.

86. *Oration* 2, *18, 21,* and *43*.

87. *Oration* 2, 98; *Oration* 4, 78; *Oration* 21, 10; *Oration* 30, 15, 21; *Oration* 37, 4; *Oration* 38, 16.

88. *Oration* 11, 4.

89. *Oration* 40, 40.

90. *Oration* 2, 95; *Oration* 20, 4.

> rather let us go on sacrificing throughout every day and at every moment.[91]

Nearly always, when alluding to the priesthood of all Christians, Gregory of Nazianzus quotes 1 Pet 2:9, but various indeed are the contexts. He alludes to 1 Pet 2:9 when appealing for sympathy in respect to his own basic life decision:

> So, help me, each of you who can, and stretch out a hand to me who am pressed down and torn asunder by regret and enthusiasm. The one suggests flights, mountains and deserts, and calm of soul and body, and that the mind should retire into itself, and recall its powers from sensible things, in order to hold pure communion with God. . .. The other wills that I should come forward, and bear fruit for the common good, and be helped by helping others, and publish the Divine light, and bring to God a people for His own possession, a holy nation, a royal priesthood [1 Pet 2:9], and His image cleansed in many souls. And this, because, as a park is better than and preferable to a tree, the whole heaven with its ornaments to a single star, and the body to a limb, so also, in the sight of God, is the reformation of a whole church preferable to the progress of a single soul: and therefore, I ought not to look only on my own interest, but also on that of others [Phil 2:4].[92]

Of Basil of Caesarea, he writes:

> And when he saw the great heritage of God, purchased by His own words and laws and sufferings, the holy nation, the royal priesthood [1 Pet 2:9], in such evil plight that it was torn asunder into ten thousand opinions and errors: . . . he could not content himself with quietly lamenting the misfortune, and merely lifting up his hands to God, and seeking from Him the dispersion of the pressing misfortunes, while he himself was asleep, but felt bound to come to her aid at some expense to himself.[93]

Out of Egyptian tyranny, ancient Israel was called to be "a holy people, and a portion of the Lord, and a royal priesthood.[94] "To the Emperor Julian, Gregory could say after the death of Gallus:

91. *Oration* 45, 23 (NPNF, 2d ser., 7:431).
92. *Oration* 12, 4 (NPNF), 2d ser., 7:246).
93. *Oration* 43, 41 (NPNF, 2d ser., 7:409).
94. *Oration* 6, 16, in Migne, *PG*, 35:743.

> The great inheritance, thy hereditary decoration—I mean those that are named after Christ—the nation shining out in all parts of the habitable world, the Royal Priesthood gathered together with so much blood and sweat: didst thou in so little space and brief moment of time present and deliver up unto the public murderer![95]

First Peter 2:9 can be set amid the context of Trinitarian worship and the Christian's warfare:

> Teach that we should adore God the Father, God the Son, and God the Holy Spirit, in three persons, in one glory and splendor. . . . You shall receive from greater leaders the more perfect armor, by which you will be able to extinguish the fiery darts of the devil [Eph 6:16], and to place before the Lord a peculiar people, a holy nation, a royal priesthood [1 Pet 2:9], in Christ Jesus our Lord, to whom be glory forever and ever. Amen.[96]

The same text is found when Gregory writes of love for the poor:

> But what do we, to whom has befallen that great and new name, as we are named by Christ, a holy nation, a royal priesthood, an elect and peculiar people [1 Pet 2:9] . . . what shall we, I say, who have received such an example of pity and commiseration think and do? Shall we despise them? Shall we pass them by? Shall we abandon them as if they were dead, as if accursed, as if every one of those most pernicious serpents and wild beasts? By no means, brethren![97]

In his funeral oration to the church at Constantinople, Gregory of Nazianzus connects the royal priesthood with the pilgrim people of God *en route* to the heavenly Jerusalem.

> Prepare ye the way of My people, and cast away the stones from the way [Isa. 62:10], that there may be no stumbling block of hindrance for the people [Isa. 57:14] in the divine road and entrance, now, to the temples made with hands [Acts 7:48], but soon after, to Jerusalem above [Gal 4:26], and the Holy of holies there [Heb 9:3, 24], which will, I know, be the end of suffering and struggle to those who here bravely travel on the way. Among whom are ye also called to be Saints [Rom 1:6], a people of possession, a royal priesthood [1 Pet 2:9], the most excellent

95. *Oration 4*, 35, in King, *Julian the Emperor*, 20.
96. *Oration 13*, 4, in Migne, *PG*, 35:855.
97. *Oration 14*, 15, in Migne, *PG*, 35:875.

> portion of the Lord, a whole river from a drop, a heavenly lamp from a spark, a tree from a grain of mustard seed [Matt 13:21], on which the birds come and lodge.[98]

Gregory of Nyssa frequently alludes to the clerical priesthood, as, for example, in his treatise *On Virginity:*

> How can you be a priest unto God [Rev 1:6?], anointed though you are for this very office, to offer a gift to God . . . ? How can you offer this to God, when you do not listen to the law forbidding the unclean to offer sacrifices? If you long for God to manifest Himself to you, why do you not hear Moses, when he commands the people to be pure from the stains of marriage, that they may take in the vision of God [Exod 19:15][99]

Although Gregory of Nyssa recognizes the sacrifice of praise and the sacrifice of sharing (Heb 13:15–l6),[100] and refers to "the sacrifice of praise and the incense of prayer" in the heavenly tabernacle,[101] he does not seem in his extant writings to have given any clear expression of the universal priesthood.

Thus, the Cappadocian Fathers continue and develop the Cyprianic trend toward the clerical priesthood, although Gregory of Nazianzus especially still manifests awareness of the universal priesthood in his various quotations of 1 Pet 2:9, though those contexts are usually descriptive of the people of God in general rather than interpretative of the universal priesthood.

Greek Christian Authors in Syria-Palestine

The Greek Christian writers of Syria and Palestine during the fourth century yield even fewer direct references to the priesthood of all Christians.

Eusebius of Caesarea refers to pagan priests and to the Aaronic priesthood of the Old Testament. Throughout his extensive corpus of extant writings, he frequently alludes to the high priesthood of Jesus Christ and to the Christian clerical priesthood. The martyrdom of Polycarp is described as an "acceptable burnt-offering unto God omnipotent," and Polycarp is said in his prayer to have referred to his forthcoming death as "a rich and

98. *Oration 42*, 9 (NPNF, 2d ser., 7:389).

99. Ch. 24 (NPNF, 2d ser., 5:370–71).

100. *De vita Moysis, sive De perfectione vitae ex praescripto virtutis institutae*, in Migne, *PG*, 44:383; *De occursu Domini de Deipara virgine et de justo Simeone*, in Migne, *PG*, 46:1179.

101. *De vita Moysis*, in Migne, *PG*, 44:385.

acceptable sacrifice."[102] The Emperor Constantine does not offer bloody sacrifices, "but dedicates to the universal Sovereign a pleasant and acceptable sacrifice, even his own imperial soul, and a mind truly fitted for the service of God."[103] H. Berkhof has declared that for Eusebius of Caesarea the Lord's Supper is "a spiritual sacrifice" that is "smokeless and bloodless" and " 'a spiritual worship' an element in the new spiritual conduct of Christians."[104] Rarely does Eusebius seem to be aware that all Christians have a priestly office and priestly functions. Yet, he can write:

> Who else but our Saviour has taught his followers to offer those bloodless and reasonable sacrifices which are performed by prayer and the secret worship of God?[105]

Moreover, Christians

> sacrifice, therefore, to Almighty God a sacrifice of praise. We sacrifice the divine and holy and sacred offering. We sacrifice anew according to the new covenant the pure sacrifice. But the sacrifice to God is called "a contrite heart." . . . On the one hand when we celebrate the Memorial of His great Sacrifice according to the Mysteries He delivered to us, and bring to God the Eucharist for our salvation with holy hymns and prayers; while on the other we consecrate ourselves to Him alone and to the Word His High Priest . . . Therefore we are careful to keep our bodies pure and undefiled from all evil, and we bring our hearts purified from every passion and stain of sin, and worship Him with sincere thoughts, real intention, and true beliefs. For these are more acceptable to Him, so we are taught, than a multitude of sacrifices offered with blood and smoke and fat.[106]

Cyril of Jerusalem often alludes to the high priesthood of Jesus Christ but shows no clear awareness of the priesthood of all Christians. For him, new converts are not priests but are "like Priests" in becoming "partakers of the Name of Christ" and being sealed by the Holy Spirit.[107] Epiphanius of

102. *Church History,* 4.15:32–35 (NPNF, 2d set, 1:191). As to certain martyrs and confessors at Alexandria, see ibid., 6.41:11.

103. *Oration . . . in Praise of the Emperor Constantine. . .on the Thirtieth Anniversary of His Reign,* 2:5 (NPNF, 2d ser., 1:583).

104. *Die Theologie des Eusebius von Caesarea* (Amsterdam: Uitgeversmaatschappij, 1939), 148.

105. *Oration . . . in Praise of the Emperor Constantine . . . ,* 16:9 (NPNF, 2d ser., 1:607).

106. *The Proof of the Gospel,* 1:10 (ed. and trans. W. J. Ferrar).

107. *Catechetical Lectures,* 18:33 (NPNF, 2d ser., 7:142).

Salamis differentiates "the sacrifice of praise" with its requirement of humility from animal sacrifice.[108] Theodore of Mopsuestia, who often refers to the clerical priesthood, shows no awareness in his few surviving works of the priesthood of all Christians, although he does mention the sacrifice of a broken spirit (Ps 51:17).[109]

For the Greek Christian authors of Syria and Palestine, therefore, spiritual sacrifices, but not the priestly office of all Christians, survive as a theme.

Syrian Christian Authors

The Syrian Christian literature of the fourth century seemingly makes little contribution to the preservation or the development of the concept of the priesthood of all Christians. Ephrem the Syrian may refer to it in one passage:

> The Lord willed in His love to make His servants share in His names. Priests and kings by grace clad on Thy surnames, and Moses and Joshua Thy names.[110]

Fourth-Century Latin Christian Authors

The writings of certain Latin Christian authors during the fourth century contain allusions to the priesthood of all Christians, nearly always in connection with the quotation of one of the pertinent New Testament texts. The theme, however, cannot be said to occur frequently in the works of Latin fathers of the century or to receive anything like the attention that is accorded to the clerical priesthood.

In northern Africa, Marius Victorinus, rhetor and convert from Neo-Platonism, interprets Phil 4:18c to mean that the care of Epaphroditus for the Apostle Paul "is itself a sacrifice, holy, acceptable, and pleasing to God, benevolence itself."[111] But the priesthood of all Christians does not seem to have constituted a theme for either Donatists or anti-Donatists, as the silence of Tyconius and of Optatus of Milevis would seem to indicate.

Similarly, from Gaul, the voluminous extant writings of Hilary of Poitiers, many of which were devoted to the advocacy of the Nicene

108. *Ancoratus,* 23, in Migne, *PG,* 43:57, c, d.

109. Devreese, *Le Commentaire de Theodore de Mopsuesto sur les Psaumes,* 341.

110. Morris, *Select Works of S Ephrem the Syrian,* 122.

111. *In epistolam Pauli ad Philippenses,* in Migne, *PL,* 8:1234.

theology against the Arians, are lacking in references to the universal Christian priesthood, although Hilary does frequently quote 1 Pet 2:5, 9.[112]

But in Sicily and on the Italian peninsula, fourth-century Christian authors have left evidence that the royal priesthood was acknowledged and at least in some sense accepted. Julius Firmicus Maternus, Sicilian rhetor who became a Christian apologist, in his *The Error of the Pagan Religions* does not treat, teach, or directly allude to the priesthood of all Christians. He does quote Rev 5:6–10 in the context of Jesus as the Lamb of God but does not interpret verse 10 in particular.[113] He alludes to the sacrifices in the pagan cults,[114] to the pagan priesthood,[115] and to the Old Testament's Aaronic priesthood.[116] Surprising, therefore, is the following sentence in his final admonition to the reigning Roman emperors:

> With a pure heart, a devout conscience, and incorrupt mind let your clemency ever fix its gaze upon heaven, ever look for help from God, implore the worshipful godhead of Christ, and offer spiritual sacrifices to the God of salvation for the welfare of the world and your own.[117]

Although the extant writings of the bishops of Rome during the latter half of the fourth century are silent as to the priesthood of all Christians, the concept appears in the writings of Zeno, bishop of Verona, "Ambrosiaster," and Ambrose, bishop of Milan.

Zeno of Verona, after quoting Ps 50:12b—13, sets forth a threefold classification of sacrifices: "new" or Gentile, "learned" or Jewish, and Christian. The Gentile sacrifices, he declares, are "detestable" and the Jewish are "disapproved," whereas the Christian sacrifices are "elegant."[118] Zeno proceeds to interpret the Christian sacrifice:

> For if a *bodily* sacrifice is appropriate to *bodily* gods, *certainly* also a spiritual *sacrifice is necessary* to a spiritual God. Such a sacrifice is brought forth not out of a small bag but from the heart, is compared not with stinking animals but with the most pleasant customs, is offered not with bloody hands but with

112. *Tractatus in Psalmum LI,* 3 (Corpus Scriptorum Ecclesiasticorum Latinorum, 22:98); ibid., 22 (CSEL, 22:115); *Tractatus in Psalmum CXVIII,* 9 (CSEL, 22:479).

113. 27:7 (ACW).

114. 3:4; 16:2; 27:8 (ACW).

115. 24:1 (ACW).

116. 28:4, 5 (ACW), i.e., when quoting from Baruch 6:5–10, 30–31, 50–57.

117. 29:4 (ACW, 37:117).

118. *Tractatus* I:25, 2:3 (*Corpus Christianorum*, 22:73).

> clean feelings, is not slain in order to perish but, just as Isaac, is put to death in order to live.[119]

Zeno then quotes Rom 12:1 and Eccles 34:23, "The Most High does not approve the gifts of the wicked." He admonishes his Christian brethren to "offer such sacrifices as the Holy Spirit would willingly offer, the Father would approve, and the Son, who is our Lord, would glory in that approved through the same, who is blessed forever."[120]

The Latin commentator on the Pauline epistles whom modern scholars have dominated "Ambrosiaster" was not unmindful of the priesthood of all Christians or of living sacrifices.

> Under the law priests were born from the family of the Levite Aaron. Indeed now all are from the priestly family *(genere)*, as the Apostle Peter says, "Because we are" (i.e., "you are"), he declares, "a royal and priestly family *(genus)*," and therefore priests can be made from the people.[121]

In similar terms, "Ambrosiaster" declares that God

> gave an honorable royal dwelling *(regiam)*, just as Peter the apostle says, because "we are," he declares, "a royal race *(genus)*" through spiritual unction, of which the type was in the kings of the Jews.[122]

Commenting on Rom 12:1, he states:

> For according to the ancients, a sacrifice offered was killed, that it might signify that men because of sin are subjected to death. Now, however, because through the gift of God men have been made pure and set free from the second death, they ought to offer a living sacrifice, that it might be a sign of eternal life.[123]

Although the priesthood of all Christians is not a prominent theme in the extensive corpus of extant writings by Ambrose, bishop of Milan, it is to be found in certain of these writings. Especially in expounding the Gospel of Luke and in referring to aspects of the equipment of Aaron does he quote 1 Pet 2:5 or 2:9. In interpreting the "stones" from which God was "able to raise up children to Abraham" (Luke 3:8), Ambrose quotes 1 Pet

119. Ibid., 5:9 (CC, 22:75).

120. Ibid., 5:9; 5:13 (CC, 22:75, 76).

121. *Ambrosiastri qui dicitur commentarius in epistulas Paulinas*, re:Eph 4:11 (CSEL, 81[pt. 3]:100).

122. Ibid., re 2 Cor 1:21–22 (CSEL, 81[pt. 2]:203).

123. Ibid., re Rom 12:1–2 (CSEL, 81[pt. 1]:393, 395).

2:5 with emphasis on "living stones."[124] The bishop of Milan expounds the church as mother and in that context declares that God "lifts up" the "spiritual house" into "a holy priesthood."[125] The incident in which Jesus' disciples ate the grain on the sabbath (Luke 6:1–11)—a practice which, according to Ambrose, had been limited to the Aaronic priesthood—evokes an indirect allusion to 1 Pet 2:5.[126] While dealing with Levite cities and Levite refugees, Ambrose connects 1 Pet 2:9 with the call of Christ to all men.[127] In treating the unction applied after baptism, Ambrose mentions that ointment ran down the beard of Aaron (Ps 133:2) and asserts that the purpose of such running of the ointment was "that thou mayest become *a chosen generation,* priestly, *precious*; for we are all anointed with spiritual grace unto the kingdom of God and the priesthood."[128] In a treatise that may not have been written by Ambrose, mention of the blossoming of Aaron's rod leads to the question:

> What is the people itself but priestly? To whom it was said, "But ye are a chosen generation, a royal priesthood, a holy nation," as saith the Apostle Peter. Everyone is anointed to the priesthood, is anointed to the kingdom also; but it is a spiritual kingdom and a spiritual priesthood.[129]

These references to the universal priesthood in no way diminish Ambrose's great stress on the clerical priesthood. But, in his mind, the two seem to be complementary, not contradictory. He does not frequently allude to the offering of "spiritual sacrifices" except when quoting Rom 12:1–2.[130]

In Spain, two fourth-century Christian writers gave evidence of the survival of the concept of spiritual sacrifices. Priscillian, the wealthy layman who founded the Priscillianists c. 375 and later became bishop of Avila, refers to "immaculate sacrifices" when conflating 1 Pet 2:5, Prov 9:1, and 1 Pet 1:23[131] and to "spiritual sacrifices" when conflating 1 Pet 2:5 with Rom 7:14

124. *Expositio Evangelii secundum Lucan,* 2:75 (CSEL, 32[pt. 3]:81).

125. Ibid., 2:87 (CSEL, 22[pt. 3]:91).

126. Ibid., 5:33 (CSEL, 22[pt. 3] :95).

127. *On Flight from the World, 2.6, 1* (FC, 65:284–85).

128. Strawley, *On the Mysteries*, 136.

129. Strawley, *On the Sacraments*, 81. Dudden, *The Life and Times of St. Ambrose*, 2:705–7, doubted that this six-book work was written by Ambrose and favored the view that it was written by a churchman in northern Italy "early in the fifth century."

130. *Expositio Evangelii secundum Lucan,* 5:6 (CSEL, 32[pt. 3]:180–81); *De incamationis dominicae sacramento,* 2:10 (CSEL, 79:228–29).

131. *Tractatus genesis (V),* 90–91 (CSEL, 18:68).

and 1 Pet 1:13, 22.[132] Gregory, bishop of Elvira near Granada, who defended Nicene orthodoxy and attacked Priscillianism, in a passage in which he has referred to "the sacrifice of mercy" and "the sacrifice of continence" quotes Rom 12:1 and Heb 13:15 and then says:

> Thus we offer to God our bodies [as] a sacrifice, living and well-pleasing, when we serve God in all holiness and modesty, innocence, and faith and conscientiousness.[133]

Summary

The results of investigation into the existence and the nature of the concept of the priesthood of all Christians among the Christian writers between the middle of the third century and the end of the fourth century may be summarized as follows.

Cyprian, the great exponent of the clerical (i.e., episcopal) priesthood whose members offer a physical sacrifice (i.e., the eucharist), does not specifically teach the universal priesthood and rarely quotes the New Testament texts pertaining thereto but does retain the concept of prayer and deeds of mercy as sacrifices to God. Victorinus of Petau and Methodius specifically refer to the universal priesthood, and Lactantius alludes to spiritual sacrifices.

Athanasius rarely refers to the priesthood of all Christians, whereas for Didymus the Blind, the righteousness which is through faith is a spiritual sacrifice, and the royal priesthood is seen as derived from a conflation of the priestly and the kingly offices of Christ. Macarius expounds the idea of the royal pearl and gives an eschatological interpretation to the priesthood of all Christians; Evagrius of Pontus sets silent prayer, worship, and service in a mystical context. Although Basil retains some awareness of the royal priesthood of sacrifices of repentance and of praise, Gregory of Nazianzus more explicitly derives the royal priesthood from 1 Pet 2:9, a text which he quotes in diverse theological and ethical settings, but Gregory of Nyssa retains only the sacrifices of praise and of sharing. Eusebius of Caesarea seems not to be conscious of the universal priesthood but does refer to spiritual sacrifices. No teaching of the universal priesthood can be detected in Cyril of Jerusalem, Epiphanius of Salamis, or Theodore of Mopsuestia, and the evidence in Ephrem the Syrian is scant.

132. *Tractatus exodi (VI)*, 108–9 (CSEL, 18:80).

133. *Tractatus Origenis de libris sanctorum scripturarum*, 10:8, 9 (CC, 69:77–78).

Coupled with the silence of Tyconius, Optatus of Milevis, and Hilary of Poitiers is an occasional reference to spiritual sacrifice in Marius Victorinus and in Julius Firmicus Maternus. Zeno of Verona differentiates pagan, Jewish, and Christian sacrifices and interprets the last as spiritual and superior. In "Ambrosiaster" one can clearly detect the priesthood of all Christians and spiritual sacrifices, and for Ambrose the quotation of 1 Pet 2:5 or 2:9 tends to evoke an acknowledgement of the royal priesthood. The concept of spiritual sacrifices survives in Priscillian and in Gregory of Elvira.

The present investigation invites the question as to whether John Chrysostom's treatise on the clerical priesthood opened a succeeding epoch in the history of the concept of the priesthood of all Christians wherein that priesthood and its corollaries fared as well as or less well than in the period herein studied.

II.

Evangelism and Missions

7

"Lessons from Dispersions" (1960)[1]

Acts 8:1–8 is an account of the first Christian dispersion. This term "dispersion" is more commonly used to refer to that migration of the Jews from Judea into various parts of the Roman Empire which had taken place before the advent of Jesus and the going forth of his followers. Yet, the term also accurately describes what took place after the death of the first Christian martyr—Stephen. The Christians of Jerusalem with the exception of the apostles were driven forth from the city by the hand of Sadduccean persecution and went down into the regions of Judea and Samaria. To such persecution, Saul of Tarsus was a major contributor.

This first Christian dispersion had two important characteristics. One was its involuntariness. Luke twice used the passive voice to express the fact that these Christians did not scatter themselves but *were* scattered. These brethren did not engineer an exodus from the Holy City. They were catapulted like so many spores into the hinterland. The pressure of persecution unto death cracked the seed pod of the Jerusalem church. It triggered the laity into a practical apostleship. Yet, these men doubtless knew that their Lord Jesus had commissioned his followers to "make disciples of all nations." They doubtless knew of his word, *"As the Father hath sent me, even so send I you."*[2] Yet, these disciples had been slow and reluctant to respond. They lived too soon to be able to debate with the critics whether the Great Commission was a genuine utterance of Jesus. Their Lord had sent forth the seventy, but it took persecution of the Jerusalem congregation to start the expansion of the gospel. This dispersion was a compulsive eviction, a dispossessing of the possessed. Indeed here was the first instance of that

1. This article first appeared in *Western Recorder* (April 7, 1960) 3.
2. John 20:21.

principle classically described by Tertullian, *"The blood of Christians is seed (of the church)."*[3]

A second characteristic of this dispersion was its invincibility. The living Christ through the Holy Spirit wrought victory out of seeming defeat. Extremity was turned to opportunity. This dispersion led to the taking of the Christian gospel by a deacon to the despised half-breeds who had their own cult of Mount Gerizim, to the radical turning of the arch persecutor, to the turning of the leader of the Jewish Christian mission to the Gentiles who were no longer "unclean," and to the tendering by the church of Antioch of Barnabas and Saul of the Jews of the Jewish dispersion and the Gentile world. Once outside the local precincts of Jerusalem, the seed of the gospel was planted by those who themselves had been driven forth like seed.

This first Christian dispersion was by no means the last. Christian history has evidenced the recurrence of this pattern.

In the sixteenth century, the Christian brethren called Anabaptists, hounded by savage persecution instigated by Catholics and state church Protestants, were scattered throughout Western Europe, and going forth into exile, they became witnessing pilgrims and lay preachers. The Anabaptists took the Great Commission seriously as obligatory upon all Christians of all the Christian centuries. Their leaders even gathered in Augsburg in 1527 in a missionary convention to plan a strategy of evangelizing Europe, and in Moravia the missionary impulse was widely extended.[4]

In the seventeenth century, constricted by the heavy hand of the English state church, a band of thoroughgoing Separatist Puritans made their way to Holland and ultimately to the shores of New England, where they joined in time with the state church Puritans of Massachusetts Bay. In the spirit of their Separatism Roger Williams, himself driven out from Puritan ranks, carved out the lines of a new commonwealth, and another, John Eliot, took the gospel to the Indians. The suffering of its servants is the seed of the church.

In our own twentieth century, Southern Baptist and other Christian missionaries who planted their lives in China and learned one of its difficult dialects after World War II were exiled by the falling of the Bamboo Curtain, but a great majority of these were redeployed as Christian missionaries in the varied nations of Southeast Asia and elsewhere with a resultant extension of the Christian message. The suffering of its servants, the ministration of its missioners, the blood of its martyrs is still the seed of the church! We have no

3. Tertullian, *Apology*, 50.

4. Littell, *The Anabaptist View of the Church*, 109–37, and Little, "Protestantism and the Great Commission," 26–42.

reason to believe that God has declared a moratorium on such dispersions. Indeed, behind the Iron Curtain there are continued evidences of the same.

Are there any alternatives to God's providential dispersion of his saints? Yes, at least two. By our deliberate refusal to be willing to be used by God we can find ourselves bypassed in the redemptive purpose of God. Israel, the holy people of the covenant, commissioned to bear God's light to the Gentiles, was tragically lacking in obedience. The Jewish Christians, in the center of the Christian movement in the first flush of dawn, faded from the scene, and Pella is a stark reminder of their disappearance from the plan of the ages.[5] North Africa, once the location of a vigorous Christian movement known for its confessors and martyrs and as the homeland of the great Augustine, through Arian concessions and Islamic conversions became a "has been" in the march of the Christian gospel. Nestorians, who planted the cross over vast reaches of Asia for nearly a millennium, today are a tiny remnant hardly to be identified with Christianity itself.[6] The people of God in any generation or area can refuse to rise to or to continue in the high destiny of being fellow workers with the Eternal and his Son Jesus Christ.

The other alternative is that of free, ready obedience to the redemptive will of God. It is hearing and heeding before the constraints of providence or the hand of persecution should begin. It means taking seriously the Great Commission of Jesus Christ our Lord. It means defying the irrational and un-Christian distribution of 450 Southern Baptist preachers for 2,000,000,000 of the earth and 28,000 for the 170,000,000 of the continental United States, ministering to 9,000,000 Southern Baptists in particular.[7] It means living on the frontiers of Christian discipleship AD 1960—in a mountain community where reaping comes slowly, in the teeming cities where secularism and ecclesiastical religion seem almost to choke out the Christian gospel and way, in the front-line of Christian communication and witness through television, drama, and the written word, in eliciting the witness of Christians—we say "laity"—by life and by lip in the human precincts where "men of the cloth" get no hearing. Yes, it means turning from running in the ministerial derby for the established First Church with its "plush" and security or for Church Suburbia, the "plum" of contemporary pastorates, when these have a strong ministry to the minister. Not *"Zion Stands with Hills Surrounded"* but *"The Son of God Goes Forth to War"* must predominate in life as well as hymnody. Whether being scattered or going forth, our mission is to proclaim to men, as did Philip, Jesus as the Christ.

5. Schlatter, *The Church in the New Testament Period*, 272f.

6. Latourette, *A History of the Expansion of Christianity*, II:263–85.

7. Cauthen, *By All Means*, 128.

8

"Authority for the Christian World Mission" (1963)[1]

John 20:21; Matt 28:18–20; Acts 1:8

These texts state the claim of a Christian world mission. The word "mission" means not merely the aggregation of mission boards and societies and vocational missionaries now serving. It embraces the task and goal of sending and going, of witnessing and discipling, which belongs to the total Christian community. The word "world" is meant to signify universality so that in the Space Age its scope may not necessarily be earth-bound. By "authority" is meant the origin, the legitimacy, and the dynamic of the Christian world enterprise. "Authority" thus includes both the *exousia* (right to rule) of Matthew 28:18 and the *dunamin* (power or strength) of Acts 1:8.

Christians have not always readily recognized and accepted the Christian world mission as authoritative and, therefore, as obligatory upon themselves. The apostles, under the initial dynamic of the Holy Spirit, responded to the Great Commission of the risen Christ. Later missionaries, often with a mixture of motives, took the Christian gospel to pagan peoples.

The major classical Reformers such as Luther and Calvin, strange as it may seem, regarded the Great Commission as binding upon the apostles and their contemporaries and as having been fulfilled prior to the sixteenth century. Thus Protestants, preoccupied with other concerns, initially assumed no direct responsibility for the evangelization of non-Europeans. The

1. This chapter first appeared in *Christ for the World*, edited by G. Allen West Jr. Nashville: Broadman Press 1963.

notable exception to this was among the Anabaptists, who viewed the Great Commission as obligatory upon all Christians of all centuries and, amid severe persecution, sent forth missioners throughout Europe. "No proof-text was more frequent in the Anabaptist testimonies, and no command attributed to the Lord was taken more seriously than the Great Commission."[2]

The Moravians were actively engaged in the missionary enterprise and so were certain Anglican and Lutheran missioners. It was not, however, until the time of the English Baptist, William Carey (1761–1834), that Protestant Christians on a widespread scale were aroused to responsible overseas missionary participation. Then followed what K. S. Latourette has called "the great century" of Protestant missions—the nineteenth century.

In the second half of the twentieth century, those of us who profess allegiance to Jesus as Lord need to reassess the authority that inheres in the Christian world mission in the face of present-day challenges. Communism with a worldwide goal, a totalitarian method, an atheistic philosophy, and a "missionary" zeal ever challenges Christians to all-out competition for the allegiance of men. Oriental religions, long quiescent, are actively resurgent and seek converts even in America and Europe. An affluent American society, with increasingly affluent churches, militates against sacrifice for the redemption of mankind. Racial prejudice in utter denial of the reconciling power of the cross of Jesus Christ arises with serpentine erectness to hinder the advance of Christian witness. What then is the basis for assuming responsibility for a worldwide Christian witness in the 1960s?

I

First, the author of the authority for the Christian world mission is the triune God. The mission is not a projection of human cosmopolitanism; it is the purposive movement of the eternal God—Father, Son, and Holy Spirit.

The authority is manifested in the purpose of the Father. From patriarchal covenant (cf. Gen 12:2f.) to great prophetic utterances about Israel's light bearing and servanthood to the nations (cf. Isa 42:1, 6f.; 43:8–13; 49:5f.), the universal purpose of Yahweh, the God of Israel, was increasingly revealed. Yahweh, out of love, had chosen and called forth a distinctive people, "a kingdom of priests and a holy nation" (Ex 19:6, RSV). "He made known his ways to Moses, his acts to the people of Israel" (Ps 103:7, RSV). This eternal, divine purpose manifested in time found its center in Jesus Christ, who, as George Johnston has said, "reconstituted" the Israel of God. Christ's new Israel was to embrace Gentiles as well as Jews. This unfolding

2. Littell, "Protestantism and the Great Commission," 30.

of the divine purpose Paul called the revelation of "the mystery" (cf. Eph 3:1–6). This purpose was a redemptive, reclamatory, and saving purpose. The Creator is the Redeemer. Thus, not merely the "Lord God Almighty" who "didst create all things," but "the Lamb . . . slain" who "didst ransom men for God from every tribe and tongue and people and nation" is worthy of worship (cf. Rev 4:11; 5:8–9). "The Old Testament's revelation of the God who is the Father of Jesus Christ is a vital part of the scriptural basis for the Church's mission. That basis . . . is the doctrine of God, the God who himself is the mission."[3] The New Testament witnesses to him who was "the Word made flesh" and anticipates the final consummation of God's purpose.

The divine authority for the Christian world mission is likewise manifested in the *propitiation* of Jesus Christ the Son. Contemporary theologians stumble over and reinterpret the New Testament usage of this word, lest it suggest the rendering favorable of an unwilling deity. Paul spoke of justification in Christ "whom God set forth to be a propitiation, through faith, in his blood, to show his righteousness . . . that he might himself be just, and the justifier of him that hath faith in Jesus" (Rom 3:25–26, ASV). John declared that "Jesus Christ the righteous . . . is the propitiation for our sins; and not for ours only, but also for the whole world" (1 John 2:1–2, ASV). At any rate, the Son of God has made provision for all men to be reconciled to the Father, according to God's righteousness. God resists sin as the righteous God; as the righteous God he loves men with an agape or self-giving kind of love. To provide for human sin, the Son necessarily came into our human and mundane order. This coming is described as a mission. "For this I was born, and for this I have come into the world, to bear witness to the truth" (John 18:37, RSV). The Son's own mission is the ground of his commissioning disciples. "As the Father has sent me, even so I send you." His mission, centered in death-resurrection, expresses the essential nature of the Father who sent him. "For God so loved the world that he gave his only Son" (John 3:16, RSV).

Authority for the Christian world mission is also made known in the powerful presence of the Holy Spirit. The Holy Spirit's particular advent on the day of Pentecost was indeed a mission. "But the Counselor, the Holy Spirit, whom the Father will send in my name, he will teach you all things, and bring to your remembrance all that I have said to you" (John 14:26, RSV). "But when the Counselor comes, whom I shall send to you from the Father, even the Spirit of truth, . . . he will bear witness to me" (John 15:26, RSV).

3. Wright, "The Old Testament Basis for the Christian Mission," 26.

Ancient controversies about the Spirit's procession are meaningful only if procession is coupled with mission. The Holy Spirit brings the twin gifts of God's presence and power. Fleeing from the presence of God's Spirit is impossible (cf. Ps 139), but the post-Pentecostal presence is a gift. Not just any kind of power suffices, for the power of the divine Spirit is essential (cf. Zech 4:6; Acts 1:8). The Spirit is not merely concerned with the legitimacy of the mission but rather with the dynamic for the mission. To advance the Christian mission as instruments of God, the dynamic must be had. The dynamic in turn authenticates the mission.

The Christian world mission is, therefore, initially, essentially, and finally the mission of the triune God. Its goal is nothing less than "adoration of the Triune God."[4]

II

A second consideration is the *extent* of the authority for the Christian world mission. What is the scope of "all authority" (Matt 28:18)? The scope may be described in terms of persons (humanity), time (temporality), and means (methodology).

The Christian mission is directed to all men—to "all nations" (Matt 28:19), "the world" (John 3:16), "the whole creation" (Mark 16:15, RSV), and "the uttermost part of the earth" (Acts 1:8). The apostles perceived an essential intolerance in the Christian gospel, for "there is salvation in no one else, for there is no other name under heaven given among men by which we must be saved" (Acts 4:12, RSV). Christianity was neither an appendage of Judaism nor a candidate for syncretism.

But, one may ask, what of the twentieth-century situation? Is it not possible that there should be an indigenous religion for each culture or each major geographical area? Is it presumptuous for Western Christians to seek to convert non-Westerns to the Christian faith? Hendrik Kraemer has declared "that for the first time since the Constantine victory in AD 312 and its consequences, the Christian Church is heading towards a real and spiritual encounter with the great non-Christian religions."[5] And shall we see, with Kraemer, evidence of God's revelation, not in the world religions themselves, but in "the human religious consciousness, manifest in the many religions"?[6]

4. Anderson, "Further Toward a Theology of Mission," 313.

5. Kraemer, *Religion and the Christian Faith*, 20.

6. Ibid., 6.

"Thou madest us for Thyself, and our heart is restless, until it repose in Thee."[7] Yet, finding rest means being found by the coming and sending God of the gospel. It means a divine unveiling in history. The Christian world mission is nothing less than God's witness by human instruments to his selfdisclosure, directed to the least, the lost, and the last of mankind. A twentieth-century witness that intends to address all the human race is far from presumptuous. Only if men confusedly seek to distribute the American way of life or Western civilization in place of the universal gospel is there presumption! There is none if men testify to him who was a Jew and an Asiatic—even the universal Christ.

Moreover, the Christian world mission is to continue "to the close" or the consummation "of the age." This is the clear implication of the Great Commission (Matt 28:20). This is specifically stated in Matt 24:14, RSV: "And this gospel of the kingdom will be preached throughout the whole world, as a testimony to all nations; and then the end will come." Worldwide proclamation of the gospel is said to precede "the end" (*telos*)—whether second advent (*parousia*), resurrection, or judgment. Various questions arise from such a passage. Is the coming of "the end" conditioned primarily by the fulfillment of the Christian world mission? Is the mission fulfilled when initiatory preaching has been undertaken in every nation and in every language and dialect? Clear answers to such questions come hard. To be sure, the mission is projected throughout the whole of "this age," even to its end.

Again, the Christian world mission calls for the utilization of all available and legitimate means for its fulfillment. Paul once declared, "I have become all things to all men, that I might by all means save some" (1 Cor 9:22, RSV). God and his witnesses must use all the means at their disposal in fulfillment of the universal mission. This principle is especially needed for the challenges of the twentieth century. "By all means" calls upon men to give vigorous leadership to the Royal Ambassadors in Baptist churches. It means undertaking a discerning and ever-widening Christian witness to the international students in American universities and colleges. It should involve a greater consciousness of the missionary potential of Christians who for business purposes, military service, or voluntary travel spend time in other nations. It must embrace a continued and expanding use for the Christian world mission of the means of communication—television, radio, the printed page, and so on.

At the completion of his theological course in the Nigerian Baptist Theological Seminary in Ogbomosho, Samuel Akande, and his wife Comfort, came to the United States to complete his college education and a year

7. Pusey, *The Confessions of St. Augustine*, 3.

of study at the Southern Baptist Theological Seminary in Louisville. Nigerian students had been enrolled in the Seminary in Louisville before, but the Southern Baptist churches of the city had not been willing to accept them into full membership. At least the fear of being rejected had prevented their seeking membership. Sensitive to the situation, John R. Claypool, pastor of the Crescent Hill Church near the Seminary campus, carefully consulted with the leaders of his congregation as to their willingness to receive the Akandes into full fellowship. Hence, since the members were prepared for such an eventuality, in September 1961, the Akandes were received as regular members of the Crescent Hill Church and continued as members until returning to Nigeda in June 1962. Members of the church indicated that the Akandes' coming had enabled them to realize more clearly than ever before the nature of the ecclesia of Christ and the relation of its nature to its mission. Who knows but that this action may have contributed more to the extension of the mission of our God than the thousands of dollars given by this church to missionary causes that year?

The Christian mission embraces all humanity until "the end of· the age," and its fulfillment depends on the use of "all means."

III

A final consideration about the authority for the Christian world mission pertains to the human agents or instruments of the mission. Christian witnesses are agents or doers in that the witness must be actively, as well as unconsciously, given. They are, however, never agents in their own strength or with their own message. They are instruments of the redeeming God who serve his world mission. They testify to what he has done for and to them.

Who then are the proper agents or instruments for such universal witness? The biblical answer is clear. All Christians are to be agents of our Lord Christ's world mission. Those upon whom the Holy Spirit has come are to be his witnesses (cf. Acts 1:8). All who belong to "a chosen race, a royal priesthood, a holy nation, God's own people" are, according to the divine intention, to "declare the wonderful deeds of him who called" them "out of darkness into his marvelous light" (1 Pet 2:9, RSV). The mission ought to have as its agents the whole "people of God" (1 Pet 2:10).

Tragic indeed is the fact that the term "laity" ever became the antonym of "clergy." The implication of the apostle Peter's usage of people (*laos*) of God is that not to be in the "laity" is not to be a Christian! No ordained minister who has thoughtfully read 1 Pet 2:10 in his Greek New Testament should ever object to being reckoned among the "laity." Likewise, no "layman" who has ever perceived his own essential involvement in the ministry and mission of his Lord should be offended by being asked whether he is a minister or a missionary.

Indeed, the apostle Paul seemed to envision the ministry as inclusive as sainthood and sainthood as embracing all Christians. The "gifts" of "apostles," "prophets," "evangelists," and "pastors and teachers" were given "for the equipment of the saints, for the work of ministry, for building up the body of Christ" (Eph 4:11–12, RSV). W. O. Carver, perhaps sensitive to the trichotomous misconception of Eph 4:12, which is easily derived from the English usage of commas, wrote: "The perfecting of the Body is the work, not of 'the ministry' but of 'all the saints,' and the ministers are to prepare the saints for this work."[8]

All Christians as "the people of God" ought to share in the Christian world mission. The risen Lord who claimed "all authority" (Matt 28:18) commissioned his followers to share in the exercise of this authority. It is "not as if God needed a human counselor or a human assistant. It is rather much more a sign of His greatness which condescends to man, when God not only wins men for his Kingdom but even takes them into His service, bestowing upon them and honoring them with His Spirit to be His fellow workers."[9] The participation of Christians in the mission is, therefore, an extension of the selfemptying of Jesus Christ.

The participation of all Christians in the mission of Jesus Christ toward all men is not only consistent with but an indication of the true nature of his ecclesia. As the Germans would say, the ecclesia is both "a coming together" (*Sammlung*) and "a sending forth" (*Sendung*).[10] Emil Brunner has aptly affirmed, "The Church exists by mission, just as a fire exists by burning."[11] The mission is no optional feature or sideline of the church's life which may be rightfully relegated to a handful of devout women. To be Christ's ecclesia is to accept and to engage in his world mission. Commenting on Matt 28:18, Karl Barth has interpreted "go therefore and make disciples" as follows: "Make them what you yourselves are! Have them learn here, with me, where you yourselves have learned! Call them into the twelve of the eschatological Israel! Let them share in its place and task in the world."[12]

Among Baptists, the obligation of lay witness has been no strange truth. J. G. Oncken, pioneer in establishing Baptist churches in Germany,

8. Carver, *The Glory of God in the Christian Calling*, 150.

9. Anderson, *op. cit.*, 304.

10. Ibid.

11. Brunner, *The Word and the World*, 108.

12. Barth, "An Exegetical Study of Matthew 28:16–20," 63.

was fond of the motto, "Every Baptist a missionary," and labored to make it a reality among German Baptists.[13] "He was truly a gift of God to the Continent of Europe and to the world, and no modern Baptist save Carey may compare with him as the founder of a mighty and farreaching missionary movement."[14]

H. Wheeler Robinson, the Baptist Old Testament scholar at Oxford, was not content with the frequent usage of the concept of "the priesthood of all believers" but insisted also on the validity and importance of "the prophethood of all believers."[15]

Howard E. Butt Jr., well-known Southern Baptist grocery executive and preacher, has declared: "The Reformation under Martin Luther came when the Bible was opened to the common man. The modern reformation will come when the ministry is opened to the layman."[16]

One can hardly overestimate the unrealized potential of the witness of professing Christians. Great unused resources of Christian testimony and sharing lie stored in the "warehouses" of twentieth-century churches. But one should be mindful of signs of encouragement. "The apostolic vocation of laymen so evident in the churches of Korea is seldom found elsewhere. The establishment of seventy-three new churches by the staff of the Presbyterian Hospital in Taegu ought not to be so extraordinary, as it most certainly is in fact."[17] Nor should a Texas Baptist laymen's evangelistic crusade in Japan be considered unusual.[18]

Almighty God, Father, Son, and Holy Spirit, accept our gratitude for thy redemptive mission to all thy human creatures and for our privilege of being among thy agents in thy continuing mission. Forgive our failures. Quicken our zeal and courage. Set our feet into new paths. Endow us with thy powerful presence that we may obey thy universal Commission. In the name of thy Son Jesus. Amen.

13. Hughey, *Die Baptisten: Lehre, Praxis, Geschichte*, 107.

14. Rushbrooke, *The Baptist Times*, January 11, 1934, as quoted in Lord, *Baptist World Fellowship*, 76.

15. Quoted in Cook, *What Baptists Stand For*, 80.

16. Attributed to Trueblood, *Your Other Vocation*, 31ff.

17. Beaver, "The Apostolate of the Church," in Anderson, *op. cit.*, 260.

18. McGregor, "Texas Goal: Take Japan for Christ," 6–8.

9

Evangelism for Discipleship (1963)[1]

Preface

These chapters constitute a revision in form, though not in content, of five addresses delivered to the Kentucky Baptist Evangelistic Conference, assembled in the edifice of the Walnut Street Baptist Church, Louisville, January 15–17, 1962.

Theologies of evangelism, at least among Baptists, have commonly utilized an *ordo salutis* drawn principally, if not exclusively, from the writings of the Apostle Paul. In these addresses an effort has been made to give some stress also to the non-Pauline literature of the New Testament. Hence such themes as "new life" and "discipleship" are treated in place of "justification" and "faith." Such a choice of topics has been designed to bring together the gracious gift of God's grace and the duty of disciplined Christian discipleship.

The author wishes to express his gratitude to the following publishers who have granted permission for quotations from their publications to be included in the pages that follow: Moody Press, Chicago; Harper and Row, New York; The Macmillan Company, New York; University of Chicago Press; University Press, Edinburgh, Scotland; and Frederick A. Praeger Company, New York.

The author is indebted to Mr. A. B. Colvin, secretary, department of missions and evangelism, Kentucky Baptist Convention, both for the

1. This work consists of "five addresses delivered to the Kentucky Baptist Evangelistic Conference" at Walnut Street Baptist Church, Louisville, KY, on January 15–17, 1962.

invitation to deliver these addresses and for encouragement and assistance in transforming them from oral to written form. He is also grateful to Mr. Roger Ray for assistance in completion of the footnotes, to Mr. Jack N. Willett for assistance in proofreading, and to Miss Edith Killip, Mrs. Glenn Hinson, Mr. Kenneth L. Thrasher, and Mrs. Ronnie Fairbairn for the typing of the manuscript.

James Leo Garrett, Jr.
Southern Baptist Theological Seminary
November 1963

Repentance[2]

John the Baptist and Jesus came preaching, "Repent, for the kingdom of heaven is at hand" (Matt 3:2; 4:17). The apostles called for repentance and connected it with the forgiveness or remission of sins (Acts 2:38; 5:31; 8:22), even as the risen Jesus had instructed them (Luke 24:47). The principal New Testament word for repentance, μετάνοια, is rooted in both the Old Testament šuv, "to turn," and nacham, "to sigh, grieve," although nacham is used most frequently of God rather than of men. Yet, μετάνοια also has its distinctive connotation. An awareness of the meaning and significance of repentance is essential to the effective proclamation of the Christian gospel to unbelievers.

I

Sorrow or Contrition: The "Vestibule" of Repentance

The experience of sorrow, regret, or contrition is nearly always connected with repentance by the average person who uses the word. Yet, sorrow or contrition is not the basic meaning of μετάνοια, and hence it cannot be taken as the primary meaning of repentance. A classic differentiation of sorrow and repentance occurs in 2 Cor 7:8–11:

> For, although I did cause you sorrow (ἐλύπησα) by that letter, I do not now regret (μεταμέλομαι) it; although I did regret (μετεμελόμην) it then. I see that the letter caused you sorrow (ἐλύπησεν) only for a time. I am glad of it now, not because you had such sorrow (ἐλυπήθητε), but because your sorrow led

2. Chamberlain, *The Meaning of Repentance*; Taylor, "*Unum Necessarium*, or The Doctrine and Practice of Repentance," VII:1–491; Dirksen, *The New Testament Concept of Metanoia*.

> you (ἐλυπήθητε) to repentance (μετάνοιαν), for you took your sorrow (ἐλυπήθητε) in accordance with the will of God, so that you should not suffer any loss at all from me. For the sorrow (λύπη) that comes in accordance with (the will of) God results in repentance (μετάνοιαν) that leads to salvation and leaves no regrets (ἀμεταμέλητον), but the sorrow (λύπη) the world produces results in death. For see what this very sorrow suffered (λυπηθῆναι) in accordance with the will of God, has done for you! How earnest it has made you, how concerned to clear yourselves, how indignant, how alarmed, how much it made you long to see me, how loyal to me, how determined to punish the offender![3]

As the sorrow which accorded with God's will led to the repentance of the Corinthian Christians in respect to some failure in relation to the Apostle Paul, so we may consider that contrition is preparatory to true repentance. The seventeenth-century Anglican, Jeremy Taylor, was very close to the truth when he declared that "godly sorrow" is the "porch" or vestibule of repentance.[4] Contrition is not the "house" of repentance, but it is the way of entry.

The truth that "godly sorrow" or contrition is preparatory to true repentance has been perverted by the error of perpetuating sorrow or regret per se throughout one's Christian experience. This is the error of most Roman Catholic interpretations of repentance in terms of penance. The "vestibule" has been taken into the house. Contrition is elongated and canonized as an experience not to be terminated or supplanted on this side of death or even prior to deliverance from purgatory. Such perpetuity of regret is joined with audible, sacramental confession to a priest and the performance of works of "satisfaction" to provide a major alteration from the New Testament μετάνοια. Such an alteration robs God's grace of its transforming power and the Christian life of its essential joy. But, for all its error, Roman Catholic penance does not lose sight of the truth that sorrow or contrition for sin is somehow related to repentance.

Do those who are to be confronted today with the Christian gospel perceive the proper relation of contrition to repentance? It is not likely to be so unless the messenger of the gospel is crystal clear at this point. People often have a "the sin is in getting caught" attitude, applied both to breaches of civil law and to sin against God, which may be accompanied by a temporary profusion of tears. At this point, medieval theology is instructive, for

3. Williams, *The New Testament*.

4. Taylor "*Unum Necessarium*, or, The Doctrine and Practice of Repentance," 40.

Western medievalists distinguished between a higher attitude called "contrition," or a deeply rooted sorrow due to an awareness of the reality and awfulness of sin itself, and a lower attitude called "attrition," or a sorrow rooted in some secondary motive such as the fear of hell. The medieval Romanist was wrong in giving such sanction to attrition but right in recognizing a distinction between such higher and lower motivations. We should be sensitive to the probability that much of the tearless, regretless, emotionless church joining of the 1960s may be lacking in genuine contrition. Jesus "came not to call the righteous, but sinners to repentance" (Matt 9:13).

II

Turning: The Threshold of Repentance

Pursuing Jeremy Taylor's metaphor of "godly sorrow" as the "porch" or "vestibule" of repentance, one may venture to say that "turning" is the threshold of repentance. The Hebrew word (šuv), translated "turn," "return, and "turn again," used frequently in the Old Testament to indicate a restored or renewed relation to the God of Israel, forms one of the major streams of influence affecting the *μετάνοια* of the New Testament. In the historical books of Samuel, Kings, Chronicles, and Nehemiah, and even more frequently in the prophetic books, especially, Joel, Hosea, Jeremiah, and Ezekiel, the word šuv recurs.

Solomon, in dedicating the temple, prayed:

> When thy people Israel are defeated before the enemy because they have sinned against thee, if they turn and make supplication to thee in this house; then hear thou in heaven, and forgive the sin of thy people Israel, and bring them again to the land which thou gavest to their fathers. When heaven is shut up and there is no rain, . . . if they pray toward this place, and acknowledge thy name, and turn from their sin, when thou dost afflict them, then hear thou in heaven, and forgive the sin of thy servants, thy people Israel . . . (1 Kgs 8:33–36a, RSV).

Then came the divine answer:

> When I shut up the heavens so that there is no rain, or command the locust to devour the land, or send pestilence among my people, if my people, who are called by my name humble themselves, and pray and seek my face, and turn from their wicked ways, then I will hear from heaven, and will forgive their sin and heal their land (2 Chr 7:13, 14, RSV).

In Joel's prophecy we read:

> "Yet, even now," says the Lord, "return to me with all your heart, with fasting, with weeping, and with mourning; and rend your hearts and not your garments." Return to the Lord your God, for he is gracious and merciful, slow to anger, and abounding in steadfast love, and repents of evil (Joel 2:12, 13, RSV).

The testimony reported by Hosea is, "I will go and return to my first husband" (2:7c, RSV), and the call of Hosea is "Come, let us return to the Lord" (6:1, RSV). Yet, Hosea also poignantly reported, "The pride of Israel witnesses against him; yet they do not return to the Lord their God, nor seek him, for all this. . . . They turn to Baal" (7:10, 16a, RSV).

Jeremiah's repeated plea to the covenant-breakers in spiritual adultery was "turn" and "return."

> Return thou backsliding Israel, saith the Lord, and I will not cause mine anger to fall upon you. . . . Turn, O backsliding Israel, saith the Lord; for I am married to you. . . . Return, ye backsliding children, and I will heal your backslidings (3:12b, 14a, 22a, KJV). Why then has this people turned away in perpetual backsliding? They hold fast to deceit, they refuse to return (8:5, RSV). And if that nation . . . turns from its evil, I will repent of the evil that I intended to do to it . . . and if it does evil in my sight, . . . then I will repent of the good which I intended to do to it (18:8, 10, RSV). But they did not listen or incline their ear, to turn from their wickedness and burn no incense to other gods (44:5, RSV).

Similar indeed were the invitations and declarations of Ezekiel:

> Repent and turn away from your idols; and turn away your faces from all your abominations (14:6, RSV). But if a wicked man turns away from all his sins . . . he shall surely live; he shall not die. . . . Have I any pleasure in the death of the wicked, says the Lord God, and not rather that he should turn from his way and live (18:21, 23, RSV)? If I say to the wicked, O wicked man, you shall surely die, and you do not speak to warn the wicked to turn from his way, that wicked man shall die in his iniquity, but his blood I will require at your hand (33:8, RSV).

The mission of John the Baptist was to "turn (ἐπιστρέψει) many of the sons of Israel to the Lord their God" (Luke 1:16, RSV), and Paul's Gentile mission was in order "to open their eyes, that they may turn (ἐπιστρέψαι) from darkness to light and from the power of Satan to God" (Acts 26:18, a, b, RSV).

The whole heritage of "turning" and "returning" forms the backdrop to μετάνοια. Such "turning" is no mere incidental or temporary or occasional adjustment. It is not the proverbial "turning over a new leaf" of the New Year's resolution variety. It is no mere human turning to a new direction without regard for God. It is no cheap and easy "believism" of the sentimental type peddled by pious but erroneous Christians! The New Testament mentions at times both repentance and faith (cf. Mark 1:15; Acts 20:21), at times only repentance (cf. Acts 2:38), and at times only faith (cf. Acts 16:31). Yet, true faith is necessarily joined with genuine repentance. Repentance is nothing less than a life-changing destiny-determining volte-face.

Yet, in the fullest sense, there is not only a turning by man, but a being turned by God. The obverse side of repentance is conversion.[5] Elijah prayed over his water-drenched burnt offering, "Answer me, O Lord, answer me that this people may know that thou, O Lord, art God, and that Thou has turned their hearts back" (1 Kings 8:37, RSV). "Turn us again, O God," The Psalmist petitions, "and cause thy face to shine: and we shall be saved" (Ps 80:3, KJV). To the query of his disciples about greatness in the kingdom of heaven, Jesus replied, "Unless you are turned"—the RSV's "unless you turn" fails to convey the passive voice of the verb—"and become like children, you will never enter the kingdom of heaven" (Matt 18:3, RSV).

III

A New Mind: The Living Room of Repentance

To extend Jeremy Taylor's metaphor a step further, "the living room" of repentance is a "new mind." This aspect of repentance is manifested especially by the use of μετάνοια and μετανοέω as the principle terms for repentance in the New Testament. Derived from μετά, "after," and νοέω, "to perceive with the mind" or "to understand," the word μετάνοια has the general or etymological meaning of a "renewal of the mind." Neither the Hebrew word nacham, "to pant, grieve" and in the piel "to comfort," nor the Hebrew word šuv, "to turn" or "return," conveys the idea of a new mind. This comes with the New Testament μετάνοια. Neither does the New Testament μεταμέλομαι always have this meaning. Judas, when he "saw that he was condemned, . . .

5. The English word "conversion" is derived from *conversio*, a Latin noun meaning "a turning around" and from *conversus*, the perfect passive participle of the Latin verb *convertere*, "to turn around."

repented (μεταμεληθεὶς) and brought back the thirty pieces of silver to the chief priests and the elders . . . and he went and hanged himself" (Matt 27:3, 5b, RSV). Judas obviously regretted, but he seems to have had no new mind. The need for the new mind is clearly described by the Apostle Paul in his Roman epistle:

> For those who live according to the flesh set their minds on (φρονοῦσιν) the things of the flesh, but those who live according to the Spirit set their minds on the things of the Spirit. To set the mind on the flesh (τὸ . . . φρόνημα τῆς σαρκὸς) is death, but to set the mind on the Spirit (τὸ . . . φρόνημα τοῦ πνεύματος) is life and peace. For the mind that is set on the flesh (τὸ φρόνημα τῆς σαρκὸς) is hostile to God; it does not submit to God's law, indeed it cannot; and those who are in the flesh cannot please God (Rom 8:5–8, RSV).

In the same epistle Paul exhorted:

> And be not fashioned according to this world: but be ye transformed by the renewing of your mind (μεταμορφοῦσθε τῇ ἀνακαινώσει τοῦ νοός), that ye may prove what is the good and acceptable and perfect will of God (Rom 12:2, KJV).

The new mind is characterized by self-giving humility. "Have this mind among yourselves (τοῦτο φρονεῖτε ἐν ὑμῖν) which you have in Christ Jesus" (Phil 2:5, RSV).

One of the finest expositions of repentance as the renewal of the mind was made by the late Professor W. D. Chamberlain of the Louisville Presbyterian Seminary. He regarded repentance as a "mental transfiguration," "mental revolution," "a pilgrimage from the mind of the flesh to the mind of Christ," "a calling of men's minds to be patterned after God's in order that their conduct may be in keeping with his will and that they may participate in his reign," "the metamorphosis of the whole man."[6] Chamberlain was somewhat influenced by the classical Greek approach of Coleridge, De Quincey, and Matthew Arnold, who, being insensitive to the Hebrew background of the New Testament, offered an intellectualistic interpretation of the new mind. This interpretation made μετάνοια too much of an academic exercise. The "new mind" signified by μετάνοια is never intellect apart from will, emotions, or conduct but rather "mind" as representing the whole man.

Moreover, the New Testament writers were not restricted to μετάνοια as a vehicle for expressing the reality of the new mind. The denial of one's self and the taking up of the cross (Matt 16:24), crucifixion with Christ (Gal

6. Chamberlain, *The Meaning of Repentance*, 46, 101, 47, 55, 223.

2:20), circumcision "of the heart, in the Spirit" (Rom 2:29, KJV), and putting off "the old man" and putting on "the new man" (Eph 4:22, 24, KJV), and other New Testament modes of expression described the same fundamental reality as the renewal of the mind, or repentance.

IV

Ethical Fruit or The Changed Life: The Window of Repentance

Jeremy Taylor's metaphor of "godly sorrow" as the "vestibule" of repentance may be extended one step more, and this with an essential aspect of New Testament repentance in view. John the Baptist declared to the Pharisees and Sadducees who came seeking baptism at his hands,

> Ye offspring of vipers, who warned you to flee from the wrath to come? Bring forth therefore fruit worthy of repentance.[7] . . . And even now the axe lieth at the root of the trees: every tree therefore that bringeth not forth good fruit is hewn down and cast into the fire (Matt 3:7b, 8, 10, ASV).

Paul said to Agrippa that his own Gentile mission was such that "the Gentiles . . . should repent and turn to God and perform deeds worthy of their repentance" (Acts 26:20). True repentance issues in moral change or ethical fruit. By such moral change or ethical fruit, the reality of contrite turning to the new mind in Christ is made known to our fellow man. The changed life—the evident transition from "the old man" to "the new man"—is the window through which the inner chamber of true repentance is made visible to the eye of unrepentant men. Repentance is described in Acts as "repentance unto life" (11:18).

The changed life which is the expected consequence of repentance is no mere man-made reform, for "repentance unto life" is dependent upon "repentance toward God" (Acts 20:21). Magnifying statistical increases in church membership today without genuine repentance may be only pulling down a dark shade over the window to keep from exposing the real barrenness within. Life-changing conversions, on the other hand, increase "the electric current" so that the true light of repentance passes through clear panes to the dark world without.

The ethical fruit of true repentance should not prevent our recognizing that in at least one New Testament book the word "repent" is used as a command addressed to Christians and implies the need for a new or fresh

7. Or "bear fruit that befits repentance." (RSV)

repentance. In the letters to the seven churches in Revelation, "repent" is used seven times in this sense (2:5 [twice]; 2:16; 2:21; 2:22; 3:3; 3:19).[8] In quite a different context and in an enigmatic and controversial text (6:6), the author of the Epistle to the Hebrews affirms the impossibility of a renewal unto repentance.

Repentance, then, is the contrite turning of sinful man in response to the initiatory grace of God in Jesus Christ to the new mind—the mind of the Spirit or the mind of Christ—the genuineness of which as religious reality is evidenced by the moral, ethical fruitage of a transformed life. Repentance's confession of sin has as its complement faith's confession of Jesus as Lord and Christ.

This "repentance and remission of sins should be preached in His name among all nations, beginning at Jerusalem" (Luke 24:47). Are we prepared, are we able to proclaim repentance to our contemporaries? Can we proclaim repentance to the Communist who rejects God toward whom repentance is due, who only is ready to be father-confessor to Western capitalists repentant of their "sins" of capitalism, and yet who is concerned in his dialectic passion for a kind of righteous justice in a world of injustice? Can we proclaim repentance to the Hindu who worships timeless deity or deities and seems to recognize no temporal demand for a "here and now" repentance, especially when transmitted by a Western Christian? Can we proclaim repentance to the Buddhist who wants to escape this life of suffering and who looks to his eightfold path and inexorable law of Karma rather than a God of suffering and holy love who rejoices in the repentance of sinners? Can we proclaim to the Muslim who readily acknowledges that God forgives sin in the sense of relaxing the punishment of sin but who stops abruptly at the call of repentance in the sense of a radical about-face and of faith in Jesus as one who is more than a prophet, even the Word of God become flesh? Can we proclaim repentance to the logical positivist who denies that any real and tenable knowledge of God is possible for contemporary man in this age of enlightenment and who finds in repentance only fodder for his semantic mill? Can we proclaim repentance to the humanist whose greater-than-average confidence in man's own savability makes no room for repentance and who works to improve on Bahá'í's plan for one amalgamated and eclectic world-religion? Can we proclaim repentance to the superpatriot who calls for the indiscriminate acceptance of national, sectional, or racial interests as consonant with the purpose of Almighty God and who in effect calls the nation to pride rather than repentance?

8. Calvin stressed that repentance should be pursued throughout the Christian life. *Institutes of the Christian Religion*, 1, 3, 20.

The God of all nations "is not slack... but long-suffering... not willing that any should perish, but that all should come to repentance" (2 Pet 3:9).

Forgiveness and Reconciliation[9]

The Christian gospel is the good news of the divine forgiveness of sins in Jesus Christ. Its annunciation of God's forgiveness is rooted in the many and oft-repeated affirmations about forgiveness under the Old Covenant. Says H. R. Mackintosh,

> Forgiveness has a fundamental significance in the teaching of Jesus. History reveals no prophet or founder of religion who came forward, as He did, with the claim to have power under God to forgive sin. His contemporaries obviously were aware that in adopting this attitude His intention was not simply to proclaim the general truth or principle that forgiveness is a possible thing, but rather to offer Himself with pronounced emphasis as the guarantee and medium of its reality. In His person, the kingdom of God is here. This He said as a Jew to Jewish hearers. But by all the higher minds of Jewish religion, forgiveness had invariably been regarded as foremost among the blessings which the advent of the Kingdom would secure.[10]

"The forgiveness of sins" constitutes an important portion of the Apostles' Creed. The Christian faith without forgiveness would be an emasculated or distorted faith.

What is the basic biblical meaning of forgiveness, and how is forgiveness related to that other biblical reality known as "reconciliation"? "Reconciliation," as used here, does not embrace in itself a broad delineation of the whole comprehensive redemptive achievement of God in Christ, including the identity of Jesus Christ and His death-resurrection and its atoning significance,[11] but rather has the more limited meaning of "reconciliation" suggested by the use of the term itself in the New Testament. Are forgiveness and reconciliation synonyms, or are they complementary?

9. Mackintosh, *The Christian Experience of Forgiveness*; Taylor, *Forgiveness and Reconciliation*; Denney, *The Christian Doctrine of Reconciliation*; Stewart, *A Man in Christ*.

10. Mackintosh, *The Christian Experience of Forgiveness*, 2.

11. cf. Karl Barth's usage of "Reconciliation" as one of the five principal divisions of his *Church Dogmatics*. IV:1, 2; Barth, *Die Kirchliche Dogmatik*.

I

Forgiveness

The Biblical Meaning of Forgiveness

The biblical doctrine of forgiveness rests on two primary presuppositions: (1) the God of holy love who has ordained that his creatures should live according to His will, (2) the reality of sin and of the consequent alienation of the sinner from God. Forgiveness cannot be operative without the personal being of God nor without his love and mercy. Forgiveness would be unnecessary if man were no sinner or if moral self-attainment were the way to be rectified before God.

Let us examine the principal biblical terms for forgiveness. In the Old Testament, the most significant words associated with forgiveness are the verbs naśa' and salach. Naśa' means "to lift up," "to bear," or "to take away" and hence "to forgive" or "to pardon."[12] The root meaning suggests the removal of some barrier or obstacle. The psalmist declares:

> I acknowledged my sin to thee, and I did not hide my iniquity; I said, "I will confess my transgressions to the Lord"; then thou didst forgive the guilt of my sin. (Ps 32:5, RSV)
>
> Thou didst forgive the iniquity of thy people; thou didst pardon all their sin. (Ps 85:2, RSV)

Moses prayed:

> But now, if thou wilt forgive their sin—And if not, blot me, I pray thee, out of thy book which thou hast written. (Exod 32:32, RSV)

Micah asked:

> Who is a God like thee, pardoning iniquity and passing over transgression for the remnant of his inheritance? (Mic 7:18a, RSV)

The word salach means "to forgive" or "to pardon."[13] This word was used when Moses after the golden calf episode prayed, "go in the midst of us, although it is a stiff-necked people; pardon our iniquity and our sin, and take us for thy inheritance" (Exod 34:9b, c, RSV). Likewise, it appears as the word for forgiveness in reference to peace offerings and burnt offerings (Lev 4:20; 5:10, l3; cf. Num 15:25f.)
Solomon prayed:

12. Gesenius, *A Hebrew and English Lexicon of the Old Testament*, 669–72.

13. Gesenius, *op. cit.*, 699.

> and forgive thy people who have sinned against thee, and all their transgressions which they have committed against thee; and grant them compassion in the sight of those who carried them captive, that they may have compassion on them. (1 Kgs 8:50, RSV)

The psalmist petitioned:

> For thy name's sake, O Lord, pardon my guilt for it is great. (Ps 25:11, RSV)

The prophet declared:

> Let the wicked forsake his way, and the unrighteous man his thoughts; let him return to the Lord, that he may have mercy on him, and to our God, for he will abundantly pardon. (Isa 55:7)

Through Jeremiah the Lord declared:

> I will cleanse them from all the guilt of their sin against me, and I will forgive all the guilt of their sin and rebellion against me. (Jer 33:8)

Both naśa' and salach are used in Num 14:19:

> Pardon (salach) the iniquity of this people, I pray thee, according to the greatness of thy steadfast love, and according as thou has forgiven (naśa') this people, from Egypt even until now (RSV).

The word machah, meaning "to wipe" or "to blot out," is also employed in the Old Testament writings as a term signifying forgiveness.

> Have mercy upon me, O God, according to thy loving kindness; According to the multitude of thy tender mercies blot out my transgressions. (Ps 51:1, ASV)[/ESV]

In the New Testament, the most frequently used term translated "forgive" is ἀφίημι, "to send away."[14] The LXX has used ἀφίημι to translate both the Hebrew naśa' and salach and as well kipper, "to cover," "to make atonement for." In such LXX passages, "the objects of forgiveness are ἁμαρτία(ι) ("sin(s)" or "missing the mark"), ἀνομία ("lawlessness"), ἀσέβεια ("ungodliness"), and αἰτία ("crime").[15]

In the New Testament, ἀφίημι appears frequently.

14. The noun is ἄφεσις, "forgiveness," and appears often as ἄφεσιν ἁμαρτιῶν, "forgiveness of sins," the Latin translation of which is *remissio peccatorum*. From the latter, the English word "remission" is derived.

15. Taylor, *Forgiveness and Reconciliation*, 20.

> And forgive us our debts, as we also have forgiven our debtors. (Matt 6:12, RSV)
>
> And when Jesus saw their faith, he said to the paralytic, "My son, your sins are forgiven." (Mark 2:5, RSV)
>
> And whoever says a word against the Son of man will be forgiven; but whoever speaks against the Holy Spirit will not be forgiven, either in this age or in the age to come. (Matt 12:32, RSV)
>
> If we confess our sins, he is faithful and righteous to forgive us our sins, and to cleanse us from all unrighteousness. (1 John 1:9, ASV)

Indeed, one of the two principal Old Testament words for "forgive" and the principal New Testament term indicate a basic removal of something.

Another New Testament word for "forgive" is χαρίζομαι, "to be gracious unto," and hence "to forgive." The word appears twelve times in the New Testament in the sense of forgiveness, all in Luke and in Paul. It is used to refer to divine forgiveness only (Col 2:13), to human forgiveness only (1 Cor 2:7; 12:13), and to both divine and human forgiveness (Eph 4:32; Col 3:13). With the probable exception of χαρίζομαι, the basal biblical words for forgiveness convey the concept of removal of a basic hindrance or barrier.

One may ask, therefore, what is the barrier or hindrance that, according to the biblical writers, is "lifted up," "taken away" or "sent away" by God? The three most commonly used objects of the verbs "forgive," "pardon," and "blot out" in the Old Testament are "iniquity" ('awon), "transgression" or rebellion (peša'), and "sin" (chata').[16] The psalmist declares:

> Bless the Lord, O my soul and forget not all his benefits. Who forgiveth all thine iniquities. (Ps 103:2f.)

Likewise, in the new covenant, it is "iniquity" that is to be removed.

> For they shall all know me, from the least of them unto the greatest of them, said the Lord: for I will forgive their iniquity, and their sin will I remember no more. (Jer 31:34)

The word "transgression" also appears as the object of forgiveness. Joseph's brothers admonished him:

> Forgive, I pray thee now, the transgression of thy brethren, and their sin, for that they did unto thee evil. (Gen 50:17)
>
> I, even I, am he that blotteth out they transgressions for mine own sake: and I will not remember thy sins. (Isa 43:25)

16. Young, *Analytical Concordance to the Bible*. "blot out," 101; "forgive," 367; "iniquity," 516f.; "pardon," 730; "sin," 890f.; "transgression," 997.

All three words appear in Exod 34:6f.

> The Lord, the Lord, a God full of compassion and gracious, slow to anger, and plenteous in mercy and truth; keeping mercy for thousands, forgiving iniquity and transgression and sin. . . .

In the New Testament, the primary objects for forgiveness are ἁμαρτίαι ("sins"),[17] παραπτώματα ("trespasses," or more literally "downfalls"),[18] ὀφειλήματα ("debts"),[19] ἁμαρτήματα ("sinful deeds"),[20] βλασφημίαι ("blasphemies").[21] The New Testament teaching centers in the remission of sins, not the remission of the penalty of sin.[22]

Thus, it becomes clear that the primary object in the New Testament usage of the verb ἀφίημι, "to forgive," is not persons but sins or synonyms of sins. This further demonstrates and clarifies the truth that forgiveness in the Bible is essentially a removal of something. The psalmist used a geographical simile when he said:

> As far as the east is from the west, so far does he remove our transgression from us. (Ps 103:12).

Even though the English New Testament reads "forgive him" or "forgive them," we must not forget that these pronouns are in the dative case in Greek. "Lord, how often shall my brother sin against me, and I forgive him?" (Matt 18:21, RSV) is literally "forgive to him," and our Lord's prayer' "Father, forgive them; for they know not what they do" (Luke 23:34, RSV) is literally, "forgive to them." The same applies to Luke 17:3, 4.

Applications of Divine Forgiveness

Now that the biblical meaning of forgiveness has been established, let us inquire briefly as to the most pertinent applications of the truth of forgiveness. First, forgiveness is an act of divine grace. It is not an expected action, but unexpected. Forgiveness is needed. Realistically, God in forgiving addresses both the reality of sin and the possibility of sin's removal as barrier

17. Mark 2:5ff.; Luke 5:20ff.; Matt 9:2, 5; 12:31; Luke 7:47ff.; 11:4; Rom 4:7; Jas 5:15; 1 John 1:9, 2:12.

18. Cf. Matt 6:14ff.; Mark 11:25.

19. Cf. Matt 6:12.

20. Cf. Mark 3:28.

21. Cf. Mark 3:28.

22. Cf. Mackintosh, *The Christian Experience of Forgiveness*, 24–29; Conner, *The Gospel of Redemption*, 167.

between God and men. Forgiveness is possible, for no law of Karma binds the sovereign Lord of biblical religion. Forgiveness is moral, for God's gracious removal of human sin transcends all the codes.[23]

Secondly, divine forgiveness is dynamically related to human forgiveness of one's fellow man. Matthew records words of the model prayer as:

> And forgive us our debts, as we also have forgiven our debtors.
> (ὡς καὶ ἡμεῖς ἀφήκαμεν τοῖς ὀφειλέταις ἡμῶν) (6:12, RSV)

Luke's rendition is:

> and forgive us our sins, for we ourselves forgive every one who is indebted to us.
> (καὶ γὰρ αὐτοὶ ἀφίομεν παντὶ ὀφείλοντι ἡμῖν) (11:4, RSV)

Neither the "for" of Luke nor the "as" of Matthew should be interpreted in a strict causal sense, as if human forgiveness were to divine forgiveness as cause to effect. Yet, divine forgiveness is productive of human forgiveness. God removes the barrier, and the forgiven, who are the recipients of the great gift of God, reproduce this forgiveness by removing barriers on the human level. The unforgiving brother beclouds the certainty that he himself has received God's forgiveness.

Thirdly, divine forgiveness is normally operative through the proclamation of the gospel by the Christian community, at first done by the apostles. Jesus said,

> Truly I say to you, whatever you bind on earth shall be bound in heaven, and whatever you loose on earth shall be loosed in heaven. (Matt 18:18, RSV)

The grammatical problem here is how to translate a future perfect (passive) periphrastic construction. J. R. Mantey, W. D. Chamberlain, and other Greek grammarians have insisted on the translation "shall have been bound" and "shall have been loosed."[24] The proclamation of the gospel of God's forgiveness in Jesus Christ is not the source, but the providential channel, of the divine forgiveness of the sins of men. The RSV of John 20:23 reads:

> If you forgive the sins of any, they are forgiven; if you retain the sins of any, they are retained.

According to Mantey, the literal translation is:

23. Mackintosh, *The Christian Experience of Forgiveness*, 7–18.

24. Mantey, *Was Peter a Pope?*, 47–57; Chamberlain, *An Exegetical Grammar of the New Testament*, 80.

> Whose soever sins ye forgive, they have been forgiven. Whose soever sins ye retain, they have been retained.

Moreover,

> repentance and forgiveness of sins should be preached in his name to all nations, beginning from Jerusalem. (Luke 24:47, RSV)

Fourthly, modern theologians and preachers have expanded the biblical meaning of forgiveness beyond its primary biblical meaning, i.e., removal of sins as a barrier, so that modern Christians, both liberal and conservative, understand by "forgiveness" also the reconciliation of man to God and his restoration to fellowship with God. This is the thesis of Vincent Taylor's discussion of forgiveness in his book entitled Forgiveness and Reconciliation.[25] Taylor traces this expanded modern meaning to Albrecht Ritschl's fusion of justification and forgiveness and his interpretation of both of these as restoration.[26] Taylor points out both disadvantages and advantages to the modern enlargement of the meaning of forgiveness. Yet, contemporary preachers and teachers should not "slur over" the distinction between biblical and modern usage.[27] The man whose sins are forgiven in Christ is also a reconciled and restored man. But the larger meaning was not specifically conveyed by the terms "forgive" and "forgiveness" as used in the Bible.

The removal of the sin barrier makes possible a new relation between God and sinners. One of the biblical terms used to describe this relation is "reconciliation. "

II

Reconciliation

The New Testament uses three Greek words, all from the same stem, which English versions commonly translate by the words "reconcile" and "reconciliation." The first is the verb καταλλάσσειν, a verb meaning "to change" or "to exchange" and hence "to reconcile" estranged parties. It was used in classical Greek of the exchange of coins for others of equal value, and of the change of a person from enmity to friendship.[28] The stem includes the adjective ἄλλος, which means "another of the same kind." The verb καταλλάσσειν appears three times in 2 Cor 5:18–20 and once in Rom 5:10, while the noun

25. Taylor, *Forgiveness and Reconciliation*, ch. 1.

26. Ibid., 100ff.

27. Ibid., 24–26.

28. Liddell, George, Scott, *A Greek-English Lexicon*, 1, 899.

καταλλαγή appears twice in 2 Cor 5:18–20. The third word involves the addition of another prefix: ἀποκαταλλάσσω. It carries the meaning "to reconcile completely" and appears in Col 1:20, 22, and Eph 2:16. Almost all New Testament usages of the specific terms "reconcile" and "reconciliation" are in Paul's epistles.

Reconciliation implies that sinful men are alienated or estranged from God and need to be related once again rightfully to God. Reconciliation is God's termination of the estrangement or alienation and restoration to fellowship. Reconciliation presupposes forgiveness, or the removal of sin as barrier, and issues in the fellowship of Christian life. Reconciliation, a term drawn from the area of commerce, is God's exchange of our estrangement for our restoration, of our alienation for our fellowship. Those other peculiarly Pauline words, "justification" and "adoption," drawn from the judicial order, despite all the objections of modern theologians who have resisted it, meant, to Paul at least, a right standing and a filial relation to the God and Father of Jesus Christ effectuated by God Himself.

Probably the most important issue connected with the biblical doctrine of reconciliation is whether reconciliation is mutual or reciprocal or whether it is singular. Does "reconciliation" mean both man's being reconciled to God and God's being reconciled to man, or does it mean only man's being reconciled to God? The former view has been held by various theologians such as James Denney,[29] Peter Taylor Forsyth,[30] and Walter T. Conner[31] and appears in the four centuries-old third article of the Augsburg Confession and the second article of the Thirty-Nine Articles of the Church of England, that Christ is "to reconcile the (His) Father to us." Denney argued that in Rom 11:28, "as regards the gospel they (i.e., the Jews) are enemies of God for your sake; but as regards election they are beloved for the sake of their forefathers," the word "enemies" (ἐχθροί) must be understood in the passive sense of "hated," since "beloved" in the same verse is clearly passive. This concept of being "hated" is then applied to reconciliation so that God in some sense must be reconciled to man. Denney also contends for this reciprocal or dual view on the basis of the terms "propitiation" and "wrath of God."[32] Forsyth affirms that reconciliation affects both man and God, yet

29. Denney, "St. Paul's Epistles to the Romans," II:684. Denney, *The Christian Doctrine of Reconciliation*, 230–85.

30. Forsyth, *The Work of Christ*, 81–90.

31. Conner, *The Gospel of Redemption*, 180f.

32. The writer takes seriously the biblical terms "propitiation" and "wrath of God" and does not concur in C. H. Dodd's definition of the same, *The Epistle to the Romans*, 20–24, 54f. For a contrary view, cf. Morris, *The Apostolic Preaching of the Cross*, 125–85. Yet, such a consideration as Denney makes should not outweigh the exegetical evidence

we cannot say that Christ reconciled God. Other theologians such as James S. Stewart[33] and Vincent Taylor[34] contend for the opposite view, a singular direction in reconciliation. No New Testament passage clearly states that God is "reconciled" to man, for this is pagan thought, and God is always portrayed as the Reconciler. Stewart declares,

> But we cannot agree with Denney's contention that because there is this changed situation for God as well as for man, we should go beyond the New Testament usage and speak of God being reconciled.[35]

If the evidence seems to favor the singular view, one may ask whether holding to a singular view of reconciliation can be harmonized with an objective view of our Lord's atonement. The answer is "yes," provided that we do not attempt to make the word "reconciliation" an all-inclusive term for all that God in Christ does in our behalf and instead confine its usage to the more restricted meaning found in Paul. Our Lord's atoning work makes possible a change in God's relation to repentant, believing, forgiven sinners. Yet, we have no apostolic statement, "God is or has been reconciled to man."

Reconciliation with God calls for reconciliation on the human level. The ethical and the doctrinal, the human and the divine are conjoined. Therefore, Jesus said:

> So if you are offering your gift at the altar, and there remember that your brother has something against you, leave your gift there before the altar and go; first be reconciled (διαλλάγηθι) to your brother, and then come and offer your gift. (Matt 5:24, RSV)

Paul declared that Christ Jesus was at work "to reconcile (ἀποκαταλλάξῃ) us (i.e., Jews and Gentiles) both to God in one body through the cross, thereby bringing the hostility to an end" (Eph 2:16, RSV). Has our Lord abandoned His reconciling purpose among men? Can he not reconcile white and Negro, Northerner and Southerner, Easterner and Westerner, rich and poor as he did Jew and Gentile?

Some years ago, the late Pastor R. C. Campbell of North Carolina told about two Southern Baptists, Pastor Solomon of Florida and I. E. "Ike" Reynolds, the musician, engaged in an evangelistic meeting in Cleveland, Mississippi. They went to talk with "the worst sinner in town," the murderer of Sheriff Williams, one John Wakefield, a blacksmith. Hesitatingly at first,

---

drawn from the actual uses of καταλλάσσειν and its cognates in the New Testament.

33. Stewart, *A Man in Christ*, 204–26.

34. op. cit., 74f.

35. op. cit., 221.

they talked with him about Jesus Christ; he was led to place his faith in our Lord; and the three knelt on the floor of the blacksmith shop to pray. The church was deeply stirred the next evening as Wakefield the murderer publicly confessed his faith and presented himself for membership. The first person to give the hand of fellowship to him was Mrs. Williams, the sheriff's widow. "How could you shake old John Wakefield's hand?" she was asked. "Why," she replied, "that is not the old John Wakefield; that is the new John Wakefield."[36]

This is reconciliation to God and to man. God "reconciled us to himself and gave us the ministry of reconciliation. So we are ambassadors for Christ, God making his appeal through us. We beseech you on behalf of Christ, be reconciled to God" (2 Cor 5:18b, 20, RSV).

New Life[37]

The title "New Life" has been chosen deliberately, for it seems to encompass and include a whole family of biblical words that express a common truth, namely, that in Jesus Christ we come to have new life.

E. Y. Mullins once wrote, "No teaching of Scripture brings us nearer to the heart of Christianity than the doctrine of regeneration."[38] Indeed, regeneration and sonship, which we may also refer to as adoption, are both terms drawn from the area of family life. Regeneration is the family word drawn from the realm of the biological, whereas adoption is the family word drawn from the realm of law.[39] Regeneration is primarily a Johannine and Petrine term in the New Testament. On the other hand, adoption is chiefly a Pauline word.

I

The Old Testament Background

The concept of a new heart or a new spirit is not something that began de novo with the apostles or even with our Lord Jesus, for we find in the Old

36. The writer heard Pastor Campbell tell of this occurrence, and it is narrated here by permission of Mrs. R. C. Campbell.

37. Citron, *New Birth*; Breland, *Assurance of Divine Fellowship*; Conner, *The Epistles of John*; Holliday, *Life from Above*; Spener, *Der hochwichtige Articul von der Wiedergeburt*; Simons, "The New Birth."

38. Mullins, *The Christian Religion in Its Doctrinal Expression*, 385.

39. Conner, *The Gospel of Redemption*, 182.

Testament a foregleam of the reality of the new life which God imparts and the new birth which He makes possible. Deuteronomy 30:6 (RSV) reads: "And the Lord your God will circumcise your heart and the heart of your offspring, so that you will love the Lord your God with all your heart and with all your soul, that you may live." The Psalmist expresses a similar truth in the words, "Create in me a clean heart, O God, and put a new and right spirit within me" (51:10, RSV). Jeremiah expresses it in terms of "one heart." "And they shall be my people, and I will be their God. I will give them one heart and one way, that they may fear me forever, for their own good and the good of their children after them" (32:38f., RSV). Similarly, from Ezekiel, one reads, "A new heart will I give you, and a new spirit I will put within you: and I will take out of your flesh the heart of stone and give you a heart of flesh" (36:26, RSV).

II

The New Testament Materials

In the New Testament, one finds that there is actually a larger number of terms that may be embraced under the general heading of "the new life" than one realizes at first. Of course, one should begin with the word "to beget," or "to be born," that word which, with all of its cognates, recurs so frequently and meaningfully in the writings of John and in the letters of Peter. This is the verb γεννάω. It occurs in John's Gospel (1:12f., RSV) in the familiar words, "But to all who received him, who believed in his name, he gave power to become children of God, who were born, not of blood (literally, "bloods," that is, the bringing together of the blood of parents) "nor of the will of the flesh" (that is, not through sexual desire) nor of the will of man" (literally, "from the will of the male"), "but of God" (therefore, a birth or begetting which is not of human but of divine origin).[40] In the First Epistle of John, this word γεννάω is used six times in reference to the epistle's basic truths. In connection with each of its five tests fostering assurance, a form of the word is used. In 2:29 (RSV), one reads "everyone who does right (or practices righteousness) is born of him," that is, God. 1 John 3:9 (RSV) reads, "No one born of God commits sin, for God's nature (literally, his seed) abides in him, and he cannot sin because he is born of God." A similar usage and meaning appears in 5:18 except that "He who was born of God" (Christ) keeps the "one born of God" (the Christian), and "the evil one" (Satan) "does not touch him." Notice also 4:7, "he who loves is born of

40. Robertson, *Word Pictures in the New Testament*, V:12.

God and knows God," 5:1, "Everyone who believes that Jesus is the Christ is a child of God," and 5:4, "For whatever is born of God overcomes the world." Thus, the word "born" or "begotten of God" is used in First John as the basal word for Christian salvation or discipleship. The assurance of new life in Christ Jesus rests upon such evidences as practicing righteousness, not habitually sinning, loving, believing against the Gnostics that Jesus is the Christ come in the flesh, and overcoming the world.[41]

In addition to the participial use of the word γεννάω, as in First John, the word is combined with the adverb, ἄνωθεν, which means either "again" or "anew" or means "from above." It does not seem that there is great theological significance in the grammatical issue as to what ἄνωθεν means in the third chapter of John's Gospel. Whether it means "begotten from above," or whether it means "begotten anew" or "again," the truth is essentially the same, for a new birth must necessarily be more than another natural birth. Thus, one finds the declaration in our Lord's discourse with Nicodemus, "unless one is born anew, he cannot see the kingdom of God" (3:3b, RSV). Then follows that very emphatic word, "Ye must be born anew" (3:7b, RSV).

In First Peter, there are two uses of a compound verb, ἀναγεννάω, "to be begotten again." Here the idea of the new birth is represented in the verb in the form of a prefix. Thus, 1:3 (RSV) reads, "Blessed be the God and Father of our Lord Jesus Christ! By his great mercy, we have been born anew to a living hope through the resurrection of Jesus Christ from the dead. . . ." Likewise, in 1:23 (RSV), one finds the expression, "begotten," or "born anew," "not of perishable seed (not of "the spores of mortality") but of imperishable, through the living and abiding word of God."

In the Epistle to Titus (3:5, RSV), a noun based on this same root, παλιγγενεσίας, appears in the expression, "by the washing of regeneration and renewal in the Holy Spirit." Thus, the noun, "beginning again," and the verb "to be begotten or born" in participial forms, with an adverb, and with a prefix, constitute a whole family of terms used to express the concept of a new begetting or a new birth.

Furthermore, especially in Paul's writings, the idea of the new creation is another way of expressing the same basic truth. Paul declares in 2 Cor 5:17: "Therefore, if anyone is in Christ, he is a new creation," literally, "there is a new act of creation" (κτίσις). Perhaps the emphasis of the word is more upon the act of creating than upon the resultant creature. "If any man be in Christ, there is a new act of creation occurring." Again, one finds in Gal 6:15 (RSV), "For neither circumcision counts for anything nor uncircumcision, but a new creation."

41. cf. Conner, *The Epistles of John.*

Likewise, in the uses of the verb κτίζειν, "to create," the same truth is conveyed. In Eph 2:10 (RSV), Paul speaks of Christians as being "created in Christ Jesus for good works," and in 2:15 (RSV) of Christ creating "in himself one new man in place of the two." Or, to be a little more literal, the text may be rendered, "in order that he might in himself create or make the two unto one new man." In the Ephesian letter (4:24 ASV), Paul speaks of putting on "the new man, that, after God, hath been created in righteousness and holiness of truth."

Also, notice the verb ἀνακαινέω, "to renew" which is used in Col 3:10 (ASV): "(Ye) have put on the new man, that is being renewed unto knowledge after the image of him that created him."

In a list of New Testament expressions about new life, Paul's reference to the circumcision of the heart, "spiritual, and not literal" (Rom 2:29, RSV), should be included.

Likewise, mention should be made of those Pauline expressions that point to a spiritual resurrection as distinct from a future or bodily resurrection. Compare Rom 6:3f. (RSV), "all of us . . . were baptized into his death, . . . buried with him by baptism into death, so that . . . we too might walk in newness of life." In Eph 2:1, the expression, "And you be made alive" (RSV) or "quickened" (KJV)—the verb is understood or implied in the Greek—refers to those, who "were dead through trespasses and sins" and thus signifies new life in Christ. The same thought is found in Col 2:12f. (RSV): "You were buried with him in baptism, in which you were also raised with him through faith in the working of God, who raised him from the dead. And you, who were dead in trespasses and the uncircumcision of your flesh, God made alive together with him. . . ."

It matters not whether one takes John's characteristic use of γεννάω in the passive "to be born" or "to be begotten" or whether one follows the use of Peter in the compound form," to be begotten anew," or whether one takes Paul's expressions about a new creation, renewal, circumcision of the heart, or spiritual resurrection, the truth is nevertheless the same, namely, that the New Testament witnesses to what God does for us in Jesus Christ in terms of new life.

III

Some Modern Baptist Definitions

It may be instructive to notice some of the definitions which representative Baptist theologians have given to the doctrine of regeneration. Perhaps it is more than a coincidence that in the three definitions about to be quoted there is one theme that recurs. Augustus Hopkins Strong defined regeneration as "that act of God by which the governing disposition of the soul is made holy, and by which, through the truth as a means, the first holy exercise of this disposition is secured."[42] William Newton Clarke wrote: "The beginning of the divine life, being an entrance into personal union and fellowship with Christ and so with God, is a moral change; it is a change of character, and ruling disposition. It is not a gift of new faculties, or a creation of something additional in man, but an awakening of new dispositions which prepares him for fellowship with God."[43] According to E. Y. Mullins, "Regeneration may be defined as the change wrought by the Spirit of God, by the use of truth as a means, in which the moral disposition of the soul is renewed in the image of God."[44] In each of these definitions, the word "disposition" recurs. A new begetting, a new creation, inevitably involves a new disposition, the hallmark of the "new man."

IV

The Need for New Life

Now to the larger context of an interpretation of the doctrine of new life. First, the whole biblical emphasis, particularly the New Testament emphasis, on new life stems from the need for a rebirth or recreation. This need is implied in the universality of sin, in the reality of depravity. The whole stream of biblical witness-stretching from the Genesis statement that "every imagination of the thoughts of his heart was only evil continually" (6:5, RSV) through the statements of 1 Kings (8:46) and Job (14:4; 15:14) to the Psalmist's word, "There is none that does good . . . they have all gone astray, they are all alike corrupt; there is none that does good, no, not one" (14:1, 3, RSV) and down through our Lord's parenthetical statement," If you then, who are evil, know how to give good gifts . . . ," (Luke 11:13a, RSV) to Paul's quotation of Ps 14 in Rom 3:10–18 is a kind of consentient testimony to the reality of human depravity and of the need of new creation.

Not only in the Bible but in nonbiblical sources, evidence may be found of the need for recreation. In the widespread sense of guilt, and even modern man's reconstruction of guilt in terms of guilt consciousness, there is strong evidence of a need for a power that man does not have. Likewise,

42. Strong, *Systematic Theology*, 809.

43. Clarke, *An Outline of Christian Theology*, 396.

44. Mullins, *The Christian Religion in Its Doctrinal Expression*, 378.

the recurrence of the practice of sacrifice in various religions throughout the world, a widespread and well-nigh universal practice in the history of religion, is another evidence pointing in the direction of the universality of sin and the need of man for some kind of a settlement in regard to moral evil or man's relation to God or ultimate reality.

The need for a new begetting, a new creation, is implied in even more pointed evidence drawn from the pagan non-Christian religious communities of the world. A. C. Underwood in *Conversion: Christian and Non-Christian*, after interpreting a large body of data taken from East African rites, Fiji Island ceremonies, Indian Parseeism, Sufism and the mystery cults of the Graeco-Roman world, concluded:

> Widespread rites of initiation testify to an almost universal conviction that man needs to be born again before he is fit for the spiritual kingdom. They appear to point to some permanent need in the human spirit, which Christianity alone can adequately meet. In it alone we find the idea of rebirth conceived in moral and spiritual terms, untainted by magic and unhampered by restrictions of tribe, caste, or sex.[45]

John S. Whale put it in these terms:

> The congenital weakness of human nature is the submerged rock on which the complacent claims of an optimistic humanism are shipwrecked."[46]

Moreover, not only in the fact of the sin of all men is need for rebirth implied but also in the religious and ethical standards which our Lord taught with his idea of righteousness based on the heart and the motivations of the heart. In other terms, the need of rebirth is made necessary by a serious comparison between the Sermon on the Mount and daily human living.[47] How can we be the salt of the earth and the light of the world? How can we have in reality a righteousness that exceeds that of the scribes and pharisees, whether ancient or modern? How can we live without hate, lust, swearing, and revenge? How can we be free from religious pretense and hypocrisy? It is impossible after the manner of "the old man" and possible only after the reality and power of "the new man" in Christ Jesus. Therefore, it is exceedingly appropriate to conclude on the basis of all these evidences that there is confirmatory support to that direct declaration of our Lord as

45. Underwood, *Conversion: Christian and Non-Christian*, 114f.
46. Whale, *Christian Doctrine*, 40f.
47. Conner, *The Gospel of Redemption*, 184.

to the necessity of a recreation, of a new birth, "You must be born anew" (John 3:7b, RSV).

V

The Nature of the New Life

Not only the need for the new life but the nature of the new life calls for attention. What does it mean to declare that there is a new birth? Some of our theological vocabulary needs to be translated two or three times before it is absolutely clear to those who are not familiar. How important it is that regeneration or the reality of the new life in Christ be interpreted so as to be faithful to its biblical character and at the same time relevant to the thought patterns of modern man.[48] One needs to confess in the outset that, as with so many other great realities of the Christian faith, there is in the new life in Christ a mystery. It was this mystery to which our Lord bore witness when he compared it with the wind. We are not to destroy or play down this element of mystery. With all of the techniques to be employed, with all the witness to be borne, with all the human efforts to be undertaken, there is still a wondrous and awesome mystery involved in the new creation in Christ Jesus. Yet, that which is mystery has been revealed; at least it has been partly disclosed. God has drawn the curtain and Christians are able to confess that to an extent they do perceive and understand what God has done when represented under the terms "a new begetting," or "new creation."

What is the essence of this new creation? It is not a destruction of man's created nature, that is, it is not a destruction of the order of being and life which God has created in original creation. Rather it is a recreation of sinful human life, of nature after the order of sin. It is not the addition of some new metaphysical entity which God somehow incorporates in man, or some new physical organ to correspond to the prophet's graphic term "a new heart." But, there is a spiritual and moral renewal of man after the likeness of his Creator.

48. Cf. Paul Tillich's emphasis upon "the New Being in Jesus as the Christ." The ontological significance and the Christological (more than soteriological) interpretation of "the New Being" are factors essential to an evaluation of Tillich's view. According to Tillich, "Regeneration is a state of things universally. It is the new state of things, the new eon, which the Christ brought; the individual 'enters it,' and in so doing he himself participates in it and is reborn through participation. The objective realitv of the New Being precedes subjective participation in it. . . . Regeneration is the state of having been drawn into the new reality manifest in Jesus as the Christ." *Systematic Theology*, II:177. Tillich, *The New Being*.

Who, then is the Agent in this new birth? The Agent is God or the spirit of God. "Born, not of blood nor of the will of the flesh nor of the will of the male, but of God (John 1:13, writer's own translation)!" "That which is born of the Spirit is spirit. . . . The wind blows where it wills. . . ; so it is with everyone who is born of the Spirit" (John 3:6b, 8a, 8c, RSV). Paul speaks of the "renewal in the Holy Spirit" (Titus 3:5c, RSV). God is the one who recreates. He is the creator in the first instance, and he is the Recreator in and through the divine Spirit.

What are the conditions? On man's part, there has to be some kind of response if man is to be man. The New Testament terms "repenting" and "believing" are the commonly given answers to the question as to what are man's essential responses and attitudes. The old issue of the Calvinist versus the Arminian was joined at this point. The Arminian said, "Faith must come first, and then comes regeneration; otherwise, man is reborn without his consent." The Calvinist retorted, "No, regeneration is first, and then comes faith, for a dead man cannot act in response to God."[49] One could pursue that issue considerably beyond that point, but perhaps it is better not to try to set these realities in a time sequence. Since renewal is the work of God and since faith and repentance are the responses of men, it would be better to set regeneration or re-creation above and the conditions of repentance and faith below, thus stressing the divine and human aspects.

What are the means which God employs? First Peter teaches that God uses "the living and abiding word of God" as the means through which he accomplishes his divine act of the begetting anew of man. What is the meaning of the term "the word of God" as found in 1 Pet 1:23? John F. Holliday in his book, Life from Above,[50] comes to the immediate conclusion that Peter must mean the Bible. Look carefully. Does Peter mean to say that men are begotten anew by the Old Testament or by the New Testament which had not yet really come fully into being? Or does he mean the word of God in the sense of the Gospel as the proclaimed saving deeds of God in Jesus Christ which stands behind and gives meaning to the New Testament? In whatever form it may be expressed, the preaching of the apostles or the recorded witness of the New Testament writings, it is this living and abiding Word of God that is the instrument or the means of God's regenerative miracle.

This raises the question as to what extent human influences and agencies are a part of the divine work of renewal. More than a century ago, Baptists in this country had to give ear to the "Hardshell" or Primitive Baptist objections to human agency in this matter of the new life. The question of

49. Conner, *The Gospel of Redemption*, 191.

50. Holliday, *Life from Above*, 58f.

organized missionary work in fulfilment of a missionary obligation seemed to rest in part at least upon the question as to whether the sovereign Spirit of God uses human agencies for the salvation of men or for the renewal of men. But our situation is quite different from that of our early nineteenth century forefathers! We no longer are faced with the Hardshell Baptists' objection as a major consideration. This has been largely dissipated through the years, and in its place is a different situation.

On the contrary, today there is a great confidence in the legitimacy and the efficacy of our human witness and our church and denominational organization. So one may easily forget that these are after all only means and are never the agency! They, if effective, are always means used by Almighty God. Even as Missionary Baptists tended to remind the Primitives of another generation that they should recognize the legitimacy of human agency as instrumentality used by God, perhaps today's Baptists need to be reminded that with all of the human agencies, with all of the institutions, with all the means for the proclamation of the gospel, the renewal or the recreation of men in Christ Jesus is still the work of God.

VI

Two Errors

Although there are various misconceptions of and errors about the new life, two of these should be noted briefly. One is the error of the sacramentalist, who identifies rebirth with the performance of the sacrament of baptism. He may do this in one of at least three revels. First, he may say that the sacrament itself is the means of the accomplishment of regeneration, and thus the sacrament, when properly performed by the ordained clergy who have proper jurisdiction, efficaciously brings about the regeneration of men. This, of course, does not seriously trouble most Baptists, but it still is a major teaching in a large segment of "the Christian world." Accordingly, regeneration, at least for infants, comes simply by the act and efficacy of baptism. A slight deviation from the view just described is that which says that not only is the performance of the sacrament in itself important and efficacious but along with it the attitude on the part of the recipient, especially if he be an adult or a responsible person, is also to be taken into account. Thirdly, there is the familiar viewpoint which has its roots in the nineteenth century work of Alexander Campbell and Walter Scott, namely, the idea the act of baptism somehow is necessary or mandatory for the completion and the culmination of the regenerative work of God.[51]

On the other hand, in addition to the sacramental denial and biblical understanding of regeneration, renewal, or re-creation, there is the naturalistic denial of divine rebirth. Rooted perhaps in psychology's tendency to explain regeneration or conversion totally in terms of the subconscious,[52] the naturalist may say that this is an emotional experience that has no decisive effect upon human life, that it is the projection of a desired harmony with the divine, or that it is merely an instance of the wholesale moral and religious delusion that comes with organized religion.

VII

Fruitage of New Life

Finally, a word about the fruits or evidences of new life. First John is in a sense a tract on the evidences of the new life. Doing righteousness, not having sin as the predominating pattern of one's life, one's love of God and the brethren, believing that Jesus is the Christ, the incarnate One, overcoming the world—that is the language of the first Christian century. The great German Pietist, Philipp Jakob Spencer, at the end of the seventeenth century, wrote a book on the evidences or the marks of the new birth, containing a 400–page catalog of eighteen marks of regeneration! What were they? "Love of God, fear of God, obedience to God, prayer without ceasing, regard of spiritual (matters) and disregard of earthly matters, desire of divine grace, patience, longing for a blessed end, diligence in the continual cleansing from sins, diligence in good works, self-denial, neighborly love, edifying of brethren, taking one's neighbor's dangers upon oneself, charity towards the needy, humility, and brotherly love."[53] One could well add other marks of the new life to this list. One can think of temperance, the great Puritan virtue. Baptists would tend to add Christian witnessing. Others would say

51. Campbell's language seems to have been more often that of baptism and remission rather than baptism and regeneration. Campbell in his debate with Walker (1820) said that "Baptism is connected with the promise of the remission of sins and the gift of the Holy Spirit," and in his debate with McCalla (1823) distinguished between baptism which "*formally* washes away our sins" and "the blood of Christ" which "*really* washes away our sins." Cited by Roberts-Thomson, *Baptists and the Disciples of Christ*, 50–52, 54–56. Scott developed the "five finger exercise," consisting of faith, repentance, baptism, remission of sins, and the Holy Spirit. Ibid., 74.

52. Cf. James, *The Varieties of Religious Experience*, 207f.

53. Spener, *Der hochwichtige Articul von der Wiedergeburt*, 242–654, as summarized by Citron, *New Birth*, 155f.

steadfastness of faith. Surely the Nazarene brother would add holiness. One could continue the list, but the point is that, when and where the concept of new life in Christ has been taken seriously in Christian history, some attention has been given to the characteristics, marks, or evidences of this new life.

VIII

A Contemporary Testimony

Bernhard Citron, a minister of the Church of Scotland, in his excellent book, *New Birth: A Study of the Evangelical Doctrine of Conversion in the Protestant Fathers*, includes his own testimony as to his receiving the new life in Christ. Here, in his own words, is the account of his becoming a new creature in Christ.

> Born on the 21st of September 1905, in Berlin, as the son of Jewish parents, I was brought up in the comfortable atmosphere of religious toleration, humanitarian ideals, and appreciation of science and art. My father was a physician of some renown, and my mother a member of an old-established family of bankers and lawyers. The upheaval that followed the first world war influenced my development during my adolescent years. Political radicalism and craving for amusement marked that period of my life. For some years, I was employed as a bank clerk and afterwards took up the journalistic profession, which then appeared to me as my true calling.
>
> If anyone had asked me in those days what I understood by the term "conversion," I would have answered without the slightest hesitation: "Conversion is the exchange or a loan or bond for another one, at a lower rate of interest."
>
> Though I had never firmly adhered to any particular religious creed, a general religious feeling was strong in me during my childhood and boyhood; this sense, which was early recognized by my mother, gradually decreased and reached its low watermark in my late twenties. Then, I believed in the law of political and social progress for the community and in the law of almost unfettered freedom for the individual. The beginning of the Nazi regime shattered this optimistic outlook. I left Germany in autumn 1933, and during the years of exile and wandering my life was brought to a spiritual crisis.
>
> In the utter homelessness of exile, I felt the shadow of death near me. There was nothing uncommon in the fact that a man

who was spiritually and materially uprooted should long for death.

One autumn day during my stay in Budapest, I was walking along the broad river Danube. I saw the mist moving upon the dark face of the water. Great fear fell upon me. I was afraid of the future, afraid of man, afraid of the water beneath the embankment, afraid of myself. . . . At that moment I noticed the form of a cross shining clearly through the night, with an aura of blue light around it. What I saw was the illuminated cross above a chapel at the foot of St. Gellert's hill. Suddenly I knew that the way of the Cross leads from death to life, from homelessness to the Father's house, from the terror of sin to repentance, from skepticism to faith. I decided to read the Bible. With heart beating, I entered a book shop and asked for the New Testament. With joy and awe I attended divine services, till on Good Friday of the following year I asked the minister of the Scottish Mission to instruct me in the Christian faith. I did not say that I wished to be baptized. I just said that I wished to know something about the Christian faith. As one who has starved for a long time devours the first meal which is set before him, I swallowed the word of God. At the end of my preparation, I felt an urge to confess to my instructor those doubts which had long been besetting me. It was now my greatest desire to be baptized. It was the only possible outcome of my conversion experience that I should receive the outward visible sign of the inward grace which God had wrought in me. Once more, I stood beside a broad river. This was not the river of death, but the river of life. Yet, I could not see what lay beyond. I was unable to comprehend clearly what it would mean to live the Christian life. . . .

The minister who had led me so far gave the answer: "This is not the end, but a beginning." When towards the end of the Sabbath service, after the Word of God had been proclaimed, I stepped forward and answered the questions that were put before me with a threefold "I do," I was lifted up into a sphere of new life.[54]

Discipleship[55]

The subject of "discipleship" is known even to a somewhat casual reader of the Bible as a topic of importance in the New Testament. Yet, one can search

54. Bernhard. *New Birth*, xii–xiii, 124f.

55. Bonhoeffer, *The Cost of Discipleship*; Trueblood, *The Yoke of Christ and Other*

the table of contents or indices of numerous books on Christian theology in an effort to find a sustained or careful discussion of this theme only to be disappointed by the absence of such. One can search under the doctrine of salvation or the Christian life or in works on Christian ethics without finding that much attention, if any, is paid to "discipleship." The writings of the German Christian martyr, Dietrich Bonhoeffer, particularly *The Cost of Discipleship*, have been a major factor in a renewed interest in this essential New Testament theme.

I

Discipleship as Learning

The word "disciple" (μαθητής) meant primarily a learner or pupil and was the opposite of "teacher" (διδάσκαλος). The verbal form of this work used intransitively meant "to be the disciple of one or to follow the precepts of one" (Matt 27:57, marginal reading), while the transitive use meant, as in the Great Commission (Matt 28:19) "to make a disciple, or to teach or instruct."

To be a disciple of Jesus means to be under the continued instruction of Jesus as Teacher and Lord in the attitude of learning and applying the revealed will of the Master Teacher.

Jesus demonstrated the relation of teaching to discipleship in various ways. Take three specific examples of this. He took the towel and "began to wash the disciples' feet and declared, "If I do not wash you, you have no part in me" (John 13:5, 8). Again, he declared, "A new commandment I give to you, that you love one another, even as I have loved you, that you also love one another. By this all men will know that you are my disciples, if you have love for one another" (John 13:34, 35). One of his disciples came to him with the request, "Lord, teach (δίδαξον) us to pray, as John taught his disciples," and the so-called model prayer was given (Luke 11:1ff.). If our pride and egocentric concern stand in contrast to the humility and service of our Lord, if our animosities and abrasive relations with fellow Christians become dominant, if our busy and preoccupied lives have no place for prayer, the question is obvious—are we disciples of Jesus?

Sermons; Schweizer, *Lordship and Discipleship*; Frenzmann, *Follow Me*; Trueblood, *The Company of the Committed*; Garrett, *Baptist Church Discipline*; Fletcher, *Bill Wallace of China*.

II

Discipleship as Discipline

The two English words "discipleship" and "discipline" come from the same Latin root discere, although in Greek they are different words. A closer search will reveal that between these two there is basic interrelation. Let us notice some aspects of this interrelation.

First, discipleship is discipline in that it means living under "the yoke." "Come to me, all who labor and are heavy-laden, and I will give you rest. Take my yoke upon you and learn of me; for I am gentle and lowly in heart, and you will find rest for your souls. For my yoke (ζυγός) is easy and my burden is light" (Matt 11:28f.). Jesus spoke of a yoke. A yoke was an instrument of submission and of labor. As Elton Trueblood has said, Jesus used the yoke in relation both to "the call for comfort and rest" and "the call for disturbance." Paradoxically, our Lord "offers rest to the burdened by asking them to share his burden." The symbols of the Christian religion are not a pillow but a yoke and a cross! "My yoke is easy," Jesus declared, but it was a yoke![56]

Secondly, discipleship is the discipline of continuance in Christ. "If ye continue in my work, you are truly my disciples, and you will know the truth and the truth will make you free" (John 8:31). Not every usage of the word "disciple" in the Gospels is equivalent to full and continued and genuine discipleship. "After this many of his disciples drew back and no longer went about with him" (John 6:66). No true discipleship was possible apart from an intimate relation with the Disciplizer. "Abide in me" as the branches must necessarily abide organically in the vine (John 15:4–7).

Living under the yoke and abiding in Christ are expected to result in fruit bearing. "By this my Father is glorified, that you bear much fruit and so prove to be my disciples" (John 15:8). The vine was expected to produce grapes. Followers of Jesus are expected to produce recognizable fruit because of their living dependence upon the Lord.

Discipleship as discipline is not confined to the individual Christian's relation to his Lord. The early Christian community accepted as normative the corporate discipline of discipleship. This meant positively "continuing steadfastly in the apostles' teaching and the fellowship, in the breaking of bread and prayers" (Acts 2:42). It meant, negatively, the brotherly rebuke or admonition and excommunication. The Anabaptists and early Baptists believed and practiced the disciplined community of disciples. The burden of proof rests on twentieth century Baptists as to whether the opposite of this is New Testament Christianity.

56. Trueblood, *The Yoke of Christ and Other Sermons*, 17–21.

What many Christian congregations have abandoned, the Communist Party adopted in a realistic, if grossly perverted, fashion. When the Social Democratic Party met in 1903 in Russia, a split occurred between the Bolsheviks led by Lenin and the Mensheviks. Lenin insisted that the party

> must be the "vanguard of the proletariat." . . . The party must be a band of "professional revolutionaries," bound by an iron discipline . . . No one must be admitted to the party who would not completely subject himself to its leaders and put the claims of the party on his time and efforts before all others.[57]

Discipleship as discipline, according to the Epistle of the Hebrews (12:5–11), involves a divine chastening. In fact, whereas the King James Version renders the term "chastening," the Revised Standard Version translates it "discipline." It is a discipline that befits sonship. The disciple is also a child or son of God. As son, he is to expect the parental discipline of the Almighty Father. Such discipline means suffering. This reminds us of another dimension of discipleship.

III

Discipleship As Cross-Bearing

Our Lord clearly taught that coming after him involved denying oneself, taking up one's cross, and following Jesus (Mark 8:34f.). To be a disciple of Jesus is to deny or renounce the rule of self. This is one aspect of what we call "repentance." In this sense, repentance is a turning from self-rule to the dominion of Christ.

Jesus warned prospective disciples that they must count the cost of following Him. "If anyone comes to me and does not hate his own father and mother and wife and children and brothers and sisters, yes, and even his own life, he cannot be my disciple." (Luke 14:26) This is no sanction for neglect of children or parents, but it does make clear that allegiance to Jesus should be to other loyalties as love is to hate. Count the cost like a wise tower builder or a king about to go to war. "Whoever does not bear his cross and come after me cannot be my disciple." (Luke 14:27).

Many have confused cross-bearing much as the boy who was asked by his father what he had learned in Sunday School. "We learned about a cross-eyed bear," the boy said. "About a what?" "Yes, sir, we sang 'Gladly the Cross I'd Bear.'"

57. Seton-Watson, *From Lenin to Melenkov*, 24.

Bonhoeffer has called us to the rediscovery of the costliness of grace. The works of this Lutheran martyr are relevant to Baptists and indeed to all Christians.

> Cheap grace is the deadly enemy of our church. We are fighting today for costly grace . . . Cheap grace is the preaching of forgiveness without requiring repentance, baptism without church discipline, communion without confession. . . . Cheap grace is grace without discipleship, grace without the cross, grace without Jesus Christ, living and incarnate. [On the contrary,] Costly grace is the treasure hidden in the field . . . the pearl of Christ . . . Such grace is costly because it calls us to follow, and it is grace because it calls us to follow Jesus Christ.[58]

Discipleship is cross-bearing in that Christians are called upon to be faithful even to persecution and martydom. The work "to make disciples" (μαθητεύω) stands in close proximity to the word "bear witness" (μαρτυρέω). It is no accident that the word for "witness" (μαρτύς) in the Apocalypse means "martyr." For Jesus said, "A disciple is not above his teacher, nor a servant above his master." (Matt 10:24). At least four times this saying appears in the Gospels, once in Mattthew, once in Luke, and twice in John. Luke (6:40) locates it in the Sermon on the Mount. John (13:16) uses it in reference to Jesus' washing of the disciples' feet. Both in John (15:20) and in Matthew (10:24f.) it is specifically connected with persecution and suffering. Felix Mantz, that remarkable young Swiss who had entered the circle of Brethren in Christ (known as Anabaptists), after four imprisonments was taken out to the Limmat. He was bound and about to be drowned for the "crime" of rebaptism. It was January 5, 1527. Bullinger, no sympathetic reporter, records that the mother of Mantz on the shore admonished him not to recant and Mantz cried out, "In manus tuas domine commendo spiritum meum."[59] This is discipleship.

Not only individual Christians, but also churches and denominations must take up the cross if their common discipleship be fulfilled. This is true unless a comfortable kind of religiosity that is easily compatible with a pagan, godless society be substituted for Christianity. Southern Baptists have been providentially blessed. One does not have to have an exceptional memory or a very lengthy experience or be an expert historian to recognize this.

After World War I, during the Seventy-Five Million Campaign under the leadership of Lee R. Scarborough, who established the word "cooperation" (or as he liked to say, "cooperancy") in the Baptist vocabulary, and

58. Bonhoeffer, *The Cost of Discipleship*, 35–37.

59. Krajewski, *Leben und Sterben des Zürcher Täuferführers Felix Mantz*, 147f.

with the inauguration of the Cooperative Program, Southern Baptists were led into new ventures of stewardship. Nor should one forget the peerless leadership during the same decade of E. Y. Mullins, who in his younger days had led Southern Baptist Theological Seminary forward after the Whitsitt Controversy. In the 1920s, at the pinnacle of his influence, President Mullins helped to guide the denominational ship through the troubled waters of conflict between science and religion. Then came the dark days of the 1930s, but again there was a sense of direction and leadership, divine and human. In those years of depression and debt, Southern Baptists were called upon to make contributions "above and beyond" their regular offerings to the Hundred Thousand Club so that the debts of the denomination might be honorably paid.

Out of the upheaval of World War II, came the projected vision of M. Theron Rankin who led Southern Baptists to attempt a great new unprecedented advance in world missions with the result that the compassion of Jesus and world-wide responsibility came to be shared more extensively by Southern Baptists. Concurrently, courageous Southern Baptists with remarkable initiative and with the assistance of the Home Mission Board made new pilgrimages of faith and new ventures of sacrifice and service in the West and in the North. Then, in the 1950s, Southern Baptists joined hands with fellow Baptists throughout North America in common objectives pointing toward the sesquicentennial of the establishment of the "Triennial" Convention to be observed in 1964. C. C. Warren's challenge to Southern Baptists to establish 30,000 new churches and missions by 1964 was undertaken with determination. These events evidence the blessing of God and a sense of mission.

But what of the mid-60s? Can and will Southern Baptists find and follow the will and the mission of Jesus the Lord for these years? Could it be that a new dimension of depth is the supreme need of Southern Baptists today? Could it be a new commitment, a new discipleship, a new discipline? Southern Baptists have told the world that they believe in a regenerate church membership. They have declared in favor of the historic Baptist testimony to believer's baptism. They espouse a committed churchmanship. They have affirmed and re-affirmed the authority of the New Testament. Yet, practice and performance seem often to belie these claims. Other concerns have dissipated the concern that true and genuine discipleship be characteristic of the churches and the denomination.

Discipleship means bearing a cross, and denominational discipleship is no exception. It may mean the acknowledgment of grave faults, of pseudo-devotion. It may mean coming down from the stations of pride and prejudice to the bended knee of humility. It may mean new commitments, new standards of fellowship, and new concerns one for the other. It may mean a new openness to fellowship with all who confess in sincerity Jesus as Lord. The Holy Spirit may be calling Southern Baptists to new depths of discipleship for the era of the new South and for a challenging, changing world. A new discipleship may be prerequisite to a new advance in evangelism, for we must go deeper before we can go further.

IV

Discipleship as Evangelism

Discipleship, according to Jesus, means involvement in the making of other disciples. "Follow me, and I will make you fishers of men" (Matt 4:19b, RSV). In the Matthean form of the Great Commission (Matt 28:19f.), the only finite verb is "make disciples" (μαθητεύσατε), while "go," "baptizing," and "teaching" are participles (πορευθέντες, βαπτίζοντες, διδάσκοντες). The principal action of this commission is the making of disciples or "disciplizing." Those on whom the Holy Spirit has come in power are to be witnesses of Jesus (Acts 1:8). All who are privileged to be among "a chosen race, a royal priesthood, a holy nation, God's own people" are responsibly to "declare the wonderful deeds of him who called" them "out of darkness into his marvelous light" (1 Pet 2:9, RSV). Witness for the sake of making disciples belong to the whole "people of God" (λαὸς θεοῦ) (1 Pet 2:10).

The disciplizing responsibility of all Christians has not been alien to Baptists. The pioneer of German Baptists, J. G. Oncken, was fond of the motto, "Every Baptist a missionary" and labored to make it a reality among German Baptists.[60] H. Wheeler Robinson, the Old Testament scholar at Oxford, in addition to emphasizing the "priesthood of all believers" insisted on the validity and importance of the "prophethood of all believers."[61] Howard E. Butt Jr., well-known Southern Baptist grocery executive and preacher, has declared, "The reformation under Martin Luther came when the Bible was opened to the common man. The modern reformation will come when the ministry is opened to the layman."[62] Great unused resources of Christian witness and sharing lie stored in the "warehouses" of twentieth century churches. To be a disciple of him who "came to seek and to save the lost" (Luke 19:10b, RSV) is to be engaged in the making of other disciples.

60. Cf. Moore, "Beginning in Europe—Oncken in Hamburg, 1834," 55.

61. Quoted by Cook, *What Baptists Stand For*, 80.

62. Butt attributes the thought to Trueblood, *Your Other Vocation*, 31f.

Ministers and missionaries alone can never fulfill the task of disciplizing. The great new era of the witness of all believers may be at hand.

May God give to us a new vision of Christian discipleship and may we dedicate ourselves anew to Christian discipleship as learning, as discipline, as cross-bearing, and as evangelism.

Sanctification[63]

"You shall be holy; for I the Lord your God am holy" (Lev 11:44, 45; 19:2, RSV). These are words originally set thrice in the very center of the Levitical legislation. These are also words applied by the Apostle Peter to the moral and ethical needs of Christians in the first century (cf. 1 Pet 1:16). Becoming "holy" is not a mere marginal note or a subsidiary adjunct to our Christian evangel. It is veritably its goal and end.

I

The Relevance of Sanctification

There are at least two reasons for focusing attention on sanctification. One is the confusion and the misunderstanding that is widespread in regard to the biblical teaching concerning sanctification. There are those who affirm that to be a saint is to be one of those extra-pious souls in heaven who have been canonized by the church on earth and listed on its calendar of saints and who are to be the objects of the petitionary prayers of those who are now upon the earth that they in turn may convey these petitions to Christ and to God. Or, there are others who hold that to be sanctified is to have a second crisis experience like that of becoming a Christian in which one is enabled to live above all sin, to have the perfect love of God, and to be religiously different from other ordinary Christians. There are yet others who would measure the reality or extent of sanctification either by the absence of cosmetics or by the practice of speaking in tongues. But, in contrast to all of these previously noted, there are on the other hand millions of others who are inclined to say that they want nothing to do whatever with any sanctimonious Phariseeism and who are ready to flee "at the drop of a hat" from any association with "holy Joes." There is, therefore, need for clarifying once again the biblical understanding of what it means to be sanctified. For everyone who has grossly misinterpreted this doctrine, there have probably

63. Berkouwer, *Faith and Sanctification*; Conner, W. T. *What Is a Saint?*; Flew, *The Idea of Perfection in Christian Thought*; Barabas, *So Great Salvation*; Neill, *Christian Holiness*.

been many others who have neglected it. For every world-fleeing ascetic who has had the ridicule of men there have been many world-compromising religionists who have been quite acceptable to men. Some have cried against worldliness and for holiness, but many have been willing to rest sanctification in the archives of their grandfathers and to relegate it to the history of the nineteenth century. After all, we are too busy in America greasing the wheels of twentieth century activities to pause and ask, "Who is the Holy One, what direction would He have us follow, and what would He have us to become?" A renewed rook at the biblical understanding of sanctification is imperative.

II

Sanctification as Dedication

First of all, sanctification has as its primary meaning what may be called "dedication." The whole biblical concept of sanctification is rooted in the truth that God is holy. In the Song of Moses, these words are to be found: "Who is like thee, O Lord, among the gods? Who is like thee, majestic in holiness . . . ?" (Exod 15:11, RSV). The antiphon of a seraphic group is recorded in the words, "Holy, holy, holy is the Lord of Hosts; the whole earth is full of his glory" (Isa 6:3, RSV). What the righteousness of God is to justification, the holiness of God is to sanctification. Therefore, going back to the term "holy," one finds therein a religious term which is the Old Testament is almost synonymous with deity. Perhaps best rendered by the modern word "transcendent," this word "holy" applied to the very being and nature of God. We misinterpret its meaning if we say that it is basically a word for purity, or even a word for perfection after human standards. Rather, to be "holy" is to be the very God of Israel. Thus, twenty-four times in the book of Isaiah we have the reference to "the Holy One of Israel" as the God of Israel.[64] God's uniqueness or distinctiveness is suggested by the probably root meaning of this word, namely, "to cut off" and thus "to separate." God as holy is the distinctive, other One. It is the very deity of God that is bound up in this great Old Testament word.

Of course, this word came not only to be applied to God and also to men. That which was dedicated to Almighty God was called "holy." In the original sense, He alone is holy; but because there were those men and things that were dedicated to the worship and the service of the Holy One, in a derived sense these men and things could be called holy. Consequently,

64. Baab, *The Theology of the Old Testament*, 35f.

the Bible abounds in examples of those human beings and those institutions that are described as "holy." Thus, the nation of Israel is holy (Exod 19:6), the ground where God confronted Moses is holy (Exod 3:5), the tabernacle and its furnishings are holy (Exod 40:9f.), the offerings are holy (Lev 6:17), the Sabbath is holy (Lev 27:30), the temple is holy (Ps 79:1), Jerusalem is holy (Neh 11:1), the promise is holy (Ps 105:42), the covenant is holy (Dan 11:28, 30; Luke 1:72), the law is holy (Rom 7:12), the Scriptures are holy (2 Tim 3:15), angels (Mark 8:38), apostles and prophets (Eph 3:5) are holy, and the new Jerusalem is holy (Rev 21:2). In this derived sense, men and things are called "holy" not because they are perfect, not because they are pure, not by virtue of any specific degree of obedience to God or ethical attainment, but rather because they are dedicated to God. Thus, the primary meaning of sanctification is being dedicated or set apart to the Holy God, the Eternal one. As W. T. Conner pointed out in his little book, *What is a Saint?*,[65] one misinterprets this great truth if he begins with purification or some other meaning. Take, for example, John 17:19 in which our Lord said, "I sanctify myself." If sanctification be primarily purification, then arises a strange problem of interpreting what our Lord would mean by saying "I purify myself." But, if sanctification means primarily dedication, the meaning of that text comes alive. Accordingly, Jesus meant "I dedicate myself. "

III

The Scope of the Sanctified

A second truth about sanctification is that sanctification is in the New Testament ascribed to all Christians. In Paul's letters, the familiar word "saints" connotes the totality of Christians in a given place, not a group of specially pious ones who have segregated themselves from the body of believers. Such present saints Paul identified with the body of Christians. Even to Corinth, he could write about saints and to saints, some of whom were living in a most unsaintly manner.

This truth that all Christians are saints, of course, is denied on two or three sides. It is denied by the Roman Catholic doctrine of sainthood, which is after all a strange and somewhat incongruous mixture of two teachings. The Roman Catholic Church says on the one hand that saints are those who, beholding the beatific vision, are in heaven. To be in heaven is to be a saint and to be a part of the church triumphant.[66] On the other hand, the Ro-

65. Conner, *What is a Saint?*, 9.

66. The saints are "the Elect, those who have attained the end for which they were

man Church says in another breath that those are saints who, being assuredly in heaven, have been specially beatified and canonized by the Roman Church, because of their exceptional virtue and piety and because miracles supposedly have been wrought when their particular intercession has been sought. Therefore, one may ask the question, how does the Roman church reconcile these two? On the one hand, saints are those whose names are on the church's canonized calendar, and on the other hand the saints are all those who are in heaven. Are these groups identical in number? Has not the doctrine of purgatory created this problem?

The truth that all Christians are indeed to be called "saints" is denied from a different standpoint by the modern doctrine of entire sanctification or perfection, the modern doctrine of holiness, having its foundation in Wesleyanism and having as one of its exponents Charles G. Finney. This doctrine has been in numerous instances taken beyond both Wesley and Finney with a resultant strong emphasis upon an instantaneous, crisis experience, subsequent to becoming a Christian but possible before death, in which the Christian comes to be freed from all sin and characterized by the perfect love of God. This experience has been variously described as "the second blessing," "the second work of grace," "entire sanctification," "Christian perfection," etc. Does the New Testament give us any ground for saying that the number of the sanctified ones is fewer than the number of the justified ones? Can we so separate these great terms as to say that the one stands for one distinct experience and the other an altogether separated act of divine grace? Paul wrote in the First Corinthian letter (6:11, RSV), "But you were washed, you were sanctified, you were justified in the name of the Lord Jesus Christ and in the Spirit of our God." If Paul had followed the fashion of the modern doctrine of holiness, he would have corrected that poor order in that he surely would have said "justified" before he said "sanctified." Sometimes there is a failure to distinguish when the meaning of maturity appears in the New Testament word usually translated "perfect" (τέλειος). Moreover, a lowered concept of sin may actually be implicit in the doctrine of entire sanctification or perfection. It is usually defined in terms of the absence of overt sins or conscious and identifiable sins, so that the deeper involvements of sin in the human personality and in human society may sometimes be obscured. Such a claim to realized perfection stands in marked contrast to the claims of some of the greatest followers of Jesus Christ across the centuries who in the very hours of their spiritual triumphs have not hesitated to say, as did Paul (Phil 3:12–14), that they had not yet arrived, that they had not yet attained to Christlikeness. G. C. Berkouwer,

made, in the Kingdom of God," according to Myers, "The Mystical Body of Christ," 685.

the Dutch Reformed theologian, has wisely observed, "Perfectionism is a premature seizure of the glory that will be."[67]

While all Christians are "saints," all Christians obviously are not equally godlike or mature; all do not stand at the same mark in spiritual growth. Martin Luther it was who said in a very classic way that a Christian man was *simul justus et peccator*, "at the same time a justified man and a sinner," thus pointing to the truth that the justified man is not completely free from the reality of sin and that he still must struggle against it in his present life. If Luther was right in saying that Christians are at the same time justified persons and sinners, it would also seemingly be proper to say that we are "at the same time sanctified persons and sinners."

Indeed, ordination to the Christian pastoral ministry is no guarantee of mature sainthood. Some may recall that the Apostle Paul admonished Timothy to "rekindle (or stir up) the gift of God that is within you through the laying on of my hands (2 Tim 1:6, RSV). There may be today some un-stirred gifts, some charisms that have not been kindled. Being ordained ministers of Jesus Christ is no guarantee of maturity, of depth of dedication to God, of Christlikeness. The history and theology of the Russian Orthodox Church holds a fact that seems to be like a strange thread running all through Russian history. It is a fact that goes back to the ninth century when those missionary translators, Cyril and Methodius, first put the Slavic language into an alphabet. Lacking the sounds of the Slavs and the letters of the Greeks, they made a written language, and from the earliest days of Christianity in their midst the Slavic peoples heard the Gospel and worshipped in their own tongue. This is different from what happened in the Latin West. There Latin, not the vernacular, was the language both of the Bible and of the liturgy. The clergy could, therefore, come into a place of peculiar preeminence and status so that there was a wider gulf between the clergy and the laity in the West that never existed in the East. Perhaps this is why in the history of Russian Orthodoxy a strange preeminence has been given to laymen. Therefore, it is no accident that in the days of Muscovite Empire the rulers of Moscow, when wanting advice concerning the spiritual destiny as well as the political affairs of the nation, turned to the monastery to a "lay" monk for their answer. It is no strange event, likewise, that in the nineteenth and twentieth centuries some of the clearest expressions of the soul of Russian Christianity have come from laymen, men like Alexei Khomyakov, Fyodor Dostoevsky, Vladimir Soloviev, and Nicholas Berdyaev. Being an officiating minister of Jesus Christ is not in itself a certificate of mature sainthood. Our generation may indeed be conscious of the genuine

67. Berkouwer, *Faith and Sanctification*, 67.

sainthood of some of the saints that are not "ministers" in the Southern Baptist Convention than they will be of some of us who are.

IV

Sanctification the Work of God

Thirdly, sanctification according to the New Testament is the work of God, the Triune God. First Thessalonians 5:23 (RSV) reads, "May the God of peace himself sanctify you wholly at the corning of our Lord Jesus Christ." Here "the God of peace" is obviously the Father. In 1 Cor 1:30 (RSV),the same Paul wrote: "He is the source of your life in Christ Jesus, whom God made our wisdom, our righteousness and sanctification and redemption." Jesus Christ, then, is made our sanctification! Second Thessalonians 2:13, RSV, contains another Pauline statement about sanctification: "But we are bound to give thanks to God always for you, brethren beloved by the Lord, be-cause God chose you from the beginning to be saved, through sanctification by the spirit and belief in the truth." It is common to emphasize the unique role of the Holy Spirit in sanctification. This is right and proper. But it is not amiss to recognize that the work of sanctification is in a sense also the work of Father and Son. It is the work of the Triune God. Sanctification as the work of God is emphasized by the fact that throughout the New Testament the passive form of the verb "to sanctify" (ἁγιάζειν) predominates. The Old Testament often says "Sanctify yourselves." The New Testament almost uniformly says, "Be ye sanctified." Sanctification as the work of God is not something that occurs contrary to man's consent to be sure, but God is the Sanctifier.

At this point, one may question what has been called the Keswick doctrine of sanctification. Such a doctrine seems to make sanctification dependent entirely upon one's prior willingness to be sanctified and regards the Holy Spirit as being, as it were, employed instrumentally by us; that is, we counteract "the flesh" by the Holy Spirit who aids us and serves us as we sanctify ourselves. Contra Keswick, we do not use the Holy Spirit in that instrumental sense. The Holy Spirit rather works to make us like Jesus Christ.[68] All the ascetical systems and schemes of self-cultivation of virtues are questionable if they lead to the notion that we can sanctify ourselves merely by using God as a kind of convenient instrument. When appeals are made in Baptist congregations for persons to "rededicate" their lives to Jesus Christ and to make a public rededication of themselves to God, is this act

68. For a statement of the Keswick doctrine, cf. Barabas, *So Great Salvation*, 1952.

interpreted to mean that somehow one does perform an act of dedication? Or is it interpreted as a response in which Christians are yielding themselves afresh to the God who has dedicated them unto Himself? Surely an act of rededication, meaningful as it may be, ought not to be interpreted as a mere human act.

V

Sanctification and Justification

In the fourth place, sanctification is not always in the New Testament related to justification as process is to act. Admittedly, the standard Reformation teaching at this point set down by Calvin and Luther and brought on down through Charles Hodge and A. H. Strong was this: we are justified as an act of divine grace in a point of time as an event, but we are sanctified through all our Christian experience as a process, to be culminated at death or beyond death. There is an element of truth, to be sure, here. That element of truth is that the Pauline doctrine of justification is never stretched out over the whole Christian life. Paul speaks of having been "justified" as if he meant that this is something that happened when men became Christians. But the other side is not so clear. In fact, the historic Reformation doctrine needs reexamination in the light of the New Testament. Such reexamination among Southern Baptists has been undertaken by Harold W. Tribble and W. T. Conner.[69]

69. Tribble's contribution was primarily to stress that dedication is the basic meaning of sanctification, as evidenced especially in John 17:19. Tribble interpreted sanctification as act rather than process. cf. *The Christian's Spiritual Life or the Doctrine of Sanctification* and *Our Doctrines*, 123. Yet, sanctification, for Tribble, in no sense begins at the time of regeneration. "Regeneration," he wrote in 1928, "comes before the sanctification of the followers of Christ . . . 'Ye must be born again' comes first" (*The Christian's Spiritual Life*, 17, 20). In the revised edition of *Our Doctrines* in 1936 (73–103), Tribble placed sanctification in the chapter on "The Human Side of Christian Experience" along with repentance, faith, and confession rather than in the chapter on "The Divine Side of Christian Experience" along with forgiveness, regeneration, justification, and adoption. Thus, Tribble interpreted sanctification primarily as a human response of the Christian rather than as a work of God.

Conner, on the other hand, agreeing with Tribble that sanctification can properly be interpreted as an act of dedication, went beyond Tribble (1) in insisting that sanctification is both "by the power of the Spirit and by . . . faith" and (2) in breaking more completely with the Reformation pattern of construing justification and sanctification as act and process, respectively. Conner distinguished "positional sanctification" and "progressive sanctification" and made the former "synonymous with justification and regeneration." cf. *A System of Christian Doctrine*, 467f.; *The Gospel of Redemption*, 193–95; *What is a Saint?*, 11.

What is this other aspect of sanctification? The Apostle Peter opened his First Epistle (1:1f; RSV) as follows: "Peter, an apostle of Jesus Christ, to the exiles of the Dispersion . . . , chosen and destined by God the Father and sanctified by the Spirit for obedience to Jesus Christ and for sprinkling with his blood," What does this mean? It means that Peter is saying that there is a sanctification "for" or "unto obedience and unto the sprinkling of the blood of Jesus." If one always interprets sanctification as a process, how can he explain Peter's statement, "sanctified unto the sprinkling of the blood of Jesus"? Did Peter mean that the "sprinkling" would occur after death? Or rather is sanctification as used by Peter more or less descriptive of our becoming Christians? Recall again Paul's statement in 1 Cor 1:30 that Christ was "made our wisdom, our righteousness and sanctification and redemption." It does not seem that Paul in that context is singling out sanctification so as to make it different from the other terms. Observe also 2 Thess 2:13b, RSV: ". . . God chose you from the beginning to be saved, through sanctification by the Spirit and belief in the truth." There it seems that sanctification occurs concurrently with belief in the truth, and both of these are instrumental to salvation. One ought not to impose on the New Testament lines of demarcation that do not grow out of the New Testament. That seems to justify some hesitation as to exact agreement with the view that sanctification is always the process and justification the act. Rather it would be clearer to say that justification is the initiatory act in nearly all of the uses of this term, but sanctification has a more flexible meaning. When Paul wrote to saints, he implied that they had been sanctified or dedicated unto Jesus Christ, but he also declares that, since there are some thorny problems in Corinth and some trouble in Thessalonia, therefore "the will of God" is "your sanctification: that you should abstain from immorality" (1 Thess 4:3, RSV). There are other texts, to be cited presently, which point beyond the present to the future, to the fulfillment of sanctification. Sanctification is not so much something which men can put into a time schedule. Its basic meaning is dedication to God and the God-likeness which comes from being truly dedicated to God.

VI

Sanctification Versus Moral Evil

In the fifth place, sanctification stands opposed to all moral impurity and unrighteousness and is God's call to absolute Godlikeness. One need not minimize the fact that sanctification has its ethical implications in the New

Testament. Paul was clear about these as he wrote in Rom 6:19, RSV: "I am speaking in human terms, because of your natural limitations. For just as you once yielded your members to righteousness for sanctification." Again, "This is the will of God, your sanctification, that you abstain from immorality . . . For God has not called us for uncleanness, but in holiness" (1 Thess 4:3, 7, RSV). Therefore, Christians are not to take lightly the ethical and moral aspects of being dedicated unto God. The lives of worshippers reflect the conception of the nature of the God or gods whom they worship. Those who worshipped the gods of Greece and Rome, the deities of Olympus, could and did follow the immoral, petulant, and conniving activities of these so-called gods. Those who were in the cult of Baal could join in the sensualities that were common to Baalite religion. Likewise, those who worship and serve "the God and Father of our Lord Jesus Christ," who confess His name and proclaim His gospel, must, in reality, become like the God whom they serve.

America's moral decline can be halted to the extent that Christians are truly dedicated by the Spirit of God and become increasingly like the God to whom and by whom they have been sanctified. Like the ermine, that has perfectly white fur and yet such a horror of filth that it would rather be captured than to be defiled, Christians are called upon to live amid the unrighteousness and the impurities of 20th-century America. But do Christians have a kindred concern that they, redeemed from sin, might become like Jesus Christ and so live in the midst of ungodliness? Do we yearn to become mature followers of Jesus Christ, to be recognized not so much as Mr. Jones, pastor of the Baptist church, or as Mr. Jones, BD, but rather Mr. Jones, a saint of God. There is much land to be possessed in laying hold of the fulness of what it means to be sanctified. One need not be afraid of our being too sanctified as Baptists if we understand what sanctification means. Baptists ought not to pass over all the responsibility for sanctification to the Church of the Nazarene and the Churches of God or to the Roman Catholic Church. The time has come for Baptists to re-examine themselves in thoroughgoing soul-searching. One application among many may be noted.

VII

A Contemporary Application[70]

If we Baptists are really mature in Christ and are becoming like Christ, if we are being renewed in the image of Him who created us and are being

70. A more pressing problem for Southern Baptists at the time of publication is

"conformed," as Paul said, "to the image (or the likeness) of his Son" (Rom 8:29, RSV), then we ought to be able to find a way to meet the challenges that are before us today. We now hear the question raised as to whether Southern Baptists will divide or ought to divide. They may sound like strange words, yet who will deny the possibility thereof? Have we counted the cost and weighed the consequences of such an occurrence? Have we measured the probable effects on the missionary enterprise to which we have been dedicated and which, perhaps more than anything else, has held us together? In a generation and a time in history when more attention has been given to Christian unity than in many centuries, when the great communions of Protestantism have found themselves closer together than in four centuries, when the Eastern Orthodox and the Roman Catholics can talk more amicably to one another than they have done since the eleventh century, does it make sense for Southern Baptists, who have said they had some convictions as to why they could not participate in the ecumenical movement, to act as if it did not matter if they should split in three or four directions? Would Southern Baptists not thereby be the laughing stock of the whole Christian world? Surely, there is a way in the midst of the stresses and the storms to find the will of God. But men who find and follow this divine pattern must find themselves conformable to His likeness and image and conscious that the great goal of sanctification is not completed. Hear the words of the Epistle to the Hebrews, "Strive for peace with all men, and for the holiness without which no one shall see the Lord" (Heb 12:14, RSV), and Paul's prayer "that he may establish your hearts unblamable in holiness before our God and Father, at the coming of our Lord Jesus with all his saints" (1 Thess 3:13, RSV).

Ours is a responsibility, first of all, to be made saints and to become saintlike, not so much by our conscious effort to enroll in sainthood as by trustful obedience as He to Whom we are dedicated makes us to be like he is. So dedicated to Him and reflecting His grace, we may lead others to become like unto Jesus Christ. This is our challenge: "Be ye sanctified." This is the goal of our Lord's evangel, bearers of which we are privileged to be.

their response to the racial crisis, which may prove to be the most critical issue faced by them during the twentieth century.

10

"Evangelism and Social Involvement" (1969/70)[1]

The relation of evangelism and social involvement is now a very acute issue in various Christian denominations, and especially is this true among Baptists. A paradigm of the current difficulties in the proper resolution of the tension between these two aspects of the mission of the Christian *ecclesia* is to be found in the report that the evangelism staff and the social action staff of the World Council of Churches find it very hard to communicate with each other meaningfully, although both are housed in the same building in Geneva.

Why is This Now an Acute Issue?

There are numerous reasons why this particular issue has come to be, especially in the 1960s, a critical issue. Some of these may be noted briefly.

First, the tides of influence have ceased to flow only in one direction from the Western or so-called "Christian" nations to other nations. At the present time, conversions to the Christian faith are not so influenced by cultural, colonial, or civilizational factors as in most of the late nineteenth and early twentieth-century era. Such a condition has evoked reconsiderations of the goals and the means of Christian evangelization.

Secondly, the growth of large blocs, even majorities, of non-Christians among the so-called "Christian" nations of the West, including those

1. This article was first presented to the missionary convocation of Spurgeon's College, London, England, on May 8, 1969. It then appeared in *Southwestern Journal of Theology* 12.2 (Spring 1970) 51–62.

persons who retain certain formal links with the institutional structures of Christianity, has made anachronistic the societal concept of the *corpus christianum*, derived from the medieval period and retained, even if in national and competing segments, in post-Reformation Europe. The Christian situation in Europe and in most of North America is such that Christians in these areas must realize that evangelism should begin at home and that the field is the whole world.

Thirdly, the wide extension of the franchise (ballot) in democratic nations has given to or placed on the average citizen, including the average Christian man and woman, greater responsibility for the shaping of the political order than his ancestors had. Contrast with this the severe limitations upon Christians in the Roman Empire in the New Testament era so far as direct influence on the political order was concerned.

A fourth factor of great importance is the urgency of the great social or societal problems of our increasingly technological world order such as poverty, overpopulation, race, war, class conflict, crime, pollution, and the like. Such problems not only baffle the wisest and ablest of the political leadership but call for the spiritual energies and loving participation of contemporary Christians.

In the fifth place, a critical evaluation of the more individualistic, "pietistic" expression of Protestant Christianity and of its understanding of Christian conversion has been in progress. Such critique has been goaded by the Marxist charges of exploitation through the promise of "pie in the sky by and by" and fostered by the recovery of the Hebraic holistic understanding of man and the validly-realized dimensions of Christian eschatology with the result that "saving of souls" has tended to be replaced by "transformation of lives."[2]

Similarly, there have been frequent and varied reassessments of the Social Gospel in American Protestantism and Christian Socialism in the United Kingdom. The Kingdom of God, for example, has been found to be not identical with any political or social reforms or programs. Moreover, critics such as Reinhold Niebuhr[3] have stressed the stubborn residual power of sin in human society as well as in individuals. Nevertheless, the critics have retained the sense of Christian responsibility for the structuring of society which the Social Gospel and Christian Socialism magnified.

2. See Davies, *Worship and Mission*, 39–46.

3. In his Niebuhr, *Moral Man and Immoral Society*, Niebuhr first advanced the thesis "that a sharp distinction must be drawn between the moral and social behavior of individuals and of social groups" according to which, while individuals are at times capable of sympathy, a sense of justice, and consideration of the interests of others, social groups are more potently driven by "collective egoism."

A seventh consideration is the relatively smaller proportion of professing Christians among the rapidly increasing total world population and the fact that such a decreasing proportion of Christians is occurring at the very time when secularist, humanist, and anti-theistic movements and influences are very potent.

Furthermore, the sterility of churches that have in the past been evangelistically effective and the somnolence of many churches to the pressing needs and concerns of mankind today have helped to make the issue under consideration crucial. One cannot only point to the meager remnant of the once mission-minded Nestorian Church and to the lands of the Near East and northern Africa now dominated by Islam where once a thriving witness to Christ prevailed, one can also point to church buildings and locations in the United Kingdom and in the United States where a nineteenth-century aggressive Christian outreach has been replaced by twentieth-century spiritual apathy. Moreover, even where missionaries are still being commissioned there has been at times a serious lack of concern as to how the Christian mission is to be related to the agonizing needs and legitimate strivings of human beings and human societies.

Finally, Baptists and others of the "Believers' Church" heritage face the contemporary dilemma of evangelism or social involvement with a special acuteness. These Christians have characteristically stressed the proclamation of the Word of God, the witness of lay people, the necessity of a voluntary, personal faith-commitment, and the miracle of regeneration by the Spirit of God. Baptists in particular have in most nations been closely identified with the underprivileged masses and sympathetic with their needs. Kenneth Scott Latourette has emphasized that believers' churches have had a distinctive role in bringing the gospel to the poor and less advantaged.[4] Exceptions to this general trend are to be found in England, where most industrial workers and their families have been outside organized Christianity since the Industrial Revolution and Baptists tend to be almost exclusively of the middle class, and the Southern states in the United States, where many white Baptists have been oblivious and even hostile to the needs and rights of Negro fellow citizens and fellow Christians. The heirs of the Believers' Church heritage need to take seriously the words of J. K. Zeman, a Canadian Baptist leader whose background is in the Lutheran and Reformed tradition in Czechoslovakia:

> A denomination which is constituted on the principle of "mixed membership" and on infant baptism can predict its numerical growth [or decrease] on the basis of national vital statistics . . .

4. Latourette, "A People in the World: Historical Background," 248f.

[but] a believers' church is only one generation away from extinction. Unless God the Spirit continues His gracious ministry of regeneration, such a church is doomed to death.[5]

What Are the Biblical Guidelines for This Issue?

From this review of some of the reasons for the acuteness of this issue, it is now in order to turn to the biblical foundations on the basis of which Christians may hopefully seek and find an adequate resolution of the issue.

Several Old Testament themes are especially pertinent to the issue under discussion. The covenant of the God of electing love and loyalty love, Yahweh, with his people Israel (Deut 7:6–10) is coupled with Yahweh's purpose through Israel to extend his salvation to all nations (Isa 49:5f) so that the faith of Israel came to include both particularism and universalism. The prophets of Israel and Judah, especially those of the eighth century BC, protested not only against an idolatrous or adulterous unfaithfulness toward God but also against the exploitation of the poor, dishonesty in business practices, and selfish luxury. The first of the Servant songs (Isa 42:1–4) anticipated the Servant's non-violent establishment of justice among the nations, while the Spirit-anointed Liberator was

> to bring good tidings to the afflicted . . . to bind up the brokenhearted, to proclaim liberty to the captives,
>
> and the opening of the prison to those who are bound;
>
> to proclaim the year of the Lord's favor,
>
> and the day of vengeance of our God to comfort all who mourn to grant to those who mourn in Zion— to give them a garland instead of ashes, the oil of gladness instead of mourning, the mantle of praise instead of a faint spirit; that they may be called oaks of righteousness, the planting of the Lord, that he may be glorified (Isa 60:1b-3, RSV)

The mission of Jesus is the foundation for the interpretation of the mission of the new People of God. That the role of Jesus was shaped by the Servant motif may be seen in the saying, "For the Son of man also came not to be served but to serve, and to give his life for the ransom of many" (Mark 10:45, RSV).[6] The Matthean interpretation of the ministry of Jesus

5. Groff, "Theological Interpretation," 60.

6. In submitting to suffering and death as the way of self-giving, Jesus thereby turned from the popular Messianism which was, at least for some, intimately connected

was threefold: teaching in their synagogues and preaching the gospel of the kingdom and healing every disease and every infirmity" (4:23, 9:35). The Johannine witness includes the saying, "As the Father has sent me, even so I send you . . . Receive the Holy Spirit" (20:21b, 22b). The disciples of Jesus are "the salt of the earth" and "the light of the world" and should let their "light so shine before men, that they may see" their "good works" and "glorify" the heavenly Father (Matt 5:13a, 14a, 16). According to Luke-Acts, "repentance and forgiveness of sins should be preached in his name to all nations, beginning from Jerusalem" (Luke 24:27) and "you shall receive power when the Holy Spirit has come upon you and you shall be my witnesses in Jerusalem and in all Judea and Samaria and to the end of the earth" (Acts 1:8). Matthew reported Jesus' post-resurrection commission as follows: "Going, disciplize all nations, baptizing them into the name of the Father and of the Son and of the Holy Spirit, teaching them to observe all that I have commanded you, and lo, I am with you all the days unto the consummation of the age" (28:19f, writer's translation).

The apostles interpreted their own role and the mission of the post-Pentecostal *ecclesia* as derivative from and expressive of the salvific or reconciling work of the crucified and risen Messiah and Lord. Thus, Paul declared, "For I am not ashamed of the gospel: for it is the power of God unto salvation to every one that believeth, to the Jew first, and also to the Greek" (Rom 1:16, ASV). Furthermore, "if anyone is in Christ, he is a new creation; . . . All this is from God, who through Christ reconciled us to himself and gave us the ministry of reconciliation . . . So we are ambassadors for Christ, God making his appeal through us. We beseech you on behalf of Christ, be reconciled to God" (2 Cor 5:17a, 18, 20, RSV). According to both Peter and Paul, the work of Christ has a corporate dimension and has had distinct social effects. "But you are a chosen race, a royal priesthood, a holy nation, God's own people, that you may declare the wonderful deeds of him who called you out of darkness into his marvelous light. . . . Maintain good conduct among the Gentiles, so that in case they speak against you as wrongdoers, they may see your good deeds and glorify God on the day of visitation" (1 Pet. 2:9, 12, RSV). Of Jews and Gentiles Paul wrote: "For he is our peace, who has made us both one, and has broken down the dividing wall of hostility . . . that he might create in himself one new man in place of the two, so making peace, and might reconcile us both to God in one body through the cross, thereby bringing the hostility to an end" (Eph 2:14, 15b, 16, RSV). Christian love and true religion were described concretely in terms of love in action. "By this we know love, that he laid down his life

---

with the revolutionary program of the Zealots.

for us and we ought to lay down lives for the brethren. But if anyone has the world's goods and sees his brother in need, yet closes his heart against him, how does God's love abide in him" (1 John 3:16f, RSV)? "Religion that is pure and undefiled before God and the Father is this: to visit orphans and widows in their affliction, and to keep oneself unstained from the world" (Jas 1:27).

What Basic Definitions Are Essential to Clarifying This Issue?

The terms "evangelism" and "social involvement" have been employed without definition, though with the implication that both are distinctly Christian activities. More precision in definition now becomes essential.

By "evangelism" is meant Christians bearing witness to the good news of God's action in man's behalf in Jesus Christ, to whom they themselves have responded believingly, with the purpose of fostering and eliciting from others this same response of repentance-faith to the regenerating work of God the Holy Spirit. The Department of Studies in Evangelism of the World Council of Churches has described the role of Christians in evangelism as striving to "bring about the occasions for men's response to Jesus Christ." Whatever the definition, the element of wooing, inviting, and appealing should not be eliminated, although it may not always be explicit and verbal. But it is also important to state some of the things that evangelism is not. It is not high-pressure salesmanship, or religious "hucksterism," or the coercion of religious commitment. Neither is it rightly defined as any Christian deed, duty, or action, in behalf of others, or a combination of these.

By "social involvement" is meant Christians individually or corporately operative in human society (or outside the churches) for the purpose of human, good or well-being. Moreover, there are at least two distinct, though related, types of social involvement open to churches and Christians. One consists of Christian ministries of helping, or *diakonal service* such as healing, caring, sharing, etc. Such diakonal involvement is the duty and privilege of Christians in whatever era or circumstance they may live, though the particular forms of this service should be shaped by actual human needs. Such service should begin with one's fellow Christians and extend into the wider circle of human associations. Hence, Paul admonished the Galatian Christians to "do good to all men, and especially to those who are of the household of faith" (Gal 6:10b, c, RSV). Protestants, including those of the more evangelistic or revivalistic type, have not been without their fruitage in the Christian helping ministries: hospitals, homes for orphan and neglected children, schools of all types, homes for unwed mothers, homes for the aged, and kindred enterprises. Roman Catholics have established a wide range of institutions of this same type and often preceded Baptists and other Protestants in doing so. The historic peace churches (Mennonite, Quaker, Brethren) have contributed wartime noncombatant service and disaster relief of many kinds. However, the question must now be raised as to how effective these institutions have been and now are in ministering to those outside the churches. For example, the Baptist home for the aged may have become the home for aged Baptists!

A second type of social involvement consists of the efforts of Christians, either corporately or individually, to change the patterns or structures of the political, economic, or social order so that these may conform more fully to what they understand to be the good and well-being of mankind in the light of the purpose of God. This may be called *social action*. Evangelical Protestantism has been more productive of social reforms than some of its critics have recognized. J. Wesley Bready's research on the societal impact of the Evangelical Revival on the United Kingdom[7] and Timothy Smith's study of revivalist influence on social reform in mid-nineteenth-century America[8] are noteworthy, while the evidence that the recent civil rights movement in the United States was born in the Negro Baptist and Methodist churches is not to be disputed.

There are churches that engage in diakonal service without any significant participation in social action; such has been true of certain Protestant congregations and denominations in the United States which have been very closely allied with the status quo in society. There are some churches that engage in social action but hardly are involved in diakonal service. American Unitarians have been active in civil rights struggles, but where does one find their hospitals or rescue homes? Some churches during the present decade have shifted their stress entirely to social action; such a stance leaves the church open to the criticism that it is asking the government to do what it is not willing itself to undertake. Some churches have had almost no diakonal service or social action, preferring to major on the pure proclamation of the gospel.

7. Bready, *England*.

8. Smith, *Revivalism and Social Reform in Mid-Nineteenth-Century America.*

What Are the Either/Or Tendencies Regarding Evangelism and Social Involvement?

Some contemporary Christians and churches are opting for the stance of "only evangelism," the view that the sole mission (not merely the primary mission) of the church is evangelism, especially in its form of verbalized witness or proclamation. The following arguments are sometimes advanced in support of this view: (1) Neither our Lord nor his apostles ever expected or promised an ideal human society within history. (2) The biblical injunctions to preach, bear witness, make disciples, etc. are obvious, unmistakable, and central. (3) The human problem at its deepest level is a sin problem, and sin must be dealt with and overcome if society is to be significantly and permanently altered. (4) A changed society depends upon changed men, i.e., reborn men, recreated men. Even Walter Rauschenbusch, best-known theologian of the Social Gospel in the United States, taught the need for the regeneration of individual persons.[9] More recently, John A. Mackay has asserted that it is "the business of the church to create the creators of the new social order." (5) Since the spiritual is more important than the physical, the need 'for spiritual food is even greater than the need for physical food. (6) Only a clear call to Christian commitment can make distinct the church and the unbelieving world and prevent a new flood of culture-religion.

Some warnings concerning the case for "evangelism only" are in order. (1) The "salvation of souls" and "winning of souls" must mean the total lives of human beings, including their bodies; for example, the word *sodzein* in the New Testament is used not only to mean "to save" but also "to make whole or heal." (2) Evangelism, employed in the strict sense, should be followed by instruction, nurture, worship, the cultivation of piety, witness, service, and growth in the Christian life. (3) An emphasis on the primacy of evangelism does not necessarily preclude Christian helping ministries or Christian action for social change. Compare Acts 1:8, 6:1–6 and Gal 2:11–14.

Other contemporary Christians and churches are opting for the stance of "only social involvement," or the view that the primary mission, if not the sole mission, of the church today is that of enactment of deeds, either in helping ministries or in societal change or in both. The following arguments are sometimes set forth in support of this view. (1) The Christian church for most of its history has put the stress on verbal proclamation or sacramental action; now in the present era what is needed is enactment by deeds of love, sympathy, helpfulness, and identification with the oppressed and less privileged. (2) The church has often become identified with the

9. Rauschenbusch, *A Theology for the Social Gospel*, 95–109.

societal status quo and has even been at times a defender of its injustices, exclusive privileges, and oppression. Compare the Roman Catholic Church in pre-revolutionary France, the Russian Orthodox Church prior to 1917, and Protestant and Roman Catholic churches in the southern United States until the present decade. The churches must now identify with the revolutionary forces of the present after the example of Martin Luther King Jr. and Helder Camara, the Roman Catholic archbishop of Olinda and Recife, Brazil. (3) Jesus is to be understood primarily as a revolutionary in the society of his day, a friend of the underprivileged, a breaker of the Jewish and Roman molds, a nonconformist and dangerous figure, whose characterization often closely resembles that of a Los Angeles hippie. (4) Jesus did not come merely to rescue men for a future heaven but to change the earthly human order in which they now live. (5) The church should always put human values above property values. (6) Non-Christians must know unmistakably that Christians do care about their agonies and concerns.

Some warnings concerning the case for "social involvement only" are in order. (1) The churches have had helping ministries and have contributed to societal change before the present era. Let all young Turks take note! (2) The "servant church," if truly based on the servanthood of its Lord, must be concerned with the reconciliation of men with God as well as with reconciliation with fellow men. (3) Churches today must carefully discern the religious or moral or human values or issues in political, economic, and social problems and proposals so as to know how to be a prophetic voice rather than merely another lobby.

The churches of the Southern Baptist Convention have historically given primary stress to evangelism but without neglect of the helping ministries; the involvement of these churches in social action has until very recent years been confined to selected issues such as alcoholic beverages, gambling, etc. Today, a small, but growing, group of pastors and churches within the Southern Baptist Convention is reacting unfavorably against the evangelism and revivalism of the past and is tending to substitute social involvement for evangelism.

Why Both Evangelism and Social Involvement Are Needed and Are Complementary, Not Contradictory

The crux of the present argument is that both evangelism and social involvement are essential to the mission and obedience of Christians today. That the "both/and" stance is to be taken rather than either of the "either/or" stances may be evident from a consideration of the alternatives.

What are the alternatives or probable consequences of the neglect of evangelism? Three very distinct and mutually-exclusive alternatives may be noted: (1) A neo-Constantinian extension of "baptized heathens,"[10] which believers' churches have long deplored, with greater disparity between the company of the baptized and the company of the disciples and a diffused religiosity without clear Christian experience of the grace of God; (2) The temporary and doubtful expedient of proselytizing those who have been evangelized through the ministry and witness of others—a strategy ultimately self-defeating for Christianity as a whole; and (3) A decadent, and ultimately dying, church—not in the sense of the defectibility of the whole People of God but in the sense of the demise of particular congregations and denominations.

What are some alternatives or probable consequences of the neglect of Christian social involvement? Three somewhat overlapping alternatives may be mentioned: (1) The reduction of the transmission and sharing of the gospel of Christ to words, sometimes ineffective words, to the neglect of the deeds of Jesus, which may serve as examples for today's Christians; (2) The implication that Christians tacitly consent to the injustices, deprivation, inhumanity, and suffering endured by their fellow men; and (3) The absence of clear and palpable evidence that Christians really do love their fellow men in all circumstances and conditions with the love that they claim to have received from their Lord and Saviour.

Today's need is for both evangelism and the social involvement of Christians, i.e., helping ministries and societal change. Christians must engage both in proclamation by word and enactment by deed. These must complement and cross-fertilize each other. Vatican Council II's dogmatic constitution on the Church, *Lumen Gentium*, keeps in balance the proclamation and the *diakonia*. Baptist writers, both in Britain[11] and in the Southern Baptist Convention,[12] have recently urged the same kind of balance. Striving

10. This term is that used by Christopher Wansey, Anglican vicar of Roydon, Essex, England, as reported in a news story, The Christian and Christianity Today, "'Baptised Heathens,'" 19. Speaking to "a conference on baptismal reform attended by some 90 pastors of the Evangelical churches of Westphalia and the Rhineland at Radewormvald, near Cologne," Wansey criticized Anglican baptismal practices stemming from the Act of Uniformity of 1662 and charged that "the medieval practice of 'drafting little conscripts' into the Army of Christ and calling them 'volunteers' was perpetuated, until it reached absurd proportions, and culminated in a nation of 'baptised heathens.'"

11. Bottoms, "Evangelism and Service," editorial page.

12. Maston, "Evangelism and Social Concern," 24; Harris, "Evangelism and Christian Social Action: Is It Either-Or?," 12f; Clinard, "Evangelism and Ethics," 12f.

for such a balance may not prove to be more difficult than the struggle of Christians in the fourth and fifth centuries to retain both the deity and the humanity of Jesus Christ or than the efforts in the Reformation and post-Reformation era to resolve the seeming conflict between divine sovereignty and human freedom.

We must be evangelistic pastors and churches. The Anglican Bishop of Coventry, Cuthbert Bardsley, after an eleven-day preaching mission in the new Coventry Cathedral during September 1968, argued convincingly in *The* [London] *Times* that the day of proclamation and mission is not past.[13] The same bishop, subsequently preaching in one of the Anglican parishes of Oxford, testified to university students and townspeople that the greatest decision of his life had been made forty years before when as an Oxford undergraduate he had responded personally to Jesus Christ.

We must be servant ministers and servant churches. It has been reported that, when Thomas Aquinas in the thirteenth century once visited the Pope, the Pope, pointing to the magnificent buildings and evident wealth of the Church of Rome, said to the learned Dominican, "The Church can no longer say, 'Silver and gold have I none.'" "That is right," replied Thomas, "but neither can the church say, 'In the name of Jesus of Nazareth, rise up and walk.'" We must not allow ourselves to be blinded by institutional success or security so as to miss God's mission of helping our fellow men to rise up and walk.

As in marriage, so in this crucial issue, "what therefore God has joined together, let no man put asunder" (Matt I9:6b, RSV).

13. Bardsley, "Day of Mission Is Far From Over," editorial page.

11

"Foreword" to *An Evangelical Saga: Baptists and Their Precursors in Latin America* (2005)[1]

Justice Anderson, historian and missiologist, has been motivated by and has written in the face of the convergence of three Christian phenomena.

First, we are becoming acutely aware that the center of gravity for Christianity is shifting from Europe and North America to the Southern Hemisphere (some would insist on adding all of Asia). My own reading of *The Coming of the Third Church* (1977) by Walbert Buhlmann, the Roman Catholic missiologist, and of *The Next Christendom: The Coming of Global Christianity* (2002) by Philip Jenkins, the Penn State historian, has constituted defining moments for my awareness of this momentous trend. Buhlmann, though too restricted to the Catholic scene, introduced the idea of the emergence of a predominant Third World Christianity after the millennium-long Eastern and Western epochs. Then Jenkins, a quarter century later, armed with a profusion of statistics, asserted convincingly that the shift had already occurred. Whether by observing the present-day internal tensions within the Anglican communion or taking note of the conclave that elected Pope Benedict XVI, one can hardly avoid the obvious new importance of Christianity south of the Equator.

Second, there is the changing face of Christianity in Latin America with its 480 million professed Christians. From earliest colonial times the Roman Catholic Church was virtually the exclusive form of Christianity

1. This chapter first appeared as the Foreword to Justice C. Anderson's *An Evangelical Saga: Baptists and Their Precursors in Latin America*. Maitland, FL: Zulon Press, 2005.

and so continued for nearly four centuries until the advent of Protestants, or Evangelicals. Although a half-century ago liberation theology with its basis in Marxist social analysis might have appeared to be the wave of the Latin American future, prior to its curtailment under Pope John Paul II, it was rather the Base Christian communities and the Catholic Charismatic movement that would significantly alter Latin American Catholicism. But the greatest change wrought during the last half of the twentieth century was the rise and exponential growth of Pentecostalism in Latin America, reaching the masses of the poor and disinherited with their practice of folk Catholicism and far outdistancing the Evangelicals in numbers. Anderson's readers will find, perhaps surprisingly, that Latin American Pentecostalism had roots in Latin American Evangelicalism as well as in North American Pentecostalism.

Third, the Baptists of North America and most of Europe until recently have had little knowledge of the origins and growth of Baptists in Latin America and the Caribbean, and the same is possibly true of most general historians of Christianity, for the entire story until recent years has been largely confined to the Spanish and Portuguese languages. Historians of the Baptist movement have tended to focus exclusively on Europe, North America, and Australia-New Zealand. Only Robert A. Baker (1958), Albert W. Wardin (1995), and Bill J. Leonard (2003), it seems, have included Latin America. Anderson has ably brought the Latin American Baptist pioneers—missionaries and nationals—into the global Baptist story.

Anderson, whose teaching ministry was situated both in South America's Southern cone and in the Southwestern region of the United States, carefully researched on site the history of Baptists in Asia, Africa, and Oceania, as well as in Latin America and the Caribbean, and brought together his findings as the third and final volume (1990) of his three-volume *Historia de los Bautistas*. Now he has, after updating for the last decade and a half, translated into his mother tongue the Latin American/Caribbean portion of that third volume. But in addition, Anderson has placed the narrative in the context of the Latin American Evangelical precursors—both "providential" and "intentional"—of the Baptists and of the burgeoning Pentecostal movement in Latin American and futurist studies relative to Christianity in Latin America. While he manifests his expertise, he maintains a collegial attitude toward all who have written about the Christian faith and Latin America.

For those who have a myopic vision of the Baptist movement, for those whose interests have not spilled over the parapets of old Christendom, and for those who are generally futurist and global in their thinking, "Doctor Justo," my distinguished and esteemed colleague, provides an exciting and informative venture in reading. For this, I am deeply grateful.

III.

Worship, Prayer, and Stewardship

12

"Is Anything Sacred?" (1955)[1]

A campfire service was drawing to a close. One eager student jumped up and proposed to the group, "Let's give fifteen *rahs* for Jesus."

A student prayer meeting in the men's dormitory on a Baptist campus was disturbed by a commotion in the hall. One of those in the prayer meeting opened the door and shouted to the offenders, "You blankety-blank guys, shut up! We're having a prayer meeting in here!"

Do such incidents as these make your Christian conscience cringe? If not, then you may have become insensitive to the *sin of sacrilege.*

(With some trepidation the writer has undertaken this report at the request of the editor, neither assuming the role of self-appointed critic of this student generation, nor regarding himself as belonging to any coterie of superior Christians. The data used has been obtained from Southern Baptist sources, and the incidents and quotations can be authenticated.)

What Is Sacrilege?

Sacrilege, according to *Webster's New International Dictionary,* is "The crime of stealing, misusing, violating, or desecrating that which is sacred or holy, or dedicated to sacred uses." The word itself is derived from the Latin words, *sacer* (holy) and *legere* (to gather or pick up). While the word has most frequently had a Roman Catholic ecclesiastical use, it is by no means merely a Roman Catholic term. Indeed, the Hebrews spoke of that which was holy *(qodesh)* to Jehovah and forbidden (*cherein*) to other gods,

1. This article first appeared in *Baptist Student* (May 1955) 12–15.

and distinguished between that which was holy (*qodesh*) and that which was common (*choi*).[2]

One of the most basic concepts of the Old Testament is that of holiness. Jehovah, or *Yahweh,* the God of Israel, was regarded as holy and was called "the Holy One of Israel." The term signified the divine otherness and uniqueness which differentiated God from men. Men and things were described as "holy" if and when they were set apart to the worship of *Yahweh.* Closely related to the holiness of God in the Old Testament is the reverence of the divine name. For the Hebrews, a name was no mere tag but rather had a significant relation to the reality itself. Thus, to take the name of *Yahweh* "in vain" (Ex 20:7) was to abuse the very person of *Yahweh.* After the Babylonian captivity, out of reverence the Jews used ADONAI or "Lord" instead of pronouncing the covenant name, YAHWEH. In the model prayer of our Lord, the first petition is "*Hallowed* be thy name" (Matt 6:9).

Contemporary Examples

From the biblical background, we turn to the problem at hand. Many are the evidences today of lessened reverence for the name and being of God. The use of "Thou," "Thee," and "Thine" has frequently been supplanted by the use of "you" and "your" in respect to God. Some, it would seem, think of God as a "Buddy" or the "Man Upstairs" rather than the great sovereign Creator and Father of our Lord Jesus Christ. A parrot in a cafe near a Baptist campus was known to have been taught to say, "Praise the Lord! Hallelujah!"

Sin and the Christian experience of salvation have been the subject of some less-than-reverent treatment. Some sing, "I was sinking deep in sin—whee!" while others sing, "One, two, three, the Devil's after me." Some seminary students have yelled, "Yea, black, yea gray, yea Seminary, let's pray." In a similar category are such expressions as "We want to get on the ball for you, Lord." A jazzy rendition of "When the Saints Go Marching In" by a Baptist college band at a football game created difficulties for the Baptist students from the rival state college campus.

A Mock Sermon

The Bible has also been involved in contemporary sacrilege. One illustration of this is a mock sermon, "The Good Samaritan." Only a brief portion of this desecration of the Scriptures is quoted.

2. Cf. Snaith, *The Distinctive Ideas of the Old Testament*, 24–44.

"The text for this sermon is taken from Generations to Revolutions.

"There was once a man, the good Samaritan, going from Jerusalem to Jericho, and he fell among thorns. The thorns rose up and choked him down a hundredfold. An angel strove with him and set him free.

"As he was going on down the road he met the Queen of Shebah. She gave him a hundred changes of raiment and fifty pieces of silver. He bought himself a chariot and drove furiously all day long until he came to a Juniper tree and caught his hair in the branches thereof. He hung there all night until in the morning Delilah came over, cut off his hair, and he fell on stony ground!"

Sacrilege in Worship Services

Another area of sacrilege is the worship service. A student commented at the beginning of one worship service, "The floor show is about to begin." Concerning the invitation, another commented, "We only want them to come in two's so we can turn in round numbers to the state Baptist paper." A youth revival preacher prayed, "Lord, we are going out there to shoot the wind. But, Lord, we want you to be with us." Preaching material has been described as "soap." A group of ministerial students imitating the late Dr. Truett, even to the point of a mock invitation, intensified the doubts of a history major standing nearby.

Another related problem is the use of religious choruses purely as a recreational technique. Sacrilege can even extend to the beliefs and practices of others. On a Baptist campus, a group of ministerial students undertook an elaborate "take-off" of Catholic mass. Statues of Mary, prayer candles, and a rosary were obtained. The episode was terminated when a Catholic student entered the room and did serious violence to the "priest."

Analyzing the Problem

Is all this sacrilege? Admittedly, it is often difficult to know at what point humor ends and sacrilege begins. The trend toward sacrilege is (a) more common on Baptist campuses than among Baptist students in state and private institutions, and (b) more common among those who have surrendered their lives for full-time Christian service.

Why such sacrilege? Undoubtedly, some of these attitudes and practices have been learned from older religious leaders. This is by no means only a student problem. They may be due to spiritual immaturity, or "finding oneself in deep water before one can swim." What are the effects of this trend? Sacrilege affects the offender. The thoughtless, careless practice tends to become a habit. One's devotional life may be affected. God is not glorified. Sacrilege also often adversely affects associates of the offender. His Christian influence may be seriously diminished; the faith of others shaken.

If tempted to become modern Nadabs and Abihus, desiring to worship God in one's own self-conceived way, or a modern Ananias or Sapphira, guilty of religious hypocrisy, we need to stand beside the princely young man of Jerusalem whose life was transformed by seeing him whom he described as "Holy, holy, holy . . . the Lord of hosts" (Isa 6:3).

13

"Prayer" (1958)[1]

Prayer, in its widest Christian meaning, is communion with God. Some form of prayer is found in the various world religions, and the study of the history of religions has focused much attention on primitive prayer. Yet, Christian prayer is unique both in meaning and in manner. The root of the principal Hebrew verb "to pray" has been variously interpreted as "to cut, decide" and "to level, arbitrate." The Greek New Testament words used almost synonymously for prayer, *deesis, proseuche',* and *enteuxis,* connote needful petition, devout entreaty to God, and confiding access, respectively. The English word "pray" is derived from the Latin *precari,* "to entreat."

Prayer is characterized by various moods such as adoration, thanksgiving, confession, petition, and intercession, no one of which can rightfully be regarded as the totality of prayer. Prayer may be either oral or silent, explicit or implicit, private or corporate.

Prayer in the Old Testament presupposed that God is personal, both transcendent and active. Motivated chiefly by human needs, prayer in Israel consisted of invocation, praise, confession, petition, intercession, thanksgiving, propitiation, benediction, and even imprecation. Significant prayers recorded in the Old Testament include those of Abraham, Moses, Hannah, Samuel, David, Solomon, Elijah, Isaiah, Hezekiah, Job, Daniel, and the Psalms. Frequently prayer was led by a national leader and was evoked by particular need, but with Jeremiah individual prayer attained great importance.

The Apocrypha, although containing some noteworthy prayers, reveals little development in prayer. Liturgical prayers in pre-Christian Judaism can be noted in the Talmud and Prayer Book.

1. This article first appeared in *Encyclopedia of Southern Baptists*. v.2, s.v. Nashville: Broadman Press, 1958.

Jesus, both by example and by teaching, emphasized the urgency of prayer. For him prayer was both daily communion with the Father and his special habit preceding the crises of his life. His prayers, as those uttered while on the cross demonstrate, were largely intercessory and not solely petitionary. The Lord's Prayer, probably designed for personal usage although containing social elements, proceeds from adoration to petition, from "Thy" to "us." Jesus stressed as essential elements in prayer sincerity without ostentation (Matt 6:5f.), simplicity without verbosity (Matt 6:7f.), humility (Luke 18:9–14), importunity (Luke 11:5–10, 18:1–8), forgiveness (Matt 6:14f), faith (Matt 17:20, Mark 11:22–24), and a vital relation with himself (John 15:7). His teaching on secret prayer, designed as a corrective for Pharisaism, was in no sense intended to discourage genuine public prayer. Prayer, "in my name" involves the willing submission of the one praying to be Christ's agent.

The early Christians for a time simultaneously participated in Jewish worship and themselves engaged in communal prayer. Prayer characterized the leadership of the apostles. Directed to Jesus, it effected the work of the Holy Spirit, preceded providential deliverance, and issued in missionary expansion. According to Paul, prayer is to be in and by the Holy Spirit. The means of conquering anxiety, it is to be strongly intercessory and unceasing. Paul's prayer for removal of his "thorn in the flesh" (2 Cor 12:8f.) is a classic illustration of the truth that, although a petition may not be granted, the prayer is answered. Hebrews stressed the new approach to God's throne of grace through Jesus' continuous work of intercession. James mentioned prayer in faith for wisdom and for healing, God's availability and prayer's efficacy, and neglected and misdirected praying. According to Peter, prayer should be offered seriously to the God who hears. Peter also pointed out that prayer can be hindered by domestic trouble. Boldness to ask according to God's will characterized John; "the prayers of the saints" and prayer for Christ's coming are found in Revelation.

The history of Christian prayer is largely the record, as Hughes asserts, of the struggle between two conceptions, the "prophetic" and the "mystical," the one leading to communion and the other to absorptive union with God. In the ancient era the formulation and usage of liturgies was marked by the decline of spontaneity in prayer. Prayer was offered for persecutors, for heretics, as propitiation, and commonly, by the fourth century, for the dead. Tertullian's *de Oratione* (AD 204) is the oldest extant commentary on the Lord's Prayer. Monasticism served to discourage petitions for temporal things and to make prayer the special continual task of its ascetical adherents. In the East, mystical prayer soon prevailed in the mysterious complex of ritual and sacrament; later in the West prayer to Mary and the saints increasingly prevailed. Augustine, according to Heiler, effected a synthesis of the contemplative and the mystical in prayer. This synthesis Thomas Aquinas sought to preserve, but mystics such as Hugo of St. Victor gave the contemplative the pre-eminence—a trend followed by John of the Cross and Frances de Sales. The Fenelon-Bousset controversy centered in the proper motive of prayer, whether man's disinterested love of God or the love for God that pertains to human salvation. The Reformation brought about a renewal of prophetic prayer. For Luther and Calvin prayer was through Christ's intercession the privilege and duty of all Christians amid their vocations. Such a prophetic type of prayer prevailed among most of the Anabaptists, the Puritans, and the Pietists, but the Quakers extended the mystical tradition. Kant anticipated the modern denial of prayer's reality. Intercessory prayer was the matrix from which the modern Protestant missionary movement was born. The Social Gospel directed prayer toward social reform.

In the contemporary period, prayer has been the object of a twofold assault. Philosophical naturalism under the guise of "natural law" and "scientific necessity" has argued the impossibility of prayer, especially petitionary prayer. From psychology have come the defective propositions that prayer is autosuggestion and that it is projection, rationalization, or wishful thinking. Modern man, to deny prayer, must nullify personality, even his own, or give assent to a solipsism which he never practices. Christian prayer cannot be adequately defined solely as a means of personality adjustment.

Practical difficulties regarding prayer often beset the Christian, viz., unanswered petitions, prayer in relation to God's will, petitions for physical healing, etc. Prayer interpreted as communion means that there can be petitions not immediately granted but not genuine prayer without "answer." Praying according to God's will may alter particular intentions or executive volitions of God but not the ultimate purpose of God for man and the world. Not all petitions for physical healing are necessarily to be granted.

Prayer is imperative for the Christian, for prayerlessness is the taproot of the Christian's sins and failures, and praying brings the believer into God's presence. It is at once privilege and duty, at once from God and by man. Prayer necessitates, as Hallesby contends, a veritable wrestling with God. Forsyth has affirmed that "it is truer to say that we live the Christian life in order to pray than that we pray in order to live the Christian life."[2]

2. Barth, *Prayer According to the Catechisms of the Reformation*; Buttrick, *Prayer*; Campbell, *The Place of Prayer in the Christian Religion*; Carver, *If Two Agree*; Forsyth, *The Soul of Prayer*; Hallesby, *Prayer*; Harkness, *Prayer and the Common Life*; Hastings, *The Christian Doctrine of Prayer*; Heiler, *Prayer*; Hughes, *Prophetic Prayer*.

14

"Christian Knowledge and Conviction" (1961)[1]

The assembling by Southern Baptists of a Child Life Conference for consideration of the theological foundations of the Christian education of children is no accidental or incidental occurrence. It is the expected and needed consequence of a succession of events some of which will be surveyed presently. Nor is it surprising that in the very center of such a conference consideration should be given to the child's Christian knowledge and conviction. The term "Christian knowledge and convictions"—whether advisedly or inadvisedly chosen—needs definition. Such knowledge may be of two kinds. One is the knowledge of objective facts, such as the names of the books of the Bible, the identity of each of the Ten Commandments or of the twelve apostles, the posting of Luther's 95 theses on the church door at Wittenberg, or the organization of the Southern Baptist Convention in 1845. The other kind of knowledge is the "faith-kind-of" knowledge, or the knowledge which is derived from a believing and obedient response to God as revealed in Jesus Christ and interpreted in the light of the Christian Scriptures and of Christian history. Both of these kinds of knowledge come within the purview of the present subject, although the importance of the "faith-kind-of" knowledge is emphasized by the addition of the term "conviction."

1. This chapter was first presented as a lecture at the Child Life Conference on January 31–February 3, 1961, which was sponsored by the Education Division of the Southern Baptist Convention Baptist Sunday School Board. It first appeared in *Book of Proceedings: Child Life Conference. January 31–February 3, 1961*. Nashville: Baptist Sunday School Board, 1961.

I

In the outset, it is necessary to gain a background for perspective in facing the present problems of teaching and training children up to twelve years of age in the Christian religion. What is the teaching aspect of the Christian gospel? How has this teaching responsibility been construed? That the Christian churches have a teaching function is recognized by both the theologian and the religious educator of the present era. Karl Barth has entitled his multi-volume work on systematic theology *Church Dogmatics*, and Emil Brunner has defined dogmatics (or theology) as extension of the teaching function of the Christian church.[2] Increasingly, Protestant religious educators are realizing that the church is not merely the habitat of their task but the reason for their task.

The sixth chapter of Deuteronomy, various passages in Proverbs, the eighth chapter of Nehemiah, and other portions of the Old Testament give evidence of the existence of teaching in ancient Israel. The disappearance of prophecy and the codification of teaching led to the legalism of scribalism and Pharisaism. Yet, the Jewish home and the synagogue school persisted. Jesus our Lord was denominated "teacher" or "rabbi" as well as "prophet," and the Synoptic Gospels frequently allude to his teaching activity. The apostles, according to Acts 5:42, "did not cease teaching and preaching Jesus as the Christ (RSV). "Teachers" were one of the "gifts" or orders of the ministry according to Paul (1 Cor 12:28; Eph 4:11). The early Christian centuries witnessed the rise of catechetical schools, while the early medieval darkness tended to restrict the light of Christian truth except in the monasteries and cathedral schools. Theology became an academic discipline in medieval universities, but only with the Reformation did instruction of the laity, Bible reading, and family religious nurture become common realities.

Despite the continuity of the teaching function in Christianity, the relation of the preaching or kerygmatic function or role to the teaching function or role has not been clear. Nor has C. H. Dodd's distinction between *kerygma*, or the preached content of the gospel, and *didache*, or the ethical instruction (and sometimes also the apologetic) of Christianity been completely adequate concept.[3] As James D. Smart has pointed out, such a distinction serves well "as a protest against the insipid moralism of a pulpit that has forgotten the kerygma," but its defect lies in its detaching "the work of teaching from all essential relation to the kerygma." According to Dodd's distinction "Acts 5:42 would need to be rewritten then to say that the

2. Brunner, *The Christian Doctrine of God*, I:3–5.

3. Dodd, *The Apostolic Preaching and Its Development*, esp. 7f.

apostles 'preached Jesus Christ and taught Christian ethics,' instead, of what is written: 'They ceased not to teach and preach Jesus Christ.'"[4]

The essential function of teaching in Christianity serves to legitimize the teaching ministry within the framework of Christian leadership. The theological character of the message to be taught makes imperative a theological undergirding of the preparation of teachers and of the teachers of teachers. The content and the communication of the Christian religion should never be put in isolation wards, for there is an interdependence and interrelatedness of the two.

Christian education in modern Protestantism may be traced from the beginnings of the Sunday school movement. Robert Raikes' "Ragged School," founded in 1780 in Gloucester, England, was essentially a school for poor illiterate children embracing both general and Christian education. Caught up into the "wind tunnel" of the Evangelical revival tradition, the Sunday school lost its function of general education, broadened its pupilage to include the children of Christian parents, and, especially in the United States, became the evangelizing arm of the church.[5] While the evangelistic purpose has persisted in many Sunday schools, including Southern Baptist, the nineteenth century witnessed the rise of forces which altered the character of many Protestant church schools in this country. Horace Bushnell, in his *Christian Nurture* (1847), severely criticized aspects of the sudden conversion-centered Sunday school and contended for the strong and well-nigh impersonal determinism of the Christian family upon the child.[6]

With the spread of liberal Protestant theology, the historical-critical approach to the Bible, and of new educational methods in public schools, a new mood regarding religious nurture appeared in many churches. This new mood crystallized with the organization of the Religious Education Association in 1903—the word "religious" rather than "Christian" being of more than passing significance. Readily appropriating the tenets of liberal theology—the immanence of God, the goodness of man, the humanity but not deity of Jesus Christ, the naturalness and progressiveness of Christian growth, and the temporal perfectability of the Kingdom of God—the new movement served to focus attention on the pupil and his maturation.[7] George A. Coe, writing in 1902, applied the concept of God's immanence so that it "dissolved the distinction between religious experience and other

4. Smart, *The Teaching Ministry of the Church*, 21f.

5. Ibid., 49–52.

6. Ibid., 52–54.

7. Ibid., 54–58. Roman Catholic and Jewish representatives were also present for the 1903 meeting.

types of experience, between the sacred and the secular; between business and devotion, between the divine and the human; between religious education and secular education.[8] Coe, writing in 1929, still defined Christianity as personality growth.[9] Harrison Elliott, writing in 1940 with a keen awareness of the growing theological challenge to religious education, sought to defend the modern religious education movement as being reconcilable with Christianity.[10] Ernest M. Ligon in his book *Their Future is Now*, with the sub-title, "The Growth and Development of Christian Personality," makes Jesus to be the supplier of the ideals for personality.[11]

The inadequacies of this dominant trend in recent Protestant religious education and its wholesale departure from the historic Christian teachings were exposed as early as 1941 by H. Shelton Smith in his book, *Faith and Nurture*.[12] Modern American Protestant religious education had drunk deeply from the two "jugs" of liberal theology and progressive education, and, being thoroughly intoxicated, many of its leaders have not been sober enough to be conscious of the distance of their departure from the primary function and essential message of Christian education.

Southern Baptist religious education has not followed the identical path just described, although influences from the new religious education movement have been more than nominal. The predominance of a conservative theology with resistance to the inroads of liberalism and a relative denominational and cultural isolation have contributed to a distinctive Southern Baptist annal in twentieth century Christian education. Southern Baptists have been slow to articulate a theology of Christian education, especially when directed to the child. Nevertheless, several characteristics of Southern Baptist religious education should be noted. Such education has to a large extent been laymen-led, as evidenced by the history of the Sunday School Board itself. It has had the Bible as the basis for its curriculum. It has been moderately conversion-centered. It has been church-controlled, in its elementary aspects if not always in the adult. It has been expansion-goaled with a greater emphasis on an increased number of pupils and teachers than upon theological competency or ethical sensitivity.

The criticisms of the prevailing Protestant religious education by Shelton Smith, James Smart, and others is largely due to the major shifts

8. Coe, *The Religion of a Mature Mind*, 6, 332, 219, 332–334, 414, 298–304, as summarized by Smith, *Faith and Nurture*, 27.

9. Coe, *What is Christian Education?*, 60.

10. Elliott, *Can Religious Education Be Christian?*.

11. Ligon, *The Future is Now*, 1, 13–35, 362.

12. Smith, *Faith and Nurture*.

in Protestant theology and churchmanship occurring in the period since World War I. The rise of Neo-Protestantism or Neo-Orthodoxy and other theological movements on the shambles of two world wars and totalitarian atrocities has produced and intensified a conflict between liberalistic religious education concepts and Neo-Orthodox theological concepts. The rise of the ecumenical movement has brought into sharp focus the atomistic and extra-churchly pattern of the Protestant religious education movement, and the renewed interest in denominational origins has whetted the appetite for a more adequate instruction of children and young people in Christian history.

Southern Baptists have not as yet experienced such a deep theological conflict between religious educators and theologians. Nevertheless, it would be unrealistic to deny that the unappreciative cry of "promotionalism" from theological circles and the undiscriminating plea of "practical religion" from religious educators betokens some basic conflict—either real or supposed. The numerical expansion of Southern Baptists and the high percentage of losses from active church membership—to say nothing of Communist and secularistic dangers—call for greater attention to the theological foundations. Southern Baptists, no less than American Protestantism in general, are desperately in need of a new and reciprocal confrontation between theologians and religious educators[13] for the sake of the churches in whose living fellowship the content and the communication of the Christian gospel must be kept in proper relationship.

II

A re-examination of the theological foundations of Christian education may affect the total appraisal of the teaching-training ministry of the church. If the Christian nurture of children involves both the child and the Christian religion, then both the nature and learning processes of children and the nature and taught content of the Christian gospel must be determinative of our goals, curriculum, methods, and measurements.

The statement of the goals of Christian education involves a basic religio-theological persuasion. On the extreme right wing, a definition of the goal of Christian education as the accumulation and impartation of a certain quantity of Biblical data is immediately recognizable as inadequate. Nor is the concept that the church's educational agencies are the instrument for achieving solely the instantaneous conversion, baptism, and church membership of all their enrollees tenable. The failure to confront professing

13. Cf. Edge, "Theological Foundations of Religious Education."

Christians and church members probingly with the ethical demands of the gospel in our generation still continues to be a weakness of our Southern Baptist Zion. Statements of the goals on the left wing may be with some greater difficulty scrutinized. Common statements of the goal have included "personality growth," "character development," "ideal behavior," and the like. Such goals may and usually do imply that the growth is inherent, the development natural, and the ideal determined by man. Such goals are the by-products of moralism and humanism rather than the goals which belong to Christianity itself.[14]

Moralism teaches that to know the good is to be able to do the good, but the Christian gospel proclaims that man, knowing the good, chooses that which is evil. Humanism establishes ideal behavior for man to be attained by human striving, while the Bible speaks not of man-established ideals but of God-given commands to which man owes but fails to render obedience.[15] Moralism and humanism speak of character development as if largely inherent in man's continuous existence, while the apostles speak of being "conformed" to the image of his (God's) Son" and "putting on the new nature, which is being renewed in knowledge after the image of its creator" (Rom 8:29; Col 3:10). The Bible indeed speaks of growth, but it more often speaks of being "justified," "reconciled," "born anew," "forgiven," and "sanctified." Let it not be forgotten that the New Testament emphasis is on "*being* sanctified" so that one's being dedicated to God issuing in Godlikeness or Christlikeness is the work of God! Furthermore, as Smart affirms, "education that aims only at character development is education for a non-evangelizing church."[16]

The major problem of curriculum building in recent religious education seems to have been the conflict between the Bible-centered and the child-centered or pupil-centered approach. Smart has contended that these two seemingly contradictory approaches are resolved by the recovery of an adequate doctrine of the church as the fellowship of persons growing in its faith and life by means of the Christian Scriptures and the secondary sources of its teaching. Both fundamentalism and liberalism have tended to bypass the church so that the schism-making orthodoxy of the one has had an effect not altogether different from the atomistic and humanistic modernism of the other.[17] Thus curriculum builders must ask not only "What can the child learn at a given age?" but also "What is the nature and content

14. Smart, *The Teaching Ministry of the Church*, 90–93, 99–103.

15. Ibid., 103–7.

16. Ibid., 102.

17. Ibid., 109–111.

of the Christian gospel which is the church's message and reason for existence?" and "Does the existing curriculum serve to produce and strengthen strong, virile Christians capable of bearing witness to and living effectively in their faith?"

The *methods* of the Christian evangelization and nurture of children must be subjected to continual or at least periodic re-evaluation in the light of the ultimate goal or goals of the teaching-training ministry of the church.[18] The messages of Dr. Chafin and Dr. Edge have focused attention on these crucial matters. Even the *measurements* we apply to our teaching-training ministry should be commensurate with our goals. Together with the number of pupils present on the same Sunday last year, we must measure our teaching-training ministry by the Christian maturity of these pupils on the same Sunday next year. Are the Primary and Junior pupils now under your responsibility being girded and guided so that as teen-agers and young adults they will not yield to Communist brainwashing, to criminal delinquency, or to secularistic humanism, but instead will wage the warfare of the Christian soldier against a "world" that rejects the light and love of God in Jesus Christ?

III

The centrality of the Bible in the Christian education of children makes imperative an adequate presentation of the nature and content of the Bible to children by adequately trained teachers. By the Junior level at least some attention may be given to the fact that the Bible is a book of religion, not a book on general or world history, nor on science or on ethics alone. The Bible's origin in God and in man must be communicated to the child. The uniqueness of the message of the Bible should be conveyed, but so should the human instrumentalities who wrote its various books. We do our children an injustice to teach or imply that the Bible is the product of a divine dictation process. More adequately, though recognizing the limitations, we must convey the truth that the Bible is the record of God's making himself known to men and that this record centers in God's making himself known through Jesus, his Son, who being divine became man.

Nor should we surmise that the canon of the Bible is always a subject to be deferred for consideration beyond elementary years. My eight-year-old son, after having moved from a predominantly Protestant neighborhood to one in which quite a number of his playmates are enrolled in Roman Catholic parochial schools, came home one day last fall to present this question to

18. Yoder, *The Nurture and Evangelism of Children.*

his father: "Is it true, Dad, that our Bible is not the true Bible?" When children become aware of foreign languages, they can be taught that the Bible was not written in English, but in Hebrew, Aramaic, and Greek. Likewise, the fact of the Bible's transmission and preservation by manuscripts long before the invention of printing may be taught. Nor should we draw back from the truth that much of this transmission was done in and through the medieval monasteries. The fact and usage of various translations of the Bible into English is another phenomenon which may be brought into the experience of Junior and Primary children, and they, more than their parents, will be less bound to usage of the King James Version.

The child's growing awareness of the structure of the Bible should be of concern to works with primary and junior children. This usually begins with the memorization of the books comprising the Old and the New Testaments but should be continued to the level of a recognition that the Psalms are poetic and hymnic, that the Gospels present the story of Jesus from birth to resurrection, and that the epistles of the New Testament are letters written to churches or to individuals.

The contents of the Bible reach the child first in Bible stories. The usage of Biblical narrative involves three basic problems. One is selectivity, another is interpretation, and the third is application. Which Bible stories will be selected for usage in the various age groups? Should the narratives always present the goodness or exemplary nature of the Bible personages? If not, when should narratives revealing sin be introduced to the child? Is it possible that the criterion of selecting only or principally the good owes more to Norman Vincent Peale and to Mary Baker Eddy than to the prophets and the apostles? If the Biblical characters are always presented as heroes choosing the right and obeying God, how do we bridge the gulf to salvation by grace or God's justification of sinners? The problem of interpretation calls for adequate knowledge of the context of the Bible story on the part of the teacher and often of Bible customs and geography as well. Both in interpretation and in application to the pupil's life the teacher's and the lesson writer's spiritual insights are extremely important.

But suppose that the child has come to know that the Bible is a book of religion, from God and yet from men, consisting of two testaments and sixty-six books, existing in different translations, and containing narratives many of which he can summarize or relate. Has the child's acquaintance with the Bible reached the highest level which it can be expected to reach in his childhood? Perhaps not. Can we convey to the Junior child that the central meaning of the Bible is to be found in its salvation history, in that it is the book of the acts of God together with the response of men? In our eagerness to make the Bible contemporaneous with the child, let us not fall into the deistic error of making the Bible a book of timeless, eternal religious, and moral truths evident from the creation of man.

IV

Any theological reassessment of elementary Christian education must eventually proceed to the question: How adequately are we conveying to our children the basic realities or the theological centralities of the Christian religion?

As teachers of children and as teachers of the teachers of the children, are we clear as to how we do know God? Let us summarize this mode of knowing God. First, knowing God is not like knowing things but like knowing human persons. There is a reciprocity in knowing persons that we do not experience in knowing things. God takes the initiative in knowing and in making possible our knowing him. This is what we call *revelation*. Secondly, knowing God is not a reasoning process or a scientific experiment but a faith encounter. Believing involves recognition that God is and that he is trustworthy but it also must include our trustful and absolute committal to the gracious sovereignty of God in Jesus Christ. Yet, thirdly, this believing *in* God is no mere mystic encounter but rather an encounter that is dependent on an historically mediated revelation of God. We believe in God as revealed in Jesus "the Word (who) became flesh and dwelt among us." We believe in Jesus the Revealer of the Father.

Who is *God* who is thus revealed "in the face of Jesus Christ? He is the Holy One of whom the prophets spoke. He stands over against man as the unique One. He is not to be entangled in the threads of pantheistic identity with nature. He is the Lord of nature and of history. He is the eternal God, the creator of time, who in his inmost nature changes not. He is the God of all-sufficient power. He is the God whose glory is manifested. He is the God of anger, jealousy, and wrath—qualities of the divine nature which must not be expunged from childhood Christian teaching. God is righteous, and the rectitude of his nature means that he commands that man be righteous, that man's unrighteousness calls for punishment, and that God's righteousness leads him to redeem sinful man.[19] "God is just (or righteous) and the justifier of him who believes in Jesus." He is not only the Holy and Righteous One but the God of love, *agape* love, self-giving, unmerited love. God who is *agape* is merciful and longsuffering, the God of grace. This God of holiness, righteousness, and love is the Father of our Lord Jesus Christ, and Father of all believers in Jesus Christ. He has revealed himself in Jesus the Son

19. Cf. Conner, *Revelation and God*, 247–53.

and through the Holy Spirit. Moreover, the way in which he has revealed himself indicates his eternal nature. God is eternally Father, Son, and Holy Spirit—not in tritheistic individuality, not in modalistic functionalism—but in the revealedness of his very Being.

God who is the Triune God is the Creator of all that exists outside himself. The Apostles' Creed, written to combat ancient Gnosticism, speaks of God as "the almighty Father, Maker of heaven and earth." He is the author/creator of all that exists, not merely the fabricator or reformulator of eternally existent matter. All the created order stands in dependence on God the creator. The Christian doctrine of *creation* stands contrary to atheistic self-origination of matter and organic life. It can hardly be adequately interpreted in terms of theistic evolution. Nor is it adequate in view of the contemporary sciences to posit a fiat instantaneous creation. God's creative work must be related to the legitimate evidence of geology and biology as to the age of the earth, the antiquity of man, and the development of organic life.

Man is uniquely the creature of God. Like God and like the animal, man is neither divine nor merely animalistic. The Bible, especially Genesis, describes man's creaturehood as being "in the image of God." This image which seemingly means in the Old Testament man's responsible existence before God the Creator is never lost. Man, though sinner, alien, and rebel, though animal-like in behavior, never ceases to be "in the image" in the Old Testament sense. Yet, the New Testament speaks of Christians as being renewed in the Creator's image or being conformed to the image of God's Son. The image, according to Paul, is the renewed, restored image, the image made possible by redemption, the actuality of being made in the likeness of God.[20] Man is also described by Biblical writers in terms of "soul," "spirit," "flesh," "heart," "body," and other related words. Contrary to the prevailing oversimplifications of a bipartite (soul-body) or tripartite (body-soul-spirit) interpretation of man, the renewed Biblical theology of today is helping to make clear the Hebrew-Christian understanding of man as a totality. Thus terms such as "soul," "spirit," "heart," and other physio-psychological terms of the Bible need to be construed as having distinctive meanings within the framework of the unity of man. Man as created in God's image is of worth and value in God's sight and so should he be for his fellow man.

But man is not only creature, he is sinner. The Christian understanding of man as creature and as sinner must be kept together lest separated they become a misinterpretation of man. What is *sin*? Shall we say with the naturalist that sin is due to creaturely weakness *per se*? Shall we say with

20. Cf. Brunner, *Man in Revolt*, 499–503.

the idealist that sin is due to man's physical appetites and instincts and thus ultimately to the possession of a body? Shall we agree with the evolutionist that sin is a carry-over or hangover from an earlier pre-human stage out of which man may expect to develop? What of answers that claim Christian authentication? Is sin lack of conformity with the divine law? Or a violation of that law? Is it selfishness or self-centeredness? Is it prideful rebellion against God? Probably the latter expresses most fully the Biblical conception of sin. Sin, according to Gen 1–3, entered human history after creation, and thus sin, while being universal among men, is not truly natural. Sin's origin in humanity poses the question of the sinner's relation to Adamic sin. Are we guilty of Adamic sin or are we merely affected by Adamic sin? Does depravity or the basic bias of man to sin involve accountability or does it only lead inevitably to sin? When, then, comes accountability? Does it occur with the first flash of the consciousness of sin? Are there degrees of consciousness? Also, are there degrees of guilt? Sin, which is both sin (singular) and sins (plural), alienates the sinner from God, disrupts his relations with this fellow man, disintegrates the selfhood of the sinner, causes the sinner and others to suffer, and issues in the certain sequel of death.[21]

Between God and man stands *Jesus* of Nazareth. Who is he and what has he done for man? Since Calvin's day it has been common to interpret the work of Jesus in terms of the threefold office: prophet, priest, and king.[22] Clustered around these three functions can be most of the other titles ascribed to Jesus in the New Testament. Jesus is called "rabbi" or "teacher," yet he taught not as "one having authority." Some called him "a prophet," "one of the prophets," and "the prophet," the latter probably in line with Jewish expectation of the prophet of the end time. Yet, unlike the prophets who bore the word or message of God, Jesus was the Word. Under the priestly office we construe Jesus as "Son of Man," "Suffering Servant," and "High Priest." Jesus, declining to employ the more common term "Messiah," used most often the term "Son of Man"—not a synonym for his humanity but originally a heavenly figure to whom sovereignty was given. Jesus interpreted himself as both humiliated and exalted Son of Man, as the Isaianic Servant of the Lord who suffers vicariously and voluntarily. The Epistle to the Hebrews adds the Melchizedekan priesthood. Jesus' kingly office involved a reinterpretation of Jewish messianic expectation—i.e., not an earthly, political, secular kingdom but a kingdom "not of this world," God's kingly rule. Jesus was confessed to be "Lord." This term was drawn from Jewish acclamation of

21. Cf. Conner, *The Gospel of Redemption*, 1–49.

22. Cf. Calvin, *Institutes of the Christian Religion*, II:15. Calvin's order was prophet, King and priest.

Yahweh as "Lord." The work of Jesus centers in his cross and resurrection. To affirm this is not to deny the importance of the incarnation, for "the Word became flesh" in the miraculous conception wrought by the Holy Spirit. Nor is it to de-emphasize his life and teaching. Jesus came into the world to bear witness to the truth, and bearing witness to the truth leads to a cross. Our Lord's saving death both vindicates God's righteousness and reveals God's love. The cross and resurrection of Jesus constitute God's decisive victory over sin, death, and Satan, God's D-Day and H-Hour.[23] This Jesus is fully man and fully God. He is uniquely the God-man. Chalcedon expressed this as "two natures in the one Person." Modern Kenoticists have expressed this as "two movements: self-emptying and self-fulfillment."

Jesus the Christ (Messiah) makes men to be *new creatures*. Becoming a new creature is conditioned upon repenting (contrition, confession, turning) and believing (trustful repose, absolute committal). No cheap and easy repentance or believism can be rightly equated with New Testament repentance and believing. The new creaturehood is described by various analogies in the New Testament: salvation, conversion, forgiveness, justification, reconciliation, adoption, union with Christ, sanctification. Each of these sheds a distinctive ray of meaning upon what Jesus Christ does for us who become Christians. As we think of children, the terms nurture and growth have unusual significance. Can there be nurture in Christianity before conversion? Does agriculture begin with germination, or does it include plowing and planting? Growth as Dr. Edge has ably emphasized, is no optional feature of the Christian life. Nor does the New Testament use words like "salvation" or "sanctification" solely to refer to past event. Whether in its beginning or its continuation, the new creation is the work of the Holy Spirit of God. He convicts, converts, instructs, motivates, develops, guides, and strengthens the Christian. The Christian's new life in Christ is one of duty as well as grace, of obedience as well as dependence, of witness and service as well as privilege. The continuity of this new creation depends on the faithfulness and keeping power of God and perseverance in faith of the new creature.

Yet, being a new creature is neither a solo flight nor living in a vacuum. It is living in the community or fellowship of God's holy people which is the *church*. Our earlier Baptist refutation of infant baptism was so often directed against pedobaptist usage of the circumcision analogy that we have maneuvered ourselves into the unbiblical position of denying the Old Testament reality of the *ecclesia* or assembly of God. The Book of Acts describes the early Christian community in terms of nominalized verbs: "believers,"

23. Cf. Cullmann, *Christ and Time*, 84.

"disciples," "brethren," "saints," etc. Paul and Peter expand the terminology of the church by metaphors: "the people of God," "the temple of God," "the bride of Christ," and "the body of Christ." The New Testament word *koinonia* stands in unequaled richness above all its English translations. Church history evidences repeatedly the corrosive institutionalization of the church and this is not exclusively the error of Roman Catholics! The institution has often survived when the fellowship has departed. Others have misconstrued the church as the edifice used for worship. Are teachers of children planting and perpetuating the growing Southern Baptist heresy of the church as an edifice when they follow *The Curriculum Guide*[24] in teaching Nursery and Beginner children that the church is a "place"? The further question as to whether the *ecclesia* according to the New Testament is both the whole body of Christian believers of all ages and the particular, local congregation confronts us again in this generation. The Landmark fathers to the contrary notwithstanding, an exclusive application of the term *ecclesia* to a particular congregation is a misinterpretation of the New Testament. We should be willing and able to confront Christians of other communions with some sense of our common bond in Jesus Christ. Such a confrontation will send us back to the roots of our Anabaptist, Puritan, Baptist, free church heritage. There we will need to ask again: Why believer's baptism and not infant baptism? What is a regenerate congregation? What is a disciplined congregation? What is the theological and not merely the political underpinning for religious liberty? What ought the Lord's Supper to mean? Such questions will not mean dispensing with our four favorite Baptist rubrics for baptism—meaning, candidate, form, and administration—but the answers may show us what a hollow mockery it would be for us to preserve the form and administration while having lost the true meaning and the proper candidates! The Lord's Supper—in many congregations reduced to the "five minutes 'till twelve" addendum—needs re-examination not only in respect to commemoration and participation in the elements but indeed in regard to communion with Christ *and with our fellow Christians*.

Christian truth includes not only what God has done and is doing but what God will do, not only what we have experienced and are experiencing but what we shall experience. The Christian *hope* means God's victorious consummation of his redemptive work. While our Lord preached that "the kingdom of heaven is at hand," the consummation of that divine kingship we await. The Christian hope begins with death, whose sting our Lord has extracted. It looks to the culmination of history, the coming or *Parousia* of our Lord Jesus in glory, the resurrection of the dead, the final judgment, and

24. Allen and Howse, *The Curriculum Guide: 1960*, 16,17.

the eternal destiny either in blessedness or in shame, either in reward or in punishment, either in fellowship or in separation. As we teach children, let us not substitute innate immortality of the soul for the Hebrew-Christian resurrection of the body—indeed the "spiritual body." Let us not literalize where we should not be literal, but let us not "demythologize" where the essential content of the Christian hope is at stake.

V

The final aspect of "Christian knowledge and conviction" calls for attention. Shall we teach our children something about the history of Christianity, and, if so, what? Let me offer the personal conviction that one of the most consistent weaknesses in our entire Southern Baptist program of Christian education in the church and in the family is Christian history. We tend to assume that ignorance of what lay between the age of the apostles and the rise of Baptists is no serious disqualification for Christian growth and service. Our curriculum is about like—I may say it, for I am a native Texan—requiring Texas history but not requiring also American history and/or world history.

We should not continue to fail to teach our children—and this is also true of those over twelve—something of the course of Christian history. Think of the spread of Christianity to the Gentile world, the persecutions by imperial Rome, the development of clergy in distinction from laity, the state church system. Recall the rise of Islam, the medieval monasteries, the great cathedrals, the Crusades. Then came the corruption of Western Roman Christendom which evoked the work and teachings of the Reformers, the rise of the various Protestant denominations, the rise and early sufferings of the Baptists. Remember the American system of church and state, the modern missionary movement, the Social Gospel movement, the German church struggle against Nazi totalitarianism, the ecumenical movement, the Dead Sea Scrolls. Who can say that many of these things and more could and should not be taught at least beginning with the Junior level? Moreover, there is the whole challenging field of Christian biography. Let us not leave the entire task to the church librarians. Is it not tragic that many children know far more about the lives of famous athletes, of Hollywood stars, and—yes—of criminals than they know about Polycarp and Irenaeus, Ambrose and Augustine, Bernard of Clairvaux and Francis of Assisi, John Wyclif and John Hus, Martin Luther and John Knox, Conrad Grebel and Roger Williams, John Wesley and William Carey, Mary Slessor and Walter Rauschenbusch, John A. Broadus and George W. Truett?

Our mission to teach and train for Christian knowledge and conviction is an enthralling many-faceted task. Its magnitude should baffle us. Our failures should humble us. Our resources should encourage us. The need should beckon us. So may it be, O Lord, in Jesus' name. Amen.

15

"A Theology of Prayer" (1972)[1]

Is it possible to translate the second-person reality of prayer into the third-person reality of theology without some contradiction or a certain distortion of prayer? Is it not inevitable that the highly subjective experience of prayer, by being objectified, will be misinterpreted? Such questions often arise from and reflect a sincere hesitation about the possibility of a theology of prayer. One may, however, ask whether a theology of conversion is possible since conversion to Christ has many of the same subjective or existential features as the life of prayer. If so, the possibility of a theology of prayer needs to be acknowledged.

Furthermore, by "theology of prayer" the writer does not mean an explanation of praying that divests it of its profundity and mystery but rather an exposition of the major Christian doctrines in their bearing upon prayer. P. T. Forsyth anticipated that "the effort to look into its [prayer's] principle may be graciously regarded by Him whoever liveth to make intercession as itself a prayer to know better how to pray."[2]

Most Protestant writers on prayer in the present century agree that prayer, in the Christian sense, is more than desire and more than asking or petition, though it includes these, and embraces fellowship or communion

1. This article first appeared in *Southwestern Journal of Theology* 15 (1972) 3–17.
2. Forsyth, *The Soul of Prayer*, 11.

with God.[3] Prayer, according to the predominant strain in Western Catholic piety, is more often defined as contemplation than as asking.[4]

Moreover, Christian prayer is characterized by several basic and distinguishable moods or acts. These are usually identified as adoration or praise, thanksgiving, confession, petition, and intercession.[5] Adoration is prayer as extolling God for who He is. Thanksgiving is prayer as expressing gratitude to God for what He has done, usually in behalf of men. Confession is prayer as the acknowledgment by man of his sin and of his need of divine forgiveness. Petition is prayer as man's asking or imploring God for specifics for himself or for those within his immediate circle. Intercession is prayer

3. Hastings, *The Christian Doctrine of Prayer*, 21–43, defined prayer as "desire," "communion," and "petition." Heiler, *Prayer*, xiii, 358, described prayer as "the central phenomenon of religion, the very earthstone of all piety" and defined prayer as "a living communion of the religious man with God, conceived as personal and present in experience, a communion which reflects the forms of the social relations of humanity." Forsyth, *The Soul of Prayer*, 11–29, identified prayer as not mere wishing "but asking" and as "both a gift and a conquest, a grace and a duty." It is "turning our will on God either in the way of resignation or of impetration," the way to God that opens and restores "free communion" with God, the highest use of speech, productive of "clearness of spiritual vision," and a "promise" and commitment to God which is also "one form of sacrifice." For Stolz, *The Psychology of Prayer*, 18, prayer is to be "defined as man's intercourse with God." Hallesby, *Prayer*, 11–34, cited the definition that prayer is "the breath of soul," called it "a means of intimate and joyous fellowship between God and man," and juxtaposed "helplessness" and "faith" for the basic understanding of prayer. Hallock, *Prayer and Meditation*, 14–26, defined prayer as "talking things over with God," "fellowship with God," "finding the mind of God," and "the quest for power." Wyon, *The School of Prayer*, 20–22, contended that "Christian prayer" is more than "the 'ascent' of the mind to God" and includes access to and boldness in God's presence. According to Hughes, *Prophetic Prayer*, 1, prayer is more than merely "the cry of man to God," for it includes "intercourse and fellowship with the Divine." Harkness, *Prayer and the Common Life*, 25–30, quoted approvingly from the Westminster Shorter Catechism, "Prayer is an offering up of our desires unto God, for things agreeable to His will," and declared that prayer is "the opening of the Soul to God so that he can speak to us."

4. Three recent examples may be noted: von Balthasar, *Prayer*, is written entirely from the standpoint of contemplation, i.e., "looking to God" or "an inward gaze into the depths of the soul and . . . beyond the soul to God" (20). Guardini, *Prayer in Practice*, subsumes intercession under "petition" and develops at some length "inward or contemplative prayer" in the sense of a drawing away "from the manifoldness of mental activity" so as "to become single-pointed" (77–87, 134–156, esp. 134). Merton, *Contemplative Prayer*, regards contemplation as "the summit of the Christian life of prayer"; it should be devoid of the gnostic or esoteric, and with it petition is "compatible" (117, 125, 142).

5. Hastings, *op. cit.*, 45–145, treated these five but placed thanksgiving last. Conner, *The Gospel of Redemption*, 237f., listed these five in the order given here.

as man's asking or imploring God for specifics for one or for those who are outside his own immediate circle.[6]

After such foundational considerations as the nature and moods of Christian prayer, it becomes possible to ask how some of the basic Christian doctrines affect and are affected by Christian prayer.

The God and Father of All Prayer

Prayer in the great monotheistic religions (Judaism, Christianity, Islam) presupposes one supreme personal God to whom the faithful pray. The roots of this supposition are in the religion of ancient Israel. According to the Old Testament, Yahweh, the God of the covenant with Israel, is the living and personal Lord of nature and of history[7] to whom Israelites prayed. He is not intertwined with the seasons and reproductive processes, as the deities of Canaanite Baalism, nor identifiable with the worship of the sun, as in Egyptian religion. Neither is Yahweh dependent upon the repeated cycles of occurrence, as in much Greek religion. Nor is Yahweh the counterpart to a co-equal and co-eternal evil deity, as in Zoroastrianism. The manifestation of the name of Yahweh (Ex 3:13–15) made it possible for Israelites voluntarily to call upon that name (Jer 33:3; Isa 55:6; Ps 50:10).[8]

But Israel's praying was prophetic, not mystical or contemplative. Walter Eichrodt has delineated this distinction in classic terms:

> Indicative of the pattern of Old Testament piety is the fact that the dominant motives of prayer never included that of losing oneself, through contemplation, in the divine infinity. There was no room in Israel for mystical prayer; the nature of the Mosaic Yahweh with his mighty personal will effectively prevented the development of that type of prayer which seeks to dissolve the individual I in the unbounded One. Just as the God of the Old Testament is no Being reposing in his own beatitude, but reveals himself as the controlling will of the eternal King, so the pious Israelite is no intoxicated, world-denying mystic reveling in the Beyond, but a warrior, who wrestles even in prayer, and looks for the life of power in communion with his divine Lord. His

6. See Hewitt, "The Theology of Intercessory Prayer: With Special Reference to Contemporary Protestant Theology," and West, "A Study of Intercessory Prayer in the New Testament: With Special Reference to the Problems of Result and Operation."

7. See Knudson, *The Religious Teaching of the Old Testament*, 61–67.

8. See Brunner, *The Christian Doctrine of God*, ch. 12, esp. 123f.

goal is not the static concept of the *summum bonum*, but the dynamic fact of the *basileia tou theou*.[9]

The Old Testament contains great prayers of adoration and praise,[10] notable prayers of thanksgiving,[11] and significant prayers of confession of sin.[12] Yet, its most distinctive prayers are probably those of petition[13] and intercession.[14] One can hardly read these Old Testament prayers without gaining the impression that those who offered and those who preserved such prayers confidently believed that Yahweh welcomed such praying. In the New Testament, prayer participates in that transformation of the doctrine of God which centers in God as Father. According to the Synoptic Gospels, Jesus prayed to God as "Father"[15] and directed his disciples to address God in prayer as "Our Father."[16] The Fourth Gospel also refers to Jesus' praying to God as "Father."[17] In both the Synoptics[18] and in John,[19] the term "Father" is used in passages related to prayer. Unlike the Jewish custom of that day Jesus addressed God as Father in prayer by use of the Aramaic term *abba*, a term of familiarity "derived from the language of small children" but, prior to Jesus, extended to use as adult language. As used by Jesus, *abba* "expresses a special relationship with God," both of "obedient trust" and submission to authority. Joachim Jeremias has suggested that the giving of the Lord's Prayer

9. Eichrodt, *Theology of the Old Testament*, 1, 176. Hughes, *Prophetic Prayer*, 2, makes the same distinction: "In mystic piety, God is passive and impassible. Higher than goodness, truth, and beauty, no attributes can be assigned to Him. In prophetic religion, He sees, thinks, feels, and acts. He is afflicted in the afflictions of His people. God plucks the soul from the mire of sin, according to prophetic religion, while, to the mystic, it is through climbing the ladder of an ecstatic union with God that man's failings are left behind. A few souls have attempted to combine these two conceptions and there are points in which they appear to have something in common, but the slight traces of similarity serve only to emphasize the differences.

10. For example, Ex 15:1–18 (Song of Moses) and Ps 146–150.

11. For example, Ps 105–107.

12. For example, Ps 32 and 51.

13. For example, the Psalms for deliverance and for vindication and 1 Kgs 18:36f. and Isa 37:15–20; 38:2–6 (also 2 Kgs 19:15–19; 20:2–6).

14. For example, Gen 18:22–32; Ex 32:11–13, 31–34; Num 14:13–19.

15. Matt 11:25f. (Luke 10:21); Mark 14:36 (Matt 26:39; Luke 22:42); Matt 26:42; Luke 23:34, 46.

16. Matt. 6:9 (Luke 11:2).

17. John 11:41; 12:27f.; 17:1, 5, 11, 21, 24, 25. Jeremias, *The Prayers of Jesus*, 54–57, has noted that Jesus' addressing God as "Father" in prayer is found in "all five strata of the Gospel tradition": Mark, Q, L, M, and John.

18. Matt 6:6, 8, 14f., 7:11 (Luke 11:13); 7:21; Mark 11:25.

19. John 15:16; 16:23, 26.

to the disciples authorized them to say "Abba" just as Jesus did and that Jesus forbade the use of "the address *abba* in everyday speech as a courtesy title (Matt 23:9)" so that the term could be reserved for God.[20] The Epistles contain prayers and allusions to prayers addressed to God as "Father"[21] and two benedictions (or blessings) addressed to God as "Father."[22]

Some of the major objections to Christian prayer during the present century have regarded it as incompatible with aspects of God's nature and activity. James Hastings, writing in 1915, identified the chief "scientific" objection as prayers violating the divinely ordained laws of the physical universe. Three of the five "philosophical" objections described by Hastings relate to God: that prayer is unnecessary in view of God's perfect providence, that prayer is inconsistent with God's unchangeable will or predetermination of all things, and that God cannot grant the conflicting petitions and intercessions of men.[23] George Arthur Buttrick, writing in 1941, was also concerned with prayer and the laws of nature but gave more attention to "defective theories" of prayer, most of which were oriented to man, not to God.[24] Today the problems attaching to Christian prayer are not so likely to be those of perfect providence and divine predetermination of all things. The baffling enigmas of pain and suffering, of unanswered petitions and intercessions, and of "the experience of the absence of God" (William Hamilton) loom much larger. Fred L. Fisher, writing in 1964, rightly called for the recognition that the life of prayer presupposes a personal God who is immanent in human affairs, of sufficient power "to make a difference," and "susceptible to influence by the prayer of men."[25]

Jesus Christ and Prayer

Christian prayer is essentially related to the work and person of Jesus Christ in at least three aspects: His own praying, His teaching concerning prayer, and His high priestly intercession.

The four Gospels are replete with evidence that prayer was paramount in the life and ministry of Jesus. Amid the demands of his Galilean ministry he prayed "in the morning, a great while before day" (Mark 1:35), "he

20. Op. cit., 63.

21. 1 Thess 1:2f.; 3:11–13; 2 Thess. 2:16f.; Eph 2:15–23 (esp. v.17); 3:14–21 (esp. v.14); Col 1:3–5 (esp. v.3); 1:11–14 (esp. v.12).

22. Eph 1:3–14; 1 Pet 1:3–5 (esp. v.3).

23. Hastings, *The Christian Doctrine of Prayer*, 217–63.

24. Buttrick, *Prayer*, 84–95, 43–53.

25. Fisher, *Prayer in the New Testament*, 13–21.

withdrew to the wilderness and prayed" (Luke 5:16), and having gone into the hill country, "all night he continued in prayer to God" (Luke 6:12). Following the feeding of the five thousand and the dismissal of the crowds, "he went up into the hills by himself to pray" (Mark 6:46; par. Matt 14:23), in the region of Caesarea Philippi "he was praying alone" (Luke 9:18), and "he went up on the mountain [of transfiguration] to pray," and "as he was praying, the appearance of his countenance was altered" (Luke 9:28f.). Just prior to the raising of Lazarus, Jesus thanked the Father for hearing him (John 11:41f.), presumably prayed for children brought to him (Matt. 19:13), and at the Last Supper gave thanks prior to distributing the bread (Luke 22:19; par. 1 Cor 11:24) and the wine (Mark 14:23; par. Matt 26:27). He promised to ask the Father for the giving of the Holy Spirit (John 14:16), and for Simon Peter he prayed that his "faith may not fail" (Luke 22:31f.). In Gethsemane, amid sleeping disciples, he prayed about the removal of or submission to the approaching "cup" of suffering (Mark 14:32–42; par. Matt 26:36–46, Luke 22:40–46). Hebrews 5:7–9 bears witness to his praying amid suffering and before death. Three of the seven utterances upon the cross were prayers to the Father (Luke 23:34; Mark 15:34 [par. Matt 27:46]; Luke 23:46).

In his teaching concerning prayer, Jesus stressed both how to pray and that for which men should pray. His disciples were not to pray, as did the scribes and Pharisees, "that they may be seen by men" (Matt 6:5f.); neither were they to "heap up empty phrases, as did the Gentiles," as if they would "be heard for their many words" (Matt 6:7f.). Christian prayer ought not thus to be marked by ostentation or verbosity. The Temple should be "a house of prayer for all the nations" (Mark 11:17; par. Matt 21:13, Luke 19:46). Jesus' followers must keep on asking, seeking, and knocking in expectancy of the Father's good blessings (Matt 7:7–11). They are to pray in faith and in forgiveness of the sins of other men (Mark 11:24f.; par. Matt 21:22; cf. Matt 6:14f.), and, according to the Fourth Gospel, in Jesus' name with confidence as to the granting of such petitions (14:13f.; 15:16; 16:23f.; 16:26).[26] Three of Jesus' parables deal specifically with prayer: the friend at midnight (Luke 11:5–13), the importunate widow (Luke 18:1–8), and the Pharisee and the tax collector (Luke 18:9–14). The first two of these teach

26. Deissman, *Light from the Ancient East*, 123f., cited the use of *eis onoma* in an ostracon from Thebes, in which the phrase meant "to the account of," but it is difficult so to understand the usage of the phrase in the Fourth Gospel. Barrett, *The Gospel According to John*, 384, interprets "in my name" as "the invocation" of Jesus' name but not in a "magical" sense. Bultmann, *The Gospel of John*, 546, 584f., also understands the phrase to refer to the invocation of Jesus but in the sense that one "prays in the confession of faith in Jesus." Brown, *The Gospel According to John*, 636, interprets the phrase as "union with Christ." Morris, *The Gospel According to John*, 646, understands the phrase as being "in accordance with all that the name stands for" so that God is glorified.

persistency or importunity in prayer, while the third stresses humility and contrition. Jesus' disciples are to pray for their persecutors and, by implication, for their enemies (Matt 5:43–45; par. Luke 6:27f.) and for "the Lord of the harvest to send forth laborers into his harvest" (Matt 9:38; par. Luke 10:2). They are to "watch and pray" in expectation of Jesus' *parousia* (Mark 13:33) and to pray that the great eschatological tribulation "may not happen in winter" (Mark 13:17–19; par. Matt 24:19–21).

By far the most important teaching of Jesus in regard to prayer, if one may judge by the history of biblical exposition and of catechetics, has been the Model Prayer, or the Lord's Prayer (Matt 6:9–13; par. Luke 11:2–4), which, according to Luke, was given at the request of the disciples. The longer Matthean rendition consists of seven petitions, the first three of which are distinctly Godward in reference (the divine Name, the divine kingdom, and the divine will) and the last four of which have manward aspects (food, forgiveness, temptation, Satan). The second and third petitions are correlatives in that they both point to happenings during or at the end of history. The sixth and seventh petitions are correlatives, especially if "temptation" be interpreted as inducement to sin or evil rather than testing and if *apo tou ponerou* be taken as a reference to Satan.

The Church Fathers who wrote treatises on prayer usually included expositions of the Lord's Prayer. Such Fathers "viewed the [Lord's] prayer as a model or outline for other Christian prayers."[27] The earliest extant treatise of this kind is Tertullian's *Deoratione* (c. AD 200). Tertullian interpreted "daily bread" as "spiritual bread" or Christ, and the "temptation" as Satanic. He summarized the prayer as follows:

> The honour of God in the 'Father;'
>
> the testimony of faith in the 'Name;'
>
> the offering of obedience in the 'Will;'
>
> the commemoration of hope in the 'Kingdom;'
>
> the petition for life in the 'Bread;'
>
> the full acknowledgment of debts in the prayer for their 'Forgiveness;'
>
> the anxious dread of temptation in the request for 'Protection.'[28]

Origen's *Peri Euches*[29] (c. AD 233) connected "Our Father" with the adoption of Christians and expounded the personal and ontological character of divine names. For Origen *epiousion* in the fourth petition did not

27. Simpson, *The Interpretation of Prayer in the Early Church*, 94.

28. Tertullian, *De oratione*, III:681–91, esp. chs. 6, 8, 9.

29. Oulton and Chadwick, *Alexandrian Christianity*, 238–329, esp. chs. 22, 24, 27.

mean daily physical bread but "the Word of God, i.e., the knowledge and the power communicated by Jesus Christ."[30] Cyprian, in his *De Dominica oratione* (c. AD 252), the third of the extant ante-Nicene expositions of the Lord's Prayer, interpreted the second petition as eschatological, the third petition as God's enablement of men to do God's will, the fourth petition as referring both to daily physical food and to spiritual bread (either Christ or eternal life as received daily in the Eucharist), and the sixth and seventh petitions as Satanic.[31] The major extant post-Nicene expositions of the Lord's Prayer are those by Cyril of Jerusalem, Ambrose, John Chrysostom, Gregory of Nyssa, Theodore of Mopsuestia, Evagrius of Pontus, Augustine, Chromatius of Aquileia, Cyril of Alexandria, Peter Chrysologus, Arnobius, Peter of Laodicea, and Maximus Confessor.[32]

Reformation expositions of the Lord's Prayer include Luther's *Large Catechism*,[33] Luther's *Small Catechism*,[34] Calvin's *Institutes of the Christian Religion*,[35] Calvin's *Geneva Catechism* of 1541,[36] Philip Melanchthon's *Loci Communes* (1555 ed.),[37] the *Heidelberg Catechism*,[38] John Craig's *Catechism*,[39] *The New Catechism of the Church of Scotland* (1644),[40] the *Westminster Larger Catechism*,[41] and the *Westminster Shorter Catechism*.[42] Recent expositions include those by Walter Lüthi,[43] John Lowe,[44] H. Van den Bussche,[45]

30. Simpson, *op. cit.*, 69.
31. Cyprian, *De Dominica oratione*, V:447–57, esp. chs. 13–21, 25–27.
32. See Simpson, *op. cit.*, pp. 175–77, or a bibliography of the patristic expositions.
33. Part III.
34. Part III.
35. III, xx:34–38.
36. Qq. 256–95.
37. Ch. XXXIII.
38. Qq. 118–29.
39. 3rd part of God's honor.
40. Qq. 119–47.
41. Qq. 186–96.
42. Qq. 99–107.
43. Lüthi, *The Lord's Prayer*.
44. Lowe, *The Lord's Prayer*.
45. den Bussche, *Understanding the Lord's Prayer*.

Christopher Francis Evans,[46] Joachim Jeremias,[47] Heinz Schürmann,[48] Ernst Lohmeyer,[49] and Charles M. Layman.[50]

According to the New Testament, Jesus the risen Lord serves as Intercessor in behalf of Christian believers. Prayer is addressed to Jesus directly only by Stephen (Acts 7:59f.). Origen, in the third century, objected to the offering of prayer to Jesus the Son of God.[51] Some exegetes regard the Johannine phrase "in my name" as indicative of the intercession of Jesus. The Epistle to the Hebrews identifies Jesus the High Priest as the sympathetic one through whom "we may receive mercy and find grace in time of need" (4:16) and the one who "ever lives to make intercession (*entugchanein*)" for those "who draw near to God through him" (7:25). In his great intercessory prayer[52] (John 17), Jesus prayed to the Father for his own glorification and that of the Father (vss. 1–5), for his present disciples that they may be one, be kept from Satan "in the world" so as not to be "of the world" and yet be "sent . . . into the world" (vss. 6–19), and for his future disciples and their unity after the analogy of the unity of the Father and the Son (vss. 20–26). First John refers to Jesus as an "advocate" (*parakleton*) with the Father (2:1).

Among the major contemporary objections to the reality of prayer are the theories of autosuggestion, of projectionism, and of community sanctions.[53] According to autosuggestion, prayer in only a soliloquy, or a speaking with oneself. As such it may allegedly serve as a "form of self-reliance" or an instrument of "self-discipline." But can a false claim to communion with God "long pose as truth"? The prayer life of Jesus exhibits the reality of prayer as genuine communion with the almighty *Abba*. According to projectionism, the roots of which are in Feuerbach, Marx, and Freud, prayer is seen to be the wishful projection of human desires upon the "screen" of the universe without any corresponding divine Person. It makes praying to be "whistling in the dark." Jesus taught and exemplified that communion in prayer with God the Father that led to an agonizing cross—anything but a hedonistic projection. According to the community sanctions of Durkheim, prayer is only directed to an idealization of humanity or a hypostatic

46. Evans, *The Lord's Prayer*.

47. Jeremias, *The Lord's Prayer*.

48. Schürmann, *Praying with Christ*.

49. Lohmeyer, *The Lord's Prayer*.

50. Layman, *The Lord's Prayer in Its Biblical Setting*.

51. Origen, *Peri Euches*, XV:1–XVI:1.

52. John 17 has seemingly been called the "High-priestly Prayer" of Jesus since the Lutheran, David Chytraeus (d. 1600), so identified it, according to Hoskyns, *The Fourth Gospel*, 494.

53. Buttrick, *op. cit.*, 45–53.

embodiment of the tribe or the clan, not to the personal God of history who is indeed realizing his purpose through a chosen people. However, Jesus' high priestly prayer (John 17) for his present and future disciples is praying by their Leader, not hypostatizing by the followers.

The Holy Spirit and Prayer

The New Testament relates the Holy Spirit and prayer in several specific ways. First, prayer is involved in respect to the forthcoming gift or bestowal of the Holy Spirit. Jesus was to "pray (*eroteso*) the Father" for the giving of "another Counselor" (*parakleton*) (John 14:16). Jesus taught his disciples that most certainly "will the heavenly Father give the Holy Spirit to those who ask (*aitousin*) him" (Luke 11:13).

Secondly, Christians are admonished to pray in the Holy Spirit. Paul joined the admonition "Pray constantly" to the admonition "Do not quench the Spirit" (1 Thess 5:17, 19). "Pray (*proseuchomenoi*) at all times in the Spirit, with all prayer (*proseuches*) and supplication (*deeseos*)" (Eph. 6:18). Jude also admonished his readers: "pray in the Holy Spirit" (v. 20b).

Thirdly, the intercession of the Holy Spirit is promised to praying Christians. The Spirit, according to Paul, "helps us in our weakness; for we do not know how to pray as we ought." Indeed "the Spirit himself intercedes (*huperentugchanei*) for us with sighs too deep for words (*stenagmois alaletois*)." Such interceding is "for the saints" and "according to the will of God" (*kata theon*) (Rom 8:26f.). He assured the Philippian Christians that through their "prayers and the help (*epichoregias*) of the Spirit of Jesus Christ" his imprisonment would result in his deliverance (1:19).

Fourthly, the power or strength of the Holy Spirit is associated with prayer. Paul prayed for the Christians at Rome that "by the power of the Holy Spirit" they might "abound in hope" (Rom 15:13). Likewise, he appealed to them "by the love of the Spirit, to strive together" with himself in their "prayers to God" in his behalf both for his "deliverance from the unbelievers in Judea" and that his "service for Jerusalem may be acceptable to the saints" (Rom 15:30f.). In an extended prayer in Ephesians, Paul asked that to his readers God would "grant . . . to be strengthened with might through his Spirit in the inner man" (3:16).

It is axiomatic to contrast the almost exclusive preoccupation of ancient Christian creeds of the patristic age with the *person* of the Holy Spirit and the explication of the *work* of the Holy Spirit, as well as of the person of the Spirit, in the confessions of faith and catechisms of the Reformation era. But even the Reformation confessions and catechisms are virtually silent on the work of the Spirit as to prayer. The *Belgic Reformed Confession* (1561) contains a lengthy article (XXVI) on Christ's intercession which contains no mention of the Spirit, and the *Heidelberg Catechism* (1563) contains twelve questions about the Holy Spirit but no mention of prayer. The *Westminster Confession* (1647) does declare in its article on "adoption" (XII) that those justified "receive the Spirit of adoption; have access to the throne of grace with boldness; [and] are enabled to cry, Abba, Father." The same confession in its article on "Religious Worship and the Sabbath-day" (XXI, 3) asserts that prayer "with thanksgiving . . . is by God required of all men; and that it may be accepted, it is to be made in the name of the Son, by the help of his Spirit, according to his will."[54] The *Second London Confession of Particular Baptists* (1677) retains these statements. The *New Hampshire Baptist Confession* (1833) in its article on "sanctification" lists "prayer" as one of "the appointed means" used in the sanctification of believers "by the presence and power of the Holy Spirit."[55] Even the *Statement of Fundamental Truths of the Assemblies of God* (1916) contains no specific statement about the Holy Spirit and prayer.[56] Not a few of the twentieth-century books on prayer, such as those cited above by Fosdick, Buttrick, and Harkness, are deficient in respect to the Holy Spirit and prayer.

The historic tension between mystical or contemplative prayer and prophetic prayer, emphasized by Heiler,[57] should be understood, at least in part, in connection with the role of the Holy Spirit in prayer. Mystical prayer in the West has its roots in Neo-Platonism with its two movements—that of proliferation of reality from the One and the reabsorptive reunion of reality with the One. The mystic sees prayer as a leading means of fostering the latter. Prophetic prayer, in contrast, has its roots in ancient Hebrew monotheism, which affirmed that Yahweh-Creator, Lord of nature and of history, is dynamically present by his Spirit, and in the *Adventus Spiritus* that followed upon the ascension of Jesus, with its transformative effects upon the disciples. In prophetic prayer, the one who prays does not so much seek an ontological refusion with the Ground of Being as he asks and boldly pleads, even regarding matters quite specific, in the strength and with the aid of God's own Spirit for God's will to be done—from regeneration to consummation.

54. Schaff, *The Creeds of Christendom*, III:413–16, 324–28, 628, 646f.

55. Lumpkin, *Baptist Confessions of Faith* (1959), 267, 281, 365.

56. Assemblies of God, *Who We Are and What We Believe.*

57. Heiler, *Prayer*, chs. 6–9.

The Person Who Prays

The history of religion affords evidence of man's universal capacity for prayer and the widespread practice of prayer in some sense and in some manner,[58] even while allowing for the growing modern phenomenon of non-prayer. Prayer is presumably a distinctive that separates man from the animal world. Christian prayer presupposes the Christian affirmations concerning man as creature, man as sinner, and man as redeemable through Jesus Christ.

The various moods of Christian prayer reflect the various needs of the one who prays. Adoration is predicated on the greatness of God in contrast to the finitude of man, the eternity of God in contrast to man's mortality, and the power of God in contrast to man's weakness. Thanksgiving presupposes the good providence of God as Creator and Sustainer and man's dependence upon the providential God. Confession acknowledges man's sinfulness amid the expectancy of God's undeserved mercy. Petition implies that God welcomes petitions and is willing to answer, however the answer may be, and that man both needs to ask and is free to ask of God. Intercession means that, according to God's will, man in and through prayer may be privileged to share in the unfolding of God's purpose.[59]

Some of the contemporary objections stem from the human perspective and situation. One of the most common, whether stated or implied, is that man himself or in his societal context is sufficient without prayer. The new humanism continues to foster this outlook. Others invalidate prayer on the ground of ungranted petitions and intercessions. Yet others question the practicability of prayer in view of what they see as a warfare of conflicting human petitions and intercessions directed to a universal God. Such objections neglect the aspect of "Thy will be done," for prayer is not a supernatural "grab-bag" at God's "state fair."

The Church at Prayer

Christian prayer has included more than private or personal prayer from the beginning of Christianity, and Jesus' admonition vis-a-vis Pharisaism as to praying in a room with a closed door (Matt 6:6) should not be taken as a

58. See Heiler, *Prayer*, chs. 1–3.

59. Buttrick, *Prayer*, 296, has declared: "By prayer men are in tune with God, both in the play of events and in the play of thought. Mary Queen of Scots said she feared the prayers of John Knox more than all the armies of Europe . . . The history of the Church gives evidence that men have worked 'miracles' by prayer . . ."

proof-text against corporate prayer. Indeed, the same Gospel juxtaposes his saying about agreement in asking and the assurance of the Father's doing (Matt 18:19) with his saying about gathering in the name and presence of Jesus (Matt 18:20).

The church in Jerusalem in its earliest history was presented as the church at prayer. The one hundred and twenty disciples following Jesus' ascension "with one accord devoted themselves to prayer" (Acts 1:14). After the day of Pentecost, the more than three thousand "devoted themselves to . . . the prayers" (Acts 2:42). Peter and John continued to attend the hour of prayer in the Temple (Acts 3:1). The Jerusalem Christians prayed that the Lord would grant boldness of speech and miracle-working power to his "servants" (Acts 5:23–31). After the execution of James the apostle and the arrest of Simon Peter, the church in Jerusalem offered "earnest prayer for him" only to be stunned by his appearance in their midst after an angelic deliverance (Acts 12:1–17). The church in Antioch of Syria engaged in prayer, worship, and fasting as they "set apart" and "sent off" Barnabas and Saul (Acts 13:2f.). The Epistle of James alluded to the practices whereby "the elders of the church" anointed and prayed for the sick and whereby Christians confessed their sins to and prayed "for one another" (5:13–16).

The Apostle Paul referred to his praying for Thessalonian (1 Thess 1:2–3; 2 Thess. 1:3; 2:13), Roman (Rom 1:8–10), Philippian (Phil 1:3–5), and Colossian (Col 1:3–5a) Christians. He alluded to his own praying for his unbelieving Jewish brothers (Rom 10:1) and urged upon Timothy that prayers of various kinds, possibly in the context of corporate worship, be offered for civil rulers (1 Tim 2:1f.). Paul also verbalized within his epistles specific prayers for the Thessalonian (1 Thess. 3:11–13; 5:23; 2 Thess. 3:5), Corinthian (1 Cor 1:4–9), Ephesian (Eph 1:15–22; 3:14–19), and Colossian (Col 1:9–12) Christians.

The relative values of liturgical and spontaneous prayer and of verbal and silent prayer have been debated among Christian communions and in various epochs. Nevertheless, as Nels F. S. Ferré has written, "The history of the Christian Church is, more than we know, the history of believing prayer."[60]

> O, where are kings and empires now,
>
> Of old that went and came?
>
> But Lord, thy church is praying yet,
>
> A thousand years the same.[61]

60. Ferré, *A Theology for Christian Prayer*, 9.

61. Quoted by Campbell, *The Place of Prayer in the Christian Religion*, 245.

Prayer and the Eschaton

Christian prayer, as indeed Christian faith and hope, has an eschatological dimension. The second and third petitions in the Lord's Prayer (Matt 6:10), as noted above, are eschatological. Christians are to "watch and pray"[62] in expectation of Jesus' *parousia* (Mark 13:33). The common Aramaic prayer of the early Christians that Paul reiterates, "Our Lord, come!" (*Maranatha*) (1 Cor 16:22a), is very probably to be understood in reference to the *parousia*, though some regard it as a reference to the incarnation, as did John Chrysostom, and translate it, "The Lord has come." As indicative of the *parousia*, the text may also be translated "Our Lord is coming" and thus be related to Phil 4:5. Only with the translation "Our Lord, come!" is the text a prayer.[63] The New Testament Apocalypse ends with an almost identical prayer, "Come, Lord Jesus" (Rev 22:20c). The eager expectation of the *parousia* led to the prayer for its imminence. After many centuries and amid the complexities of a technological and sensate culture with its humanism and Neo-Satanism, Christians may and ought still to pray, "Come, Lord Jesus."

Especially in a secularistic age Christians must remember that the believing man is a praying man, for to believe is to pray. Moreover, for P. T. Forsyth it was "truer to say that we live the Christian life in order to pray than that we pray in order to live the Christian life."[64] The purpose of a theology of Christian prayer is that Christians may pray more effectively. So may it be.

62. Note the conflicting textual evidence, some manuscripts reading "Watch and prayer" and others only "Watch."

63. Craig, *The Interpreters Bible*, X, 262. See also Fuller, *The Foundations of New Testament Christology*, 156–58.

64. Forsyth, *The Soul of Prayer*, 16.

16

"A Christian View of Material Things" (1972)[1]

The term "material things" is a rather broad and inclusive term that is understood here to include land, bodies of water, underground, atmosphere, plants, animals, houses, buildings, clothes, adornments, furnishings, machinery, investments, money, and the like. The term "Christian view" is used here so as to suggest that the best of biblical truth and contemporary insights are being sought so that the resultant statement about material things may be authentically Christian, but no claim is made or implied that this statement of the view is characterized by finality or is to be received with unanimity.

It is first necessary to inquire of and to provide a summary statement of the biblical teachings about material things.

I

The biblical doctrine of creation means that all material things have their origin in God. In the Old Testament, the divine origin of all things is conveyed by the Hebrew word *bara*, which is used only of God and of activity peculiar to God. The creation of material things other than man has a greater role in the more detailed creation account of Genesis 1 (P) than in the man-centered creation account of Genesis 2 (J). According to Gen 1–2, to Ps 104, and to Second Isaiah, the created universe has a beginning, a sustaining continuation (Ps 104:27–30), and an end. While Yahweh is eternal,

1. This chapter first appeared in *Resource Unlimited*. Nashville: Stewardship Commission, Southern Baptist Convention, 1972.

the created universe is not eternal but derived from and dependent upon Yahweh. The cosmology of ancient Israel, especially the threestory universe, Edmund Jacob has insisted,[2] did not arise from Israel's religious affirmation about Yahweh's creative activity but was shared with the other peoples of antiquity. Psalm 104 (especially v.24) presents the created universe as a unity. The creation of all things has its end—its goal as well as its termination. Second Isaiah understands the divine salvation of Israel as a new creation, and unlike the earliest affirmations about deity in the Pentateuch, moves from covenant to creation so that the idea of creation is secondary to the idea of covenant, yet covenant is only realizable within a created order. Thus, God has created "for the covenant."[3] The hope of Israel is describable in terms of "the new heavens and the new earth" (Isa 66:22).

Not only are all material things derived from and dependent upon God the Creator, according to the faith of Israel, but also these material things that make up the created universe are reckoned by God the Creator to be "good." Seven distinct pronouncements of the goodness of the created are made in Gen 1 (vv. 4, 10, 12, 18, 21, 25, 31) by the priestly writer. Then, in the commission to Cyrus, Second Isaiah presents the declaration of Yahweh: "I form the light and create darkness; I make peace (weal) and create evil (woe), I the Lord do all these things" (45:7). No Zoroastrian dualism is to creep into Jewish beliefs! What men consider "darkness" and "woe" is to be embraced in the creative activity of Yahweh, who granted to his creatures a relative freedom. Moreover, this creative work of Yahweh produced no "chaos" but an ordered and inhabited universe (45:18–19).

The Old Testament affirms the ownership of all things by Yahweh as well as his creatorship of all things. In the Psalms, the idea is found repeatedly. "The earth is the Lord's and the fulness thereof, the world and those who dwell therein" (Ps 24:1 RSV). To Israel, Yahweh declares: "I do not reprove you for your sacrifices; your burnt offerings are continually before me. I will accept no bull from your house, nor he-goat from your folds. For every beast of the forest is mine, the cattle on a thousand hills. I know all the birds of the air, and all that moves in the field is mine" (Ps 50:8–11 RSV). "For the Lord is a great God, and a great King above all gods. In his hand are the depths of the earth; the heights of the mountains are his also. The sea is his, for he made it; for his hands formed the dry land" (Ps 95:3–5 RSV). Yahweh, in answering Job and after dealing with the hippopotamus and the crocodile, declares: "Whatever is under the whole heaven is mine" (Job 41:11b RSV). In Isa 66:1 (RSV), Yahweh declares in similar fashion, "Heaven is my

2. Jacob, *Theology of the Old Testament*, 144–46.

3. Ibid., 137.

throne and the earth is my footstool. . . ." The year of jubilee is predicated on the truth that the land belongs to Yahweh (Lev 25:23). Through the prophet Haggai and in a context of the soon to be restored temple in Jerusalem, the Lord of hosts declares: "The silver is mine, and the gold is mine" (Hag 2:8).

T. A. Kantonen has called attention to the important connection between the divine ownership of all things and the divine sovereignty or rulership over all things, including the satanic rebellion and the offer to Jesus of "the kingdoms of this world," on the ground that authority over these had been "delivered" unto Satan (Luke 4:5–6) and then God's ultimate word, "The kingdom of the world has become the kingdom of our Lord and of his Christ, and he shall reign forever and ever" (Rev 11:15 RSV).[4]

What then is the relation of man the creature to material things, according to the Bible? First, it should be noted that man is said in Gen 1 to have been given "dominion" over the animal and plant creation and to have been commanded, "Be fruitful and multiply, and fill the earth and subdue it" (Gen 1:28 RSV). Genesis 2 makes no reference to "dominion" but does refer to man's giving names to the animals (v. 20). Yet, because of man's sins, the earth shall bring forth "thorns and thistles" and man shall toil for his sustenance (Gen 3:17–19). Man's dominion over plants, animals, and the resources of the material universe must always be understood as a relative or secondary dominion under the primary sovereignty of God, yet that human dominion must be recognized as real. Some have identified the image of God in which man was made (Gen 1:27) as the very capacity for and exercise of dominion. The psalmist indeed connects man's status and his exercise of dominion: "What is man that thou art mindful of him, and the son of man that thou dost care for him? Yet, thou hast made him little less than God, and dost crown him with glory and honor. Thou hast given him dominion over the works of thy hands; thou hast put all things under his feet, all sheep and oxen, and also the beasts of the field, the birds of the air, and the fish of the sea, whatever passes along the paths of the sea" (Ps 8:4–8 RSV). Similar language about man's role appears in Job 7:17–18 and Ps 144:3. The Epistle to the Hebrews quotes Ps 8:4–6 and then comments, "Now in putting everything in subjection to him [man], he [God] left nothing outside his [man's] control. As it is, we do not yet see everything in subjection to him." Yet, he declares, "We see Jesus, who for a little while was made lower than the angels, crowned with glory and honor because of the suffering of death, so that by the grace of God he might taste death for everyone" (Heb 2:6–9 RSV).

4. Kantonen, *A Theology for Christian Stewardship*, 33f.

God's ownership of all things and man's relative but real dominion over lower creatures lead in biblical thought to man's obligation to a responsible management or use of material things—a concept translated from the Greek New Testament οἰκονομία by the English term "stewardship." The latter term, derived from the Old English usage of "warden of the sty" or "sty-ward," has few exact parallels in other modern languages. Paul uses the term "stewardship" in reference to the gospel rather than concerning material things and declares: "Moreover, it is required of stewards that they be found trustworthy" (1 Cor 4:2 RSV). Jesus, speaking of material things, said: "He who is faithful in a very little is faithful also in much; and he who is dishonest in a very little is dishonest also in much. If then you have not been faithful in the unrighteous mammon, who will entrust to you the true riches? And if you have not been faithful in that which is another's, who will give you that which is your own?" (Luke 16:10–12 RSV).

The Old Testament repeatedly warns against the use of material things as images of deity or as idols to be worshipped (Ex 20:4–6, 23; 34:17; Lev 19:4; 26:1; Deut 4:15–19; 5:8–10; 27:15). The New Testament warns against *hoarding* or *absolutizing* material things. "No one can serve two masters. . . . you cannot serve God and mammon" (Matt 6:24 RSV). "Take heed, and beware of all covetousness; for a man's life does not consist in the abundance of his possessions!" (Luke 12:15 RSV). "For what will it profit a man, if he gains the whole world and forfeits his life?" (Matt 16:26 RSV). Jesus' parable of the rich man and Lazarus (Luke 16:19–31) is set in the context of the difficulty that a rich man has in hearing the gospel or entering the kingdom of God. His encounter with the rich young ruler (Mark 10:17–31 and parallels) presents even more directly and clearly the necessity of choosing between the primacy of riches and discipleship and Jesus articulated the difficulty by saying, "It is easier for a camel to go through the eye of a needle than for a rich man to enter the kingdom of God" (Mark 10:25 RSV).

According to the teaching of Jesus, man cannot possess material things *after death*. "Do not lay up for yourselves treasures on earth, where moth and rust consume and where thieves break in and steal, but lay up for yourselves treasures in heaven, where neither moth nor rust consumes and where thieves do not break in and steal" (Matt 6:19–20 RSV). In the parable of the rich fool, God asks the fool at the hour of his death: "Fool! This night your soul is required of you; and the things you have prepared, whose will they be?" (Luke 12:20 RSV).

Yet, one saying of Jesus, his conclusion to the parable of the unjust steward, seems to indicate that man can so use material things as to have effects after his death. Jesus said: "And I tell you, make friends for yourselves by means of unrighteous mammon, so that when it fails they may receive you into the eternal habitations" (Luke 16:9 RSV).

II

The Christian understanding of the relations of God and of man to material things has been repeatedly challenged in the course of Christian history by non-Christian or quasi-Christian views of material things. No attempt here will be made to enumerate or discuss all of these contrary viewpoints. However, three of these will be considered in some detail: the Gnostic and Manichaean views, the Hindu and Buddhist views, and the modern Western materialistic views.

Gnosticism so posited the evil of matter that the entire world, or total material universe, was regarded as being under evil or demonic powers and to have had its origin somewhat apart from the transcendent deity. Hans Jonas has summarized the Gnostic cosmology as follows:

> The deity is absolutely transmundane, its nature alien to that of the universe . . . : to the divine realm of light, self-contained and remote, the cosmos is opposed as the realm of darkness. The world is the work of lowly powers. . . . The genesis of these lower powers, the Archons (rulers), and in general that of all the orders of being outside God, including the world itself is a main theme of gnostic speculation. . . . The universe, the domain of the Archons, is like a vast prison whose innermost dungeon is the earth, the scene of man's life. Around and above it the cosmic spheres are ranged like concentric enclosing shells. Most frequently there are the seven spheres of the planets surrounded by the eighth, that of the fixed stars. . . . Basilides counted no fewer than 365 "heavens." . . . [Moreover,] everything which intervenes between here and the beyond serves to separate man from God, not merely by spatial distance but through active demonic force: . . . The Archons collectively rule over the world, and each individually in his sphere is a warden of the cosmic prison. Their tyrannical world-rule is called *heimarmene*, universal Fate. . . . Through his body and his soul, man is a part of the world and subjected to the *heimarmene*. Enclosed in the soul is the spirit . . . , a portion of the divine substance from beyond which has fallen into the world; and the Archons created man for the express purpose of keeping it captive there. . . . The goal of gnostic striving is the release of the "inner man" from the bonds of the world and his return to the realm of light. . . . With

> the completion of this process of gathering in . . . , the cosmos, deprived of its elements of light, will come to an end.[5]

In Gnostic religion and thought, therefore, man can in no sense be the steward of material things, for his salvation consists of separation from his physical body and the whole material universe. A prisoner of the cosmos, man cannot be a manager of a portion of the cosmos, for such is the function of the Archons.

The Manichaean system also regarded the universe as being evil but instead posited the eternality and independence of the realm of darkness (Ahriman) as well as of the realm of light (Father of Greatness). Conflict was provoked by the realm of darkness, and, in response, the Father of Greatness called forth (a) Primal man, (b) the Friend of Lights, the Great Architect, and the Living Spirit, and (c) the Messenger. Adam and Eve are formed by the Ahriman, and he deposits in them the light left in his possession. Jonas reminds us that in Manichaean thought man's body "is of devilish substance and . . . also of devilish *design*."[6] Manichaeans consequently were vegetarians, lest they consume "ensouled" animals, and were admonished to abstain from procreation, though the hearers, unlike the elect, were allowed to marry. For Manichaean thought, material things could not be separated from the great cosmic struggle between darkness and light. Man's salvation consisted in ascetic practices and deliverance from darkness. To be responsible for the management of material things, therefore, was entirely alien to the Manichaean religion.

The Gnostic viewed material things as the work of the Demiurge and man's destiny as his deliverance from a material body, and the Gnostics' debt to Greek philosophical thought for these views was considerable. The Manichee eternalized the conflict of good and evil, of light and darkness, and subordinated the material world to this cosmic conflict.

Hinduism regards the material world as "a temporary, worthless illusion (Maya)."[7] Affected by the acknowledged caste system and by Karma, the cosmic power or law of justice that functions to assign souls to their status in reincarnation, the Hindu attitude toward material things proceeds from no doctrine of the goodness of creation. The ancient religion of the Vedas centered in a nature-worship in which planets and elements were prayed to and praised. From the time of the writings known as Brahmanas, restrictions have been placed on the eating of beef; thus the cow came to be looked upon as a special sacred animal. The concept of Maya was shaped in

5. Jonas, *The Gnostic Religion*, 42–46.

6. Ibid., 227.

7. Hume, *The World's Living Religions*, 25.

the speculative philosophy of the Upanishads with its one Supreme Being or Brahma. The world has relatively less significance for the Hindu, who has a cyclical view of history, than for the Muslim, the Jew, or the Christian. Only slowly and only in recent years have Hindu statesmen been able to evoke support for projects that alter the geographical or economic status quo.

Buddhism is a religion of the extirpation of desire through ascetical practices, an eightfold ethical "path," and the hope of a state of passionless peace called Nirvana, or after death Pari-Nirvana. Buddhism retained Hinduism's law of Karma and transmigration of souls but rejected the caste system. But to be, according to Buddhism, is to be transitory, miserable, and impersonal.[8] Insofar as material things contribute to man's desires, they are presumably to be frowned upon or devaluated. Since man's body and man's activity are without specific worth in Buddhism, it is safe to conclude that man's relation to material things can have little significance at all.[9] Yet, of Cautama, Reischauer written:

> He was too much of a realist to hold that all this flux of phenomenal existence is maya, an illusion of the unenlightened mind. He accepted it as real and believed that this process of birth and death and again rebirth and death would go on indefinitely unless the Karma energy, the blind "will to be," is stopped. Just how the universe came to be what it is or whether there is some great purpose in it all, he did not pretend to know.[10]

Western man has, on the whole, taken material things to be of greater significance for human life than has the man of the Orient. This difference is somewhat explicable by the Jewish and Christian affirmation of the divine creation of all things and of the value of man, including his body. But Western civilization has also been the locus for an absolutizing of material values at the expense of other values. Materialism as metaphysics had its advocates among the ancient Greeks[11] and among the eighteenth-century French philosophers of the Enlightenment,[12] but it has reached much greater proportions in the modern era in the West. Two important examples may be noted: Marxist dialectical materialism and capitalist functional materialism.

It is commonly asserted that Karl Marx derived his dialectic from G. W. F. Hegel and his materialism from Ludwig Feuerbach. But Marx wrote his doctoral thesis on Democritus and Epicurus and insisted in his *Theses*

8. Ibid., 71.

9. Ibid., 77.

10. Reischauer, "Buddhism," 97.

11. E.g., Leucippus, Democritus, and Epicurus.

12. E.g., de la Mettrie, Diderot, and d'Holbach.

on Feuerbach that materialism had been too fatalistic and should serve the cause of social revolution.[13] Matter, for Marx, was dynamic rather than inert. Moreover, history is understood as the product of the interaction of economic forces and without the existence and involvement of God. Hence the classless and utopian society envisioned by Marxism and toward which present socialism points abounds in material things, which are, it is said, to be distributed justly through the abolition of private property and the establishment of state ownership. R. N. Carew Hunt has commented on the Marxist handling of the basic question of thinking and being:

> Marx's treatment of this problem has coloured all subsequent communist thinking. He takes it, of course, as axiomatic that the material world is the fundamental reality, and that although it is accessible to thought, it is not constituted by it. . . . The older materialists had taught that our knowledge of the external world—and at the same time our ideas about it—was obtained by the impact of sensations upon the mind, but had regarded these sensations as passive. . . . Marx teaches that these sensations, which were held to give us faithful images of the external world, did not provide immediate knowledge but only stimuli to knowledge which completed itself in action. . . . Hence, he insisted that we only perceive a thing as a part of the process of acting upon it. . . . This activist theory of knowledge—known today as Instrumentalism—which insists that knowledge is indissolubly bound up with action (*Praxis*), is the most distinctive feature of Marx's philosophy as opposed to his theories of history and economics. . . . On the other hand, Engels, . . . went back to the older theory which held the source of knowledge to be sensations.[14]

Lenin sought to "bring Marx and Engels together by arguing that they were always in agreement, though wherever there is a divergence he invariably follows Engels."[15] Thus, to act in the cause of revolution is to be able to aid stimuli in evoking knowledge. To have knowledge of ultimate reality is to share in the dialectic processes of history. Whichever the starting point, matter, dynamically conceived, is the real. Thus, for Marxism, the world of things from atom to giant jet, from bacteria to skyscraper, or from genes to an entire society is of ultimate value as the ultimately real.

13. Mayer, *A History of Modern Philosophy*, 428, 433.
14. Hunt, *The Theory and Practice of Communism*, 34f.
15. Ibid., 180.

Unlike Marxism, capitalistic materialism does not proceed from the metaphysical affirmation that the material is the real. In fact, it may have a loose alliance with idealistic metaphysics or theistic religion. But nevertheless, in its encouragement of the acquisition and accumulation of real estate and of stocks and bonds, capitalist economics seems to bear its witness in favor of the ultimacy or supreme value of material things, at least in this present life prior to death. At this point, capitalist economics stands on common ground with its arch foe: Marxism.

The Gnostic-Manichaean outlook saw material things as evil, either intrinsically, or by association with the cosmic forces of evil in conflict with the good. The Hindu-Buddhist outlook sees material things as passing and secondary phenomena, either unreal and hence illusory, or real, and yet, so far as contributing to desire, more harm than good. The Marxist-capitalist outlook sees material things as the *summum bonum*, either because they are the ultimately real, or because they are reckoned to be of highest value to living man.

III

In view of its biblical foundations and of the major contrary answers to the question of the significance of material things, what should a Christian understanding of material things mean to Christians today? Should it have the same meaning for Christians who are living amid the technology and relative affluence of the developed nations and for Christians who are living in the underdeveloped nations? The following statements constitute an effort to formulate answers.

(l) *Origin:* Christians believe, as do Jews and Muslims, that all material things were created by and derived from God. Hence material things are not eternal but are derived and temporal. Their significance, therefore, must be consonant with their origin and their destiny. Material things cannot, for Christians, be ultimate reality, but they are indeed real. Indeed, it is the reality of material things and the orderliness and purposiveness of the universe that make possible the entire enterprise of modern science. Science's debt to Judaism and Christianity for such concepts was hardly acknowledged by A. Wolf when he indicted the medieval Christian Church as the "chief obstacle in the path of science."[16]

(2) *Value:* From the perspective of Christian truth, one can hardly affirm unconditionally that material things are inherently moral. The

16. Wolf, *A History of Science, Technology and Philosophy in the 16th and 17th Centuries*, I, 8.

pronouncements of the goodness of creation in Gen 1 pertain to the goodness of the created order as brought into existence by God. They do not necessarily invest created things or beings with an independent and intrinsic goodness: The creation of man is embraced without the pronouncements, but the same book of Genesis presents man as sinner. The usage of material things by man must be considered before their morality can be defined. Whether material things are good or evil may depend on man's usage of the same. Steel may be used to make operating room equipment for saving lives or to make weapons for killing human beings. The goodness or the evil lies in the usage. But the worth of material things in general is a corollary of the doctrine of creation.

(3) *Ownership and Dominion:* Christians by implication from creation as well as by specific biblical teaching are obliged to recognize that ultimate ownership of and dominion over all material things belong to God. "For from him and through him and to him are all things. To him be glory forever. Amen" (Rom 11:36 RSV). Together with and under this primary or ultimate divine ownership and dominion, men participate in a secondary or relative ownership and dominion of material things through what has been called "the ownership of property." Such ownership may be collective (nation, group, family) or individual or joint (husband and wife). While subject to the mortality of human owners and to its possible sale, such ownership of property may transcend the deaths of individual men through inheritance or through collective ownership; Dominion, or at least a relative dominion, may be exercised more widely than ownership, as in the case of the seas and the atmosphere. During the history of Christianity, three primary challenges have been presented to the concept and practice of individual ownership of property. One was the monastic challenge, initiated as part of a reaction against the worldliness of the contemporary Christianity and maintained through the monastic vow of poverty. The history of the Josephite monasteries in sixteenth-century Russia affords clear evidence that monastic foundations can through collective ownership be marked by the same inordinate possessiveness which initially evoked the monastic vow of poverty. A second challenge was in the name of a restored Christian community in which private ownership of property by all Christians would be surrendered in favor of congregational ownership, presumably after the Jerusalem model. The Hutterian Brethren, the Moravian wing of sixteenth-century Anabaptism, have been one of several examples of such communitarian Christian movements. A third challenge has been that of socialism in the nineteenth and twentieth centuries. By the nationalization of major industries and of the means of transportation and communication, socialism has sought to remove or curtail the excessive accumulation of property

by the few or the favored. The monastic solution centered in the monastic community, the Christian communitarian solution in the communitarian church, and the socialistic solution centered in the national community. All three challenged the unlimited development of individual or private ownership of properly. Monasticism's challenge is in the name of spirituality; Christian communitarianism's challenge is in the name of neoapostolic Christianity; socialism's challenge of family and group ownership as well as of individual ownership is in the name of societal justice. Nevertheless, private ownership continues in nonsocialist states. Christians who exercise private and family ownership of property should recognize the ultimate ownership of God and their own responsible stewardship of that property.

(4) *Necessity:* Any valid assessment of the role of material things must consider man's need of basic sustenance: food, drink, clothing, shelter (and twentieth-century man would add: medicine). Such basic sustenance must of necessity be derived from the realm of material things, as the recent East Pakistan hurricane has reminded the world. From the first century AD, Christian love has been interpreted in terms of sharing of the necessities (τὸν βίον τοῦ κόσμου) with needy brothers (1 John 3:17). But Christian obedience in such instances has not always matched the needs or the mandate of love. Christians, together with many other human beings today, hold the conviction that every human being is entitled to basic sustenance and that human labor is normally the means for providing such. Such a conviction has in recent years been joined with a growing concern about an increasing world population and the availability of material resources for the sustenance of all men.

(5) *Accumulation:* The basic production or acquisition and storage of material things for the meeting of present and future needs derives from the early history of mankind, as primitive agriculture shows. Christians have reason to acknowledge the propriety of such basic accumulation. However, the protests of John Wycliffe and many others against the acquisition and ownership of much property by the medieval Western Church show that accumulation can seriously affect the well-being of the most sacred of institutions. Man, particularly in the twentieth century and especially but not exclusively in the more developed nations, is in constant danger of absolutizing material things as the *summum bonum,* either by the inordinate demand for and acquisition of the products, conveniences, and luxuries provided by modern technology or by the excessive accumulation of material things far beyond personal or family usage without exercise of responsibility to society. Christians should from time to time reassess the shape of their own obedience to God and their stewardship of material things in view of the danger that accumulation may lead to the practice of a materialism

irreconcilable with their Christian profession of faith. The saying of Jesus is relevant: "A man's life does not consist in the abundance of his possessions" (Luke 12:15 RSV),

(6) *Exploitation:* From antiquity, man has been aware of those destructive natural catastrophes (earthquake, hurricane, tornado, fire, flood, etc.) that have taken human lives in considerable numbers . . . and have devastated the realm of nature. But only in the modern period, and especially in the present generation, has mankind begun to be truly conscious of the awesome exploitation of natural resources and pollution of the environment that more populous and more technological man has brought about. Soil conservation, reforestation, replenishment of fish, and regulations to preserve wildlife have become common in the United States earlier in the present century, but now the battle against all forms of pollution and waste of natural resources has begun. Of all twentieth-century men, Christians should be most sensitive to the need for environmental ethics. Christian love for the brethren needs to express itself in care for the total well-being of one's contemporaries and of yet unborn generations. Martin Luther's call to Christians to "be a Christ to one's neighbor" is not alien to the present needs of a populous earth to make proper use of material things.

(7) *Christian Stewardship:* The stewardship of material things for Christians includes more than the right use and conservation of natural resources and the limitation of environmental pollution. Material things, when freely and gratefully dedicated and given to God and entrusted to the Christian "household of faith," can and should be so utilized by Christian persons in the service of Christ and the fellowship of his church as to be means and instruments employed and empowered by the Holy Spirit for Christian evangelization, Christian instruction and nurture, and Christian helping ministries. Such gifts sustain both the enablers who seek to equip all Christians for their ministries and the emissaries of the good news of Christ who plant the need for new fellowships of the reborn. With no Gnostic or Manichaean disdain, no Hindu or Buddhist detachment, and no Marxist or capitalist obsession, Christians as stewards of material things—as well as of the gospel and of their total lives—can participate responsibly and joyfully in the transformation of material things into spiritual reality through Jesus Christ, his gospel, his Spirit, and his church. The medieval church used the term "transubstantiation" to describe the alleged change of "substance" of the bread and wine into the actual body and blood of Christ. But in the patristic age, the offering had been produce brought by the congregation, not the wafer and the wine elevated by the priest. Can we as evangelical Christians dare to see as the true end of Christian giving of material things

(money) the "transubstantiation" by the Spirit of God of such things so given into the personal reality of redeemed humanity?

Hans Lilje, the Lutheran bishop of Hanover, wrote about World War II of the significance of Christian stewardship and declared:

> Here the insights of our American brethren in the faith have, in the perspective of church history, something like the same significance as the lessons which the German Lutheran Reformation has taught us about justification by grace, or the Communion of the Brethren [*Unitas Fratrum*] about the unity of God's children.[17]

Whether in America or elsewhere, Christians ought in the context of their possibilities as never before to practice and live out their stewardship of material things, being ever open to the ownership and dominion of the creating, redeeming God and to the needs of men and of the universe.

17. Forward to Rendtorff, *Als die guten Haushalter*. Translated and quoted by Kantonen, *A Theology for Christian Stewardship*, 1.

17

"History of the Doctrine of Prayer" (1988)[1]

Tertullian's *On Prayer* (204) is the oldest surviving postbiblical Christian treatise on prayer. Like Origen's more lengthy *On Prayer* (ca. 233) and Cyprian's *On the Lord's Prayer* (252), Tertullian's work is a commentary on the Lord's Prayer. Christians prayed to God during persecution, and, by the fourth century, apostles, the Virgin Mary, and martyrs began to be invoked as well as God. The solitaries and the monks sought a life of prayer. By the fourth century, prayer was being offered for the deceased. Liturgical development in the church resulted in the loss of spontaneity in prayer. More than a dozen other church fathers wrote treatises on prayer.

In the history of Christian prayer, the struggle between the "prophetic" and the "mystical," the one leading to communion with God and the other to absorptive union with the divine, has been paramount.[2] This was true especially during the medieval period. Augustine of Hippo had attempted a synthesis of the two and Thomas Aquinas sought to maintain that synthesis, but twelfth-century mystics such as Hugo of St. Victor and sixteenth-century mystics such as Teresa of Avila and John of the Cross gave the mystical or contemplative the preeminence. Prayer to the Virgin Mary and to the saints and for the souls in purgatory was encouraged and widely practiced.

The Protestant Reformation brought about a renewal of prophetic prayer. According to Martin Luther, John Calvin, Philip Melanchthon, and the *Heidelberg Catechism*, prayer is dependent upon the intercession of Jesus Christ and is the privilege and duty of all Christians amid their vocations.

1. This article first appeared in *Disciple's Study Bible: New International Version.*
2. Friedrich Heiler, *Prayer*, chs. 6–9.

Prophetic prayer tended to prevail among the Anabaptists, the Puritans, and the Pietists, whereas the Quakers extended the mystical tradition. A Roman Catholic controversy on prayer between Francois Fénelon and Jacques Bossuet, which led to the papal condemnation (1699) of Fénelon, centered in the proper motive of prayer, whether one's disinterested love of God (Fénelon) or the love for God that pertains to human salvation (Bossuet).

Immanuel Kant anticipated the modern denial of the reality of prayer, but prayers of confession of sin marked the great awakenings in modern Protestantism, and intercessory prayer was the matrix in which the Modern Protestant Missionary Movement was born. The social gospel directed prayer toward societal reform. Philosophical naturalism has argued the impossibility of prayer, especially petitionary prayer, and pantheism (all is divine) has found prayer to a personal God to be contrary to its doctrine of allness. From psychology and philosophy arose the objections that prayer is autosuggestion (self-suggestion) or the projection of human wishes. Christians have faced difficulties related to unanswered petitions and intercessions, prayer and God's will, prayer and modern warfare, and prayer for bodily healing. Important twentieth-century books on prayer include those by P. T. Forsyth, James Hastings, A. L. Lilley, Friedrich Heiler, O. Hallesby, George A. Buttrick, H. Trevor Hughes, Georgia Harkness, Joachim Jeremias, Fred L. Fisher, Donald Coggan, and Thomas Merton.

"The history of the Christian Church is, more than we know, the history of believing prayer."[3]

3. Ferré, *A Theology for Christian Prayer*, 9. Suggested Reading: Davis, *Life in the Spirit*; Buttrick, *Prayer*; Hunt, *The Doctrine of Prayer*.

18

"Environment: A Southern Baptist and Roman Catholic Perspective" (1993)[1]

(co-authored with Carroll Stuhlmueller)

The Bible Calls Us

The Bible opens in Gen 1 with God creating the heavens and the earth, carefully, even wondrously, and with man and woman meant to live as a peaceful, productive family. The Bible ends in Rev 20–22 with men and women by God's grace entering a new and transformed heaven and earth. Creation, therefore, provides the setting for the entire Bible story of redemption. Throughout their lives on earth, men and women are to care for the earth, so that it always reflects the glory and goodness of God (See Gen 1:28–30; Ps 8).

Yet, men and women sinned, abusing and even destroying the earth (See Gen 6–9; Isa 1). While the earth groans under the weight of sin, as Paul writes in Rom 8:22–25, God holds out hope of sending the Holy Spirit to create again a peaceful earth, according to Ps 104:30.

1. This chapter first appeared as a pamphlet in 1993. The original footnote explains: "This text was produced by the Conversation sponsored by the Interfaith Witness Department of the Home Mission Board of the Southern Baptist Convention and by the Ecumenical and Interreligious Affairs Committee of the National Conference of Catholic Bishops."

Please read again the biblical references in the previous paragraphs. Reconstruct for yourself the steps in creation, in sin and the destruction of Creation, in grace and the new creation of the universe.

I. A Godly Lifestyle

God told the Israelites: "The land is mine; for ye are strangers and sojourners with me" (Lev 25:23). All of us rent our lives and our places on earth from God. In return, we are called upon to care for the earth and to share its produce with our neighbor. Deuteronomy 26 prescribes that when God's people celebrate the harvest, they are to come to the sanctuary and recount their faith about the ways God has always cared for them. They are to share the harvest with "aliens, orphans, and widows" (26:12).

Amos, the prophet of social justice, points out in 4:6–13 how God not only regulates the seasons of the year but also turns rain into drought, a plentiful harvest into famine, peace into war, yet not simply as punishment but as a way toward repentance and a new creation for Israel. Notice how the passage ends in praise of God the Creator.

If Israel stops trampling upon the needy and forcing poor people into slavery—actions that cause the land to tremble and all who dwell on it to mourn (Amos 8:4–8)—then the vision of the prophet Isaiah (11:6, 8b) will come true:

> the wolf shall be the guest of the lamb, . . . the calf and the young
> lion shall browse together, with a little child to guide them . . .
> The baby shall play by the cobra's den.

We return to the peaceful story of paradise in Gen 1–2.

In the light of the Scriptures, how ought my lifestyle as a Christian to impact:

1. The greed in our consumer culture?
2. The prevalent desire for our comfort and pleasure at the expense of other human beings?
3. The litter and waste that clog our communities?
4. The prevailing trends in the American culture?

II. A Responsible Interdependence

The earth, we read in Deut 6, is always a gift to be shared, not an absolute and selfish possession. When Isaiah speaks of the new creation in chapter 43, the prophet hears God calling His children by name, summoning them from north, south, east, and west. Why? "Because you are precious in my eyes and I love you." God wants the entire human race to be one family. The same Holy Spirit who pours blessings on Israel pours water on thirsty ground and enables people everywhere to say, "I am the Lord's" (Isa 44:1–5)! Then God's children of faith will become a light to other people, attracting them to Jesus (Isa 42), so as "to open the eyes of the blind, to bring out prisoners from confinement." God's servants will help to carry the burden of sick and disabled persons (Isa 53:4–6). Jesus, as we read in Matt 8:1–17, fulfills these hopes by healing the sick and curing all who are afflicted. Throughout the Bible, care of the earth, healing for the body, and conversion of the soul are all serious concerns for God and, therefore, for every human being because each of the three impacts the others.

In light of the Scriptures, how should I participate responsibly both as a Christian and as a citizen in the common concerns for the well-being of all humankind, such as the following?

1. The widespread occurrence of hunger and malnutrition?
2. The prevalence of various forms of addiction?
3. The need for economic justice and opportunity for all human beings?

III. A Conserving Stewardship

Scripture places us on a mountaintop, not necessarily to be tempted, but to view the wonder of the universe. Read again Ps 104 and Job 38–41. God, in divine wisdom, carefully established laws for the waters of the sea and the seasons of the year, as we are told in Prov 8:22–31. The prophet Jeremiah, in chapter 31, associates the new covenant, inscribed on the heart, with God's way of governing the universe.

In the Sermon on the Mount, Jesus speaks of God's concern for the birds in the sky, wild flowers in the woods, and the grass in the field (Matt 6:26–34).

When we look out at our polluted and devastated earth, we hear a groaning and agony, like that heard by Paul in Rom 8.

In light of the Scriptures, how should I, both as a Christian and as a citizen, contribute to the proper care of the earth and the atmosphere rather than abuse the earth and its resources, as may be true with the following?

1. The depletion of agricultural lands?
2. The spread of industrially produced acid rain?
3. The destruction of forests?
4. The pollution of rivers and lakes?

IV. A Future Trust

Most of the prophetic books end in one way or another with a vision of a new heaven and a new earth, a lovely world of peace and fullness for our descendants: explicitly in Isa 65–66; but see also Joel 3 (4):17–21; Amos 9:11–15; Zech 14. In Ezek 47, water flows from the altar of the temple to transform even the Dead Sea into living water. Lame and outcast people belong to this new heaven and new earth in Zeph 3:14–20. All these prophetic passages allow us to see at least a partial vision of the mystery of our resurrected body, as it is strongly affirmed in Rom 6:5 and in 1 Thess 4:13–5:11. What we do now in caring for the earth somehow or other touches even the degree of happiness that will be ours for all eternity.

In light of the Scriptures, how should I as a Christian, church member, and citizen fulfill my responsibility toward future generations with respect to the earth and the atmosphere, in view of such challenges as the following?

1. The diminishing resources on planet earth?
2. The "now" mentality with its instant gratification?
3. The pattern of unrestrained development/consumption?

Suggested Reading

Austin, Richard Cartwright. *Hope for the Land.* Atlanta: John Knox Press, 1988. A comprehensive examination of biblical theology as it addresses modern environmental concerns.

Bergant, Dianne. *The World Is a Prayerful Place.* Wilmington, DE: Michael Glazier, Inc., 1987. Reflections on a spirituality informed by the creation theology of the biblical wisdom tradition.

Eschweiler, Edward. *Celebrating God's Good Earth.* Milwaukee: HI-TIME Publishing, 1991. A booklet for Catholic high school students treating nine environmental topics containing ideas for prayer, discussion, and action.

Granberg-Michaelson, Wesley. *A Worldly Spirituality: The Call to Take Care of the Earth.* San Francisco: Harper & Row, 1984. A holistic Christian theology that integrates sociological, political, and economic insights with critical biblical, theological, and ethical thinking.

Hessel, Dieter T., ed. *For Creation's Sake.* Philadelphia: Geneva Press, 1985. A series of essays that treat the connections between preaching, ecology, and justice.

Land, Richard D. and Moore, Louis A. eds *The Earth is the Lord's.* Nashville: Broadman Press, 1992.

Moltmann, Jurgen. *God in Creation: A New Theology of Creation and the Spirit of God.* Translated by Margaret Kohl. San Francisco: Harper & Row, 1985, Chapter 2.

Renewing the Earth: An Invitation to Reflection and Action on Environment in Light of Catholic Social Teaching. Washington: United States Catholic Conference, 1991. A Pastoral Statement by the Catholic Bishops.

Wilkinson, Loren, ed. *Earthkeeping: Christian Stewardship of Natural Resources.* Grand Rapids, Eerdmans, 1980. Revised 1991.

19

"Boomers and Busters Need to Hear Stewardship Call" (1996)[1]

The evidence seems to be compelling that a serious generational difference exists among members of churches regarding Christian stewardship of material possessions, especially in reference to churches. Both the researchers investigating stewardship and newspaper writers have agreed that the difference does exist.

On the one hand, the seniors of the pre-World War II generation tend to be regular givers, often tithers, who also may have included churches and Christian institutions in their wills. Shaped by the Great Depression toward frugality, by World War II toward faithfulness, and by the 1950s toward denominational loyalty, these church members provide much of the income of their churches despite the fact that many live on fixed retirement incomes.

On the other hand, the baby boomers in these churches tend to be less regular or generous givers. They may have chosen to join their churches because of the perceived spiritual benefits for members and their families. They may not have established a lifestyle of stewardship or patterns of giving essential to the future maintenance of the church and its ministries. They do give to specific projects or ministries or missions, often parachurch rather than denominational. Their credit card economics and their anxieties as to their future retirement income tend to prevail over sacrificial and generous giving of possessions for Christian causes at home and abroad.

The pattern of the baby busters may be more difficult to trace, but their giving patterns seem to be less generous or regular than those of the baby boomers.

1. This article first appeared in the *Dallas Morning News* of August 10, 1996.

There are, of course, many exceptions to these trends. We find baby boomers who are exemplary givers and seniors who are poor stewards by comparison. But the trends seem to be identifiable. Unaddressed and unchanged, the present situation may result in a crisis of stewardship for churches early in the 21st–century, when the present senior givers have left their earthly abode.

What can be done about this situation? One might assume boomers and busters will for certain become major givers when their older fellow members become fewer. But is that a safe assumption?

There are, of course, many exceptions to these trends. We find baby boomers who are exemplary givers and seniors who are poor stewards by comparison. But the trends seem to be identifiable.

One might, out of pessimism, call for a reduction of church ministries and mission in anticipation of reduced giving in the new century.

Much more positively, churches can accelerate their stewardship education of all ages. An abundance of biblical teaching is waiting to be identified and applied. Testimonies of the joy and blessing of giving can be offered by boomers and busters as well as by seniors. Churches can prune unnecessary or wasteful expenditures and use open and sound management procedures. Middle and younger adults can be encouraged to support more adequately that from which they receive blessing. Those who have engaged in diaconal ministries or missionary endeavors can share their stories. Warnings can be sounded as to the corrosive and idolatrous nature of all-out consumerism. Giving can be presented as an act of worship.

Boomers and busters, one hopes, will join the company of faithful, generous, and joyful givers.

Bibliography

Ackerman, Susan. "Who Is Sacrificing at Shiloh? The Priesthood of Ancient Israel's Regional Sanctuaries." In *Levites and Priests in Biblical History and Tradition*, edited by Mark Leuchter and Jeremy M. Hutton, 25. Atlanta: Society of Biblical Literature, 2011.

Alexander, T. Desmond. *Face to Face with God: A Biblical Theology of Christ as Priest and Mediator*. The Essential Studies in Biblical Theology. Downers Grove, IL: IVP, 2022.

Allen, Clifton J., and W. L. Howse, eds. *The Curriculum Guide: 1960*. Nashville: Convention, 1960.

Anderson, Justice C. *An Evangelical Saga: Baptists and Their Precursors in Latin America*. Maitland, FL: Zulon, 2005.

Anderson, Wilhelm. "Further Toward a Theology of Mission." In *The Theology of the Christian Mission*, edited by Gerald H. Anderson, 313. New York: McGraw-Hill, 1961.

Angel, Hayyim. "Ezekiel: Priest-Prophet." *Jewish Biblical Quarterly* 39 (2011) 35–36.

Assemblies of God, *Who We Are and What We Believe*. Springfield, MO: Gospel, n.d.

Austin, Richard Cartwright. *Hope for the Land*. Atlanta: John Knox, 1988.

Baab, Otto J. *The Theology of the Old Testament*. New York: Abingdon-Cokesbury, 1949.

Balthasar, Hans Urs von. *Prayer*. Translated by A. V. Littledale. London: Geoffrey Chapman, 1961.

Barabas, Steven. *So Great Salvation*. London: Marshall, Morgan and Scott, 1952.

Bardsley, Cuthbert. "Day of Mission Is Far from Over." *The [London] Times* (September 21, 1968) editorial page.

Barrett, C. K. *The Gospel According to John*. London: S.P.C.K., 1967.

Barth, Karl. *Church Dogmatics*. Vol. IV, Part 1, 2. Edinburgh: T. T. Clark, 1956, 1958.

———. *Die Kirchliche Dogmatik*. Vierter Band, Dritter Teil, Erste Hälfte, und Zweite Hälfte. Zollikon-Zürich: Evangelischer Verlag, 1959.

———. *Prayer According to the Catechisms of the Reformation*. Philadelphia: Westminster, 1952.

Basden, Paul A. "James Leo Garrett Jr." In *Theologians of the Baptist Tradition*, revised edition, edited by Timothy George and David S. Dockery, Kindle Edition, Page 303 of 415; Location 7937 of 12422. Nashville: Broadman & Holman, 2001.

Belcher, Richard P. *Prophet, Priest, and King: The Roles of Christ in the Bible and Our Roles Today*. Phillipsburg, NJ: P&R, 2016.

Benson, Edward White. *Cyprian: His Life, His Times, His Work*. London: Macmillan, 1897.

Berkouwer, G. C. *Faith and Sanctification*. Grand Rapids, MI: Wm. B. Eerdmans, 1952.

Bernard, John Henry. "The Cyprianic Doctrine of the Ministry." In *Essays on the Early History of the Church and the Ministry*, edited by H. B. Swete, 228. London: Macmillan, 1921.

———. *The Odes of Solomon*. Translated by J. Rendel Harris. Texts and Studies 8:3. Cambridge, 1912.

Bergant, Dianne. *The World Is a Prayerful Place*. Wilmington, DE: Michael Glazier, 1987.

Beuzart, Paul. Essai sur la Théologie d'Irénée. Paris: Le Puy-en-Velay, 1908.

Bévenot, Maurice. *De Lapsis and De Mcclesiae Catbolicae Unitate*. Oxford: Oxford University Press, 1971.

Bigg, Charles. *The Christian Platonists of Alexandria*. 2nd revised edition. Oxford: Clarendon, 1913.

Bonhoeffer, Dietrich. *The Cost of Discipleship*. New York: Macmillan, 1960.

Bonner, Campbell, ed. and trans. *The Homily on the Passion of Melito, Bishop of Sardis, with Some Fragments of the Apocryphal Ezekiel*. Studies and Documents. 12. Philadelphia: University of Pennsylvania Press, 1940.

Bottoms, W. W. "Evangelism and Service." *Baptist Times* CXIV (November 14, 1968) editorial page.

Bready, J. Wesley. *England: Before and After Wesley: The Evangelical Revival and Social Reform*. London: Hodder and Stoughton, 1958.

Breland, Clyde L. *Assurance of Divine Fellowship*. Nashville: Broadman, 1939.

Brown, Raymond E. *The Gospel According to John (XIII-XXI)*. The Anchor Bible. Garden City, NY: Doubleday, 1970.

Bruce, F. F. *The Book of the Acts*. The New International Commentary on the New Testament. Grand Rapids: Eerdmans, 1988. LOGOS software edition.

———. *The Epistle to the Hebrews*. Revised edition. Grand Rapids: Eerdmans, 1990.

Brunner, Emil. *The Christian Doctrine of God*. Volume I: *Dogmatics*. Translated by Olive Wyon. London: Lutterworth, 1949.

———. *Man in Revolt*. Translated by Olive Wyon. Philadelphia: Westminster, 1947.

———. *The Word and the World*. New York: Charles Scribner's Sons, 1931.

Bultmann, Rudolf. *The Gospel of John: A Commentary*. Translated by G. R. Beasley-Murray, R. W. N. Hoare, and J. K. Riches. Philadelphia: Westminster, 1971.

Bussche, H. Van den. *Understanding the Lord's Prayer*. Translated by Charles Schaldenbrand. New York: Sheed and War, 1963.

Buttrick, George A. *Prayer*. Nashville: Abingdon, 1942.

Cadiou, René. *Origen: His Life at Alexandria*. St. Louis: B. Herder, 1944.

Calvin, John. *Institutes of the Christian Religion*. Translated by Ford Lewis Battles, et al. Library of Christian Classics 20, 21. Philadelphia: Westminster, 1960.

Campbell, J. M. *The Place of Prayer in the Christian Religion*. New York: Methodist, 1915.

Carver, W. O. *The Glory of God in the Christian Calling*. Nashville: Broadman, 1949.

———. *If Two Agree*. Nashville: Broadman, 1942.

Cauthen, Baker J. *By All Means*. Nashville: Convention, 1959.

Chamberlain, *An Exegetical Grammar of the New Testament*. New York: Macmillan, 1941.

Chamberlain, W. D. *The Meaning of Repentance*. Philadelphia: Westminster, 1943.

Citron, Berhnard. *New Birth: A Study of the Evangelical Doctrine of Conversion in the Protestant Fathers*. Edinburgh: University Press, 1951.

Chadwick, Henry, trans. *Origen: Contra Celsus*. London: Cambridge University Press, 1953.

———. *The Sentences of Sextus: A Contribution to the History of Early Christian Ethics*. Texts and Studies n.s., 5. London: Cambridge University Press, 1959.

Chen, Kevin S. *The Messianic Vision of the Pentateuch*. Downers Grove, IL: InterVarsity, 2019.

The Christian and Christianity Today. "Baptised Heathens." *The Christian and Christianity Today* (November 8, 1968) 19.

Clarke, W. K. Lowther, trans. and ed. *The Ascetic Works of Saint Basil*. In Translations of Christian Literature, ser. 1, Greek Texts, 71. London: S. P. C. K., 1925.

———. *The First Epistle of Clement to the Corinthians*. London, 1937.

Clarke, William Newton. *An Outline of Christian Theology*. Edinburgh: T. and T. Clark, 1906.

Clinard, Gordon. "Evangelism and Ethics." *Baptist Standard* LXXX (August 27, 1968) 12f.

Coe, George Albert. *The Religion of a Mature Mind*. 2nd Edition. Chicago, IL: Fleming H. Revell, 1902.

———. *What is Christian Education?*. New York: Charles Scribner's Sons, 1929.

Conner, W. T. *The Epistles of John*. Nashville: Broadman, 1957.

———. *The Gospel of Redemption*. Nashville: Broadman, 1945.

———. *Revelation and God*. Nashville: Broadman, 1936.

———. *A System of Christian Doctrine*. Nashville: Sunday School Board of the Southern Baptist Convention, 1924.

———. *What Is a Saint?* Nashville: Broadman, 1948.

Cook, Henry. *What Baptists Stand For*. London: The Kingsgate, 1947.

Craig, Clarence Tucker. *The Interpreters Bible*. vol. X. Nashville: Abingdon, 1953.

Cullmann, Oscar. *Christ and Time*. Translated by Floyd V. Filson. London: S.C.M., 1951.

———. *The Christology of the New Testament*. Revised edition. Translated by Shirley C. Guthrie and Charles A. M. Hall. Philadelphia: Westminster, 1963.

Cyprian, *De Dominica oration*. In The Ante-Nicene Fathers, translated by Ernest Wallis, V:447–57. Grand Rapids: William B. Eerdmans, 1957; and in The Ante-Nicene Fathers, edited by Alexander Roberts and James Donaldson, translated by Ernest Wallis, V:447–57. Grand Rapids: Eerdmans, 1990.

Daly, Emily Joseph, trans. *Tertullian: Apologetical Works and Minucius Felix, Octavious*. The Fathers of the Church. Volume 10. Washington, DC: The Catholic University of America Press, 1950.

Daniélou, Jean. *Origen*. New York, NY: Sheed & Ward, 1955.

Davies, J. G. *Worship and Mission*. London: SCM, 1966.

Davis, Earl C. *Life in the Spirit*. Laymans' Library of Christian Doctrine. Vol. 11. Nashville: Baptist Sunday School Board, 1986.

Deissman, Adolf. *Light from the Ancient East*. Translated by Lionel R. M. Strachan. London: Hodder and Stoughton, 1910.

Denney, James. *The Christian Doctrine of Reconciliation*. New York: George H. Doran, 1918.

———. "St. Paul's Epistles to the Romans." In *The Expositor's Greek Testament*, edited by W. Robertson Nicoll, II:684. Grand Rapids: Wm. B. Eerdmans, n.d.

Devreese, Robert, ed. *Le Commentaire de Theodore de Mopsuesto sur les Psaumes (I-LXXX)*. Studie Tèsti 93. Vatican City: Biblioteca Apostolica Vaticana, 1939.

Dirksen, Aloys Herman. *The New Testament Concept of Metanoia*. Washington, DC: Catholic University of America, 1932.

Dix, Gregory, trans. and ed. *The Treatise on the Apostolic Tradition of St. Hippolytus of Rome*. Revised by Henry Chadwick. London: S.P.C.K., 1968.

Dodd, C. H. *The Apostolic Preaching and Its Development*. New York: Harper and Brothers, 1936.

———. *The Epistle to the Romans*. The Moffatt New Testament Commentary. London: Hodder and Stoughton, 1932.

Dudden, F. Homes. *The Life and Times of St. Ambrose*. 2 vols. Oxford: Clarendon, 1935.

Eastwood, Cyril. *The Royal Priesthood of the Faithful: An Investigation of the Doctrine from Biblical Times to the Reformation*. London: Epworth, 1963.

Edge, Findley B. "Theological Foundations of Religious Education." [Mimeographed mss.] Louisville: Southern Baptist Theological Seminary, 1960.

Eichrodt, Walter. *Theology of the Old Testament*. Translated by J. A. Baker. Philadelphia: Westminster, 1961.

Ellingworth, P. Paul. "Priests." In *New Dictionary of Biblical Theology*, edited by T. D. Alexander and B. S. Rosner, 697, LOGOS software edition. Downers Grove, IL: InterVarsity, 2000.

Elliott, Harrison. *Can Religious Education Be Christian?*. New York: Macmillan, 1940.

Elliott, John Hall. *The Elect and the Holy. An Exegetical Examination of 1 Peter 2: 4–10 and the Phrase Basileion Hierateuma*. Supplements to *Novum Testamentum* 12. Leiden: E. J. Brill, 1966.

Enns, Paul. *The Moody Handbook of Theology*. Revised and Expanded. Chicago: Moody, 2014.

Erickson, Millard J. *Christian Theology*. 3rd edition. Grand Rapids: Baker, 2013.

Eschweiler, Edward. *Celebrating God's Good Earth*. Milwaukee: HI-TIME, 1991.

Evans, Christopher Francis. *The Lord's Prayer*. London: S.P.C.K., 1963.

Evans, Ernest, trans. and ed. *Tertullian: Adversus Marionem*. Oxford: Clarendon, 1972.

———. *Tertullian's Treatise on the Incarnation*. London: S.P.C.K., 1956.

———. *Tertullian's Tract on the Prayer*. London: S.P.C.K., 1953.

Fairweather, William. *Origin and Greek Patristic Theology*. Edinburgh: T&T Clark, 1901.

Falls, Thomas B. *Saint Justin Martyr*. The Fathers of the Church 6. New York: Christian Heritage, 1948.

Ferré, Nels F. S. *A Theology of Christian Prayer*. Nashville: Tidings, 1963.

Fisher, Fred L. *Prayer in the New Testament*. Philadelphia: Westminster, 1964.

Fletcher, Jesse C. *Bill Wallace of China*. Nashville: Broadman, 1962.

Flew, R. Newton. *The Idea of Perfection in Christian Thought*. London: Oxford University Press, 1934.

Forsyth, Peter Taylor. *The Soul of Prayer*. London: Epworth, 1916; London: Independent, 1949.

———. *The Work of Christ*. 2nd edition. London: Independent, 1938.

France, R. T. *The Gospel of Matthew*. Grand Rapids: Eerdmans, 2007. LOGOS software edition.

Frankenberg, W., ed. *Evagrius Ponticus*, In "Abhandlungen der königlichen Gesellschaft der Wissenschaften zu Göttingen," Philologisch-historische Klasse, Neue Folge, 13.2:337. Berlin: Weidmannsche Buchhandlung, 1912.

Frenzmann, Martin H. *Follow Me: Discipleship According to Saint Matthew*. St. Louis: Concordia, 1961.

Fuller, Reginald H. *The Foundations of New Testament Christology*. New York: Charles Scribner's Sons, 1965.

Garrett, James Leo, Jr. "Authority for the Christian World Mission." In *Christ for the World*, edited by G. Allen West Jr., 73–82. Broadman, 1963.

———. *Baptist Church Discipline*. Nashville: Broadman, 1962.

———. "The Biblical Doctrine of the Priesthood of the People of God," In *New Testament Studies: Essays in Honor of Bay Summers in His Sixty-Fiflb Year,* edited Huber L. Dmmwright Jr. and Curtís Vaughan, 137–49. Waco, TX: Markham Press Fund of Baylor University Press, 1975.

———. "Boomers and Busters Need to Hear Stewardship Call." *Dallas Morning News*. August 10, 1996.

———. "Christian Knowledge and Conviction." In *Book of Proceedings: Child Life Conference. January 31–February 3, 1961*, 74–86. Nashville: Baptist Sunday School Board, 1961.

———. "Evangelism and Social Involvement." *Southwestern Journal of Theology* 12.2 (Spring 1970) 51–62.

———. "History of the Doctrine of Prayer." *Disciple's Study Bible: New International Version*. Nashville: Holman, 1988.

———. "Is Anything Sacred?" *Baptist Student* (May 1955) 12–15.

———. "Prayer." In *Encyclopedia of Southern* Baptists, 2:1102–3. Nashville: Broadman, 1958.

———. "The Pre-Cyprianic Doctrine of the Priesthood of All Christians." In *Continuity and Discontinuity in Church History: Essays Presented to George Huntston Williams on the Occasion of His 65th Birthday,* edited by F. Forrester Church and Timothy George, 45–61. Leiden: E. J. Brill, 1979.

———. "The Priesthood of All Christians: From Cyprian to John Chrysostom." *Southwestern Journal of Theology* 30 (1988) 22–33.

———. "Recovering My Priesthood." *Home Missions* (February 1962) 14–15.

———. *Systematic Theology: Biblical, Historical, and Evangelical*. 1st edition. Grand Rapids: Eerdmans, 1995; 2nd edition. Eugene, OR: Wipf & Stock, 2014.

Garrett, James Leo, Jr., and Carroll Stuhlmueller. "Environment: A Southern Baptist And Roman Catholic Perspective." Huntington, IN: Our Sunday Visitor, 1993.

Gesenius, William. *A Hebrew and English Lexicon of the Old Testament*. Edited by Francis Brown, S. R. Driver, and Charles A. Briggs. Boston: Houghton Mifflin, 1907.

Goldingay, John. *Hosea–Micah*. Baker Commentary on the Old Testament Prophetic Books. Grand Rapids: Baker, 2021.

Goodspeed, Edgar J., trans. *The Apostolic Fathers*. New York: Harper & Brothers, 1950.

Granberg-Michaelson, Wesley. *A Worldly Spirituality: The Call to Take Care of the Earth*. San

Francisco: Harper & Row, 1984.

Grant, Robert M., ed. and trans. *Second Century Christianity: A Collection of Fragments*. London: S.P.C.K., 1946.

Greenslade, S. L., trans. and ed. *Early Latin Theology*. Library of Christian Classics. Volume 5. Philadelphia: Westminster, 1956.

Groff, Warren F. "Theological Interpretation." In *The Concept of the Believers' Church*, edited by James Leo Garrett Jr., 59–72. Scottdale, PA: Herald, 1970.

Grudem, Wayne A. "Prophecy, Prophets." In *New Dictionary of Biblical Theology*, edited by T. D. Alexander and B. S. Rosner, 701, LOGOS software edition. Downers Grove, IL: InterVarsity, 2000.

———. *Systematic Theology*. 2nd edition. Grand Rapids: Zondervan, 2020.

Guardini, Romano. *Prayer in Practice*. Translated by Prince Leopold of Loewenstein-Wertheim. N.p.: Pantheon, 1957.

Haldar, Alfred O. *Associations of Cult Prophets among the Ancient Semites*. Translated by H. S. Harvey. Uppsala: Almquist & Wiksells Boktryckeri AB, 1945.

Hallesby, O. *Prayer*. Translated by Clarence J. Carlsen. Minneapolis: Augsburg, 1931.

Hallock, E. F. *Prayer and Meditation*. My Covenant Series. Nashville: Broadman, 1940.

Harkness, Georgia. *Prayer and the Common Life*. New York: Abingdon-Cokesbury, 1948.

Harnack, Adolf. *History of Dogma*. Translated by Neil Buchanan. New York: Dover, 1961.

Harris, James G. "Evangelism and Christian Social Action: Is It Either-Or?" *Baptist Standard*. LXXX (August 27, 1968) 12f.

Hastings, J. *The Christian Doctrine of Prayer*. New York, C. Scribner's Sons; Edinburgh, T. & T. Clark, 1915.

Heiler, Friedrich. *Prayer*. Translated by Samuel McComb. London: Oxford University Press, 1932.

Hessel, Dieter T., ed. *For Creation's Sake*. Philadelphia: Geneva, 1985.

Hewitt, T. Furman. "The Theology of Intercessory Prayer: With Special Reference to Contemporary Protestant Theology." ThD Dissertation, Southern Baptist Theological Seminary, 1968.

Holliday, John F. *Life from Above*. Toronto: Evangelical, 1957.

Hoskyns, Edwyn C. *The Fourth Gospel*. Edited by Francis Noel Davey. 2nd edition. London: Faber and Faber, 1947.

Hughes, H. Trevor. *Prophetic Prayer: A History of the Christian Doctrine of Prayer to the Reformation*. London: The Epworth, 1947.

Hughey, John David, Jr. *Die Baptisten: Lehre, Praxis, Geschichte*. Kassell: J. D. Oncken Verlag, 1959.

Hume, Robert Ernest. *The World's Living Religions*. New York: Charles Scribner's Sons, 1947.

Hunt, R. N. Carew. *The Theory and Practice of Communism: An Introduction*. 5th revised ed. New York: MacMillan Company, 1960.

Hunt, T. W. *The Doctrine of Prayer*. Nashville: Convention, 1986.

Ironside, H. A. *The Four Hundred Silent Years: From Malachi to Matthew*. New York: Loizeaux Brothers, 1914.

Jacob, Edmund. *Theology of the Old Testament*. Translated by Arthur W. Heathcote and Philip J. Allcock. New York: Harper and Brothers, 1958.

James, William. *The Varieties of Religious Experience*. New York: Modern Library, n.d.

Jay, Eric George, ed. *Origen's Treatise on Prayer*. London: S.P.C.K., 1954.

Jeremias, Joachim. *The Lord's Prayer*. Translated by John Reumann. Facet Books, Biblical Series. 8. Philadelphia: Fortress, 1964.

———. *The Prayers of Jesus*. Translated by John Bowden. Studies in Biblical Theology 6. 2nd ser. London: SCM, 1967.

Johnson, Aubrey R. *The Cultic Prophet in Ancient Israel*. 2nd edition. Cardiff: University of Wales Press, 1962.

Jonas, Hans. *The Gnostic Religion: The Message of the Alien God and the Beginnings of Christianity*. Boston: Beacon, 1958.

Kaiser, Walter. "Biblical Theology of the Old Testament." In *Foundations for Biblical Interpretation*, edited by David S. Dockery, Kenneth A. Mathews, Robert B. Sloan, 340. Nashville: Broadman & Holman, 1999.

Kang, Dae-I. "The Royal Components of Melchizedek in Hebrews 7." *Perichoresis* 10 (2012) 95–124.

Kantonen, T. A. *A Theology for Christian Stewardship*. Philadelphia: Muhlenberg, 1956.

Kay, D. M., trans. *Apology*. In *The Ante-Nicene Fathers*, edited by Alexander Roberts and James Donaldson, 10:264. New York, Christian Literature, 1896.

King, C. W., trans. *Julian the Emperor, Containing Gregory Nazianzen's Two Invectives and Libanus' Monody, with Julian's Extant Theosophical Works*. London: George Bell and Sons, 1888.

Kleist, James A., S. J., ed. and trans. *The Didache, The Epistle of Barnabas, The Epistles and Martyrdom of St. Polycarp, The Fragments of Papias [and] The Epistle to Diognetus*. Ancient Christian Writers 6. Westminster, MD: Newman, 1948.

———. *The Epistles of St. Clement of Rome and St. Ignatius of Antioch*. Ancient Christian Writers 1. Westminster, MD: Newman, 1948.

Knudson, Albert C. *The Religious Teaching of the Old Testament*. New York: Abingdon-Cokesbury, 1918.

Köstenberger, Andreas J. *John*. Baker Exegetical Commentary on the New Testament. Grand Rapids: Baker, 2004.

Kraemer, Hendrik. *Religion and the Christian Faith*. Philadelphia: Westminster, 1957.

Krajewski, Ekkehard. *Leben und Sterben des Zürcher Täuferführers Felix Mantz*. Kassel: J. G. Oncken, 1957.

Land, Richard D. and Moore, Louis A. eds *The Earth is the Lord's*. Nashville: Broadman, 1992.

Latourette, Kenneth Scott. *A History of Christianity*. New York: Harper and Brothers, 1953.

———. "A People in the World: Historical Background." In *The Concept of the Believers' Church*, edited by James Leo Garrett Jr., 241–49. Scottdale, PA: Herald, 1970.

Lawson, John. *The Biblical Theology of Saint Irenaeus*. London: Epworth, 1948.

Layman, Charles M. *The Lord's Prayer in Its Biblical Setting*. Nashville: Abingdon, 1968.

LeSaint, William P., trans. and ed. *Tertullian: Treatises on Marriage and Remarriage*. Ancient Christian Writers 13. Westminster, MD: Newman,1951.

Liddell, Henry George, and Robert Scott, compilers. *A Greek-English Lexicon*. Revised and augmented by Henry Stuart Jones with the assistance of Roderick McKenzie. Oxford: Clarendon, 1940[?].

Lightfoot, B. *St. Paul's Epistle to the Pbilippians*. London: Macmillan, 1868.

Ligon, Ernest M. *The Future is Now*. New York: Macmillan, 1955.

Littell, Franklin Hamlin. *The Anabaptist View of the Church*. Philadelphia: American Society of Church History, 1952.

———. "Protestantism and the Great Commission," *Southwestern Journal of Theology* (October 1959) 26–42.

Lohmeyer, Ernst. *The Lord's Prayer*. Translated by John Bowden. London: Collins, 1965.

Lord, F. Townley. *Baptist World Fellowship*. Nashville: Broadman, 1955.

Lowe, John. *The Lord's Prayer*. Oxford: Clarendon, 1962.

Lumpkin, William L. *Baptist Confessions of Faith*. Philadelphia: Judson, 1959.

Lüthi, Walter. *The Lord's Prayer: An Exposition*. Translated by Kurt Schoenenberger. Edinburgh: Olive and Boyd, 1961.

Macarius. *Fifty Spiritual Homilies of St. Macarius the Egyptian*. Translated and edited by A. J. Mason. London: S. P. C. K.; New York: Macmillan, 1921.

Mackintosh, H. R. *The Christian Experience of Forgiveness*. New York and London: Harper and Brothers, 1927.

Malone, Andrew S. *God's Mediators: A Biblical Theology of Priesthood*. New Studies in Biblical Theology, 43. Downers Grove, IL: InterVarsity, 2017.

Manson, T.W. *Ministry and Priesthood: Christ's and Ours*. Richmond, VA: John Knox, 1959.

Mantey, J. R. *Was Peter a Pope?* Chicago: Moody, 1949.

Marshall, Nath, ed. *The Genuine Works of St. Cyprian*. London: 1717.

Maston, T. B. "Evangelism and Social Concern." *Baptist Standard*. LXXX (August 27, 1968) 24.

Mathews, Joshua G. *Melchizedek's Alternative Priestly Order: A Composition Analysis of Genesis 14:18–20 and Its Echoes throughout the Tanak*. Bulletin For Biblical Research Supplement, 8. Winona Lake, IN: Eisenbrauns, 2013.

Mayer, Frederick. *A History of Modern Philosophy*. New York: American, 1951.

McGregor, Don. "Texas Goal: Take Japan for Christ." *Baptist Standard* (November 15, 1961) 6–8.

Merton, Thomas. *Contemplative Prayer*. New York: Herder and Herder, 1969.

Moltmann, Jurgen. *God in Creation: A New Theology of Creation and the Spirit of God*. Translated by Margaret Kohl. San Francisco: Harper & Row, 1985.

Moody, Dale. *The Word of Truth: A Summary of Christians Doctrine Based on Biblical Revelation*. Grand Rapids: Eerdmans, 1981.

Moore, John Allen. "Beginning in Europe—Oncken in Hamburg, 1834." *The Quarterly Review* XV (April-May-June 1955) 55.

Morgan, James. *The Importance of Tertullian in the Development of Christian Dogma*. London: ⊠K. Paul, Trench, Trubner, 1928.

Morris, J. B., trans. *Select Works of S. Epbrem the Syrian*. Oxford: John Henry Parker; London: F. & J. Rivington, 1847.

Morris, Leon. *The Apostolic Preaching of the Cross*. London: Tyndale, 1955.

———. *The Gospel According to John*. The New International Commentary on the New Testament. Grand Rapids: Wm. B. Eerdmans, 1971.

Mowinckel, Sigmund O. P. *Psalmenstudien, III: Kultprophetie und prophetische Psalmen*. Oslo: Jacob Dybwad, 1923.

Mullins, Edgar Young. *The Christian Religion in Its Doctrinal Expression*. Nashville: Broadman, c.1917.

Myers, Edward. "The Mystical Body of Christ." In *The Teaching of the Catholic Church*, edited by George D. Smith, 685. 2nd edition. London: Burns and Oates, 1952.

Neill, Stephen. *Christian Holiness*. London: Lutterworth, 1960.

Niebuhr, Reinhold. *Moral Man and Immoral Society*. New York: Charles Scribner's Sons, 1932.

O'Meara, John J., ed. *Origen: Prayer[and] Exhortation to Martyrdom*. Ancient Christian Writers. 19. Westminster, MD: Newman, 1954.

Ochagavia. Visibile Patris Filius: A Study of Irenaeus' Teaching on Revelation and Tradition. Orientalia Christiana Analecta. 171. Rome: Pont. Institutum Orientalium Studiorum, 1964.

Origen. *Peri Euches*. In *Alexandrian Christianity*, translated by J. E. L. Oulton and Henry Chadwick, II:238–329. The Library of Christian Classics. Philadelphia: Westminster, 1954.

Ortlund, Gavin. "Resurrected as Messiah: The Risen Christ as Prophet, Priest, and King." *JETS* 54 (2001) 761–66.

Oulton, J. E. L., and Henry Chadwick, trans. *Alexandrian Christianity*. The Library of Christian Classics II. Philadelphia: Westminster, 1954.

Palmer, Paul F, editor. "Papyrus Fragment of the Araphora of S. Mark." In *Sources of Christian Theology*, edited by Paul F. Palmer, 2:67. London: Longmans, Green & Co., 1957.

Patterson, Paige. "The Work of Christ." In *A Theology for the Church*, revised edition, edited by Daniel L. Akin, 442. Nashville: B&H, 2014.

Pusey, Edward B., translator. *The Confessions of St. Augustine*. New York: The Modern Library, 1949.

Quain, Edwin A., trans. *Tertullian: Disciplinary, Moral, and Ascetical Works*. The Fathers of the Church 40. Washington, DC: The Catholic University of America Press, 1959.

Rauschenbusch, Walter. *A Theology for the Social Gospel*. New York: Macmillan, 1917; Abingdon, n.d.

Reischauer, August Karl. "Buddhism." In *The Great Religions of the Modern World*, by Edward J. Jurji, 97. Princeton, NJ: Princeton University Press, 1947.

Rendtorff, Heinrich. *Als die guten Haushalter*. Neuendettelsau: Freimund-Verlag, 1952.

Roberts, Robert E. *The Theology of Tertullian*. London: Epworth, 1924.

Roberts-Thomson, E. *Baptists and the Disciples of Christ*. London: Carey Kingsgate, n.d.

Robertson, Archibald Thomas. *Word Pictures in the New Testament*. Volume V. New York/London: Harper and Brothers, 1932.

Robertson, J. N. W. B., ed. *The Divine Liturgies of Our Fathers among the Saints John Chrysostom and Basil the Great, with That of the Presanctified, Preceded by the Hesperinos and the Orthos*. London: David Nutt, 1894.

Schaff, Philip. *The Creeds of Christendom*. New York: Harper and Brothers, 1877/78.

Schlatter, Adolf. *The Church in the New Testament Period*. Translated by Paul P. Levertoff. London: S.P.C.K. Publishing, 1955.

Schürmann, Heinz. *Praying with Christ: The "Our Father" for Today*. Translated by W. M. Ducey and Alphonse Simon. New York: Herder and Herder, 1964.

Schweizer, Eduard. *Lordship and Discipleship*. Napierville, IL: Alec R. Allenson, 1960.

Seton-Watson, H. *From Lenin to Melenkov*. New York: Frederick A. Praeger, 1953.

Simons, Menno. "The New Birth." In *The Complete Writings of Menno Simons*, translated by Leonard Verduin and edited by John C. Wenger. Scottdale, PA: Herald, 1955.

Simpson, Robert L. *The Interpretation of Prayer in the Early Church*. The Library of History and Doctrine. Philadelphia: Westminster, 1965.

Smart, James D. *The Teaching Ministry of the Church*. Philadelphia: Westminster, 1954.

Smith, H. Shelton. *Faith and Nurture*. New York: Charles Scribner's Sons, 1950.

Smith, Joseph P., translator. *Proof of the Apostolic Preaching*. Ancient Christian Writers 16. Westminster, MD: Newman, 1952.

Smith, Timothy. *Revivalism and Social Reform in Mid-Nineteenth-Century America.* New York, Nashville: Abingdon, 1957.

Snaith, Norman H. *The Distinctive Ideas of the Old Testament.* Philadelphia: Westminster, 1946.

Spener, P. J. *Der hochwichtige Articul von der Weidergeburt.* Frankfort: a. M., 1696.

Stewart, James S. *A Man in Christ.* New York/London: Harper and Brothers, n.d.

Stolz, Karl R. *The Psychology of Prayer.* New York: Abingdon, 1923.

Strawley, J. H., ed. *On the Mysteries.* Translated by T. Thompson. London: S. P. C. K., 1950.

———, ed. *On the Sacraments.* Translated by T. Thompson. London: S. P. C. K., 1950.

Strong, Augustus Hopkins. *Systematic Theology.* 12th edition. Philadelphia: Judson, 1949.

Taylor, Jeremy. "*Unum Necessarium*, or The Doctrine and Practice of Repentance." In *The Whole Works of the Right Rev. Jeremy Taylor*, revised and corrected by Charles Page Eden, VII:1–491. London: Longman, Green, Longman, and Roberts et al., 1861.

Taylor, Vincent. *Forgiveness and Reconciliation.* 2nd edition. London: Macmillan, 1960.

Tertullian. *De oratione.* In The Ante-Nicene Fathers, translated by S. Thelwall, III:681–91. Grand Rapids: William B. Eerdmans, 1957.

Tie, Peter L. H. "*Munus Triplex* of the Trinity: The Father as the Proper Potentate, the Spirit as the Permanent Prophet, and the Son as the Perpetual Priest: Trinity and Priesthood in the Thought of James Leo Garrett Jr." *Southwestern Journal of Theology* 65:1 (Fall 2022) 107–28.

———. *Restore Unity, Recover Identity, and Refine Orthopraxy: The Believers' Priesthood in the Ecclesiology of James Leo Garrett Jr.* Eugene, OR: Wipf & Stock, 2012.

Tillich, Paul. *Systematic Theology.* Volume II. Chicago: University of Chicago Press, 1957.

———. *The New Being.* New York: Charles Scribner's Sons, 1955.

Tollinton, R. B. *Clement of Alexandria: A Study of Christian Liberalism.* 2 volumes. London: Williams and Norgate, 1914.

Torrance, T. F. *Royal Priesthood.* Scottish Journal of Theology Occasional Papers. Number 3. Edinburth, London: Oliver and Boyd, 1955.

Tribble, Harold W. *The Christian's Spiritual Life or the Doctrine of Sanctification.* Cumberland, MD: Religious, 1928, 1936.

———. *Our Doctrines.* Nashville: Sunday School Board of the Southern Baptist Convention, 1929.

Trueblood, Elton. *The Company of the Committed.* New York: Harper and Row, 1961.

———. *The Yoke of Christ and Other Sermons.* New York: Harper, 1958.

———. *Your Other Vocation.* New York: Harper & Brothers, 1952.

Underwood, A. C. *Conversion: Christian and Non-Christian.* New York: Macmillan, 1925.

United States Catholic Conference. *Renewing the Earth: An Invitation to Reflection and Action on Environment in Light of Catholic Social Teaching.* Washington: United States Catholic Conference, 1991.

Völker, Walther. *Der wahre Gnostiker nach Clemens Alexandrinus.* Texte und Untersuchungen. 57. Berlin: Akademie, 1952.

Walker, G. S. M. *The Churchmanship of St. Cyprian.* Ecumenical Studies in History. Volume 9. London: Lutterworth; Richmond, VA: John Knox, 1968.

Walton, John H. *The Lost World of Adam and Eve: Genesis 2–3 and the Human Origin Debates*. Downers Grove, IL: InterVarsity, 2015.

Watson, E. W. "The Style and Language of St. Cyprian." In *Studia Biblica et Ecclesiastica: Essays Chiefly in Biblical and Patristic Criticism by Members of the University of Oxford*, 4:257–60. Oxford: Clarendon, 1896.

Watts, John D. W. "The People of God: A Study of the Doctrine in the Pentateuch." *Expository Times* 67 (May 1956) 233.

West, Bill G. "A Study of Intercessory Prayer in the New Testament: With Special Reference to the Problems of Result and Operation." ThD Dissertation, Southwestern Baptist Theological Seminary, 1957.

Whale, John S. *Christian Doctrine*. Cambridge: University Press, 1956.

Wilkinson, Loren, ed. *Earthkeeping: Christian Stewardship of Natural Resources*. Grand Rapids, Eerdmans, 1980. Revised 1991.

Williams, Charles B. *The New Testament: A Translation in the Language of the People*. Chicago, IL: Moody, 1950.

Wilson, R. McL., trans. *The Gospel of Philip: Translated from the Coptic Text, with an Introduction and Commentary*. London: A. R. Mowbray, 1962.

Wingren, Gustaf. *Man and the Incarnation: A Study in the Biblical Theology of Irenaeus*. Philadelphia, PA: Muhlenberg, 1959.

Wolf, A. *A History of Science, Technology and Philosophy in the 16th and 17th Centuries*. 2nd ed. prepared by Douglas McKie. New York: Harper & Brothers, 1959.

Wright, G. Ernest. "The Old Testament Basis for the Christian Mission." In *The Theology of the Christian Mission*, edited by Gerald H. Anderson, 17–30. New York: McGraw-Hill Book Co., Inc., 1961.

Wright, J. Stafford. "Divination." In *New Bible Dictionary*, 3rd edition, edited by D. R. W. Wood, I. H. Marshall, A. R. Millard, J. I. Packer, and D. J. Wiseman, 279, LOGOS software edition. Downers Grove, IL: InterVarsity 1996.

Wyon, Olive. *The School of Prayer*. Philadelphia: Westminster, 1944.

Yoder, Gideon G. *The Nurture and Evangelism of Children*. Scottdale, Pennsylvania: Herald, 1959.

Young, Robert. *Analytical Concordance to the Bible*. Revised by Wm. B. Stevenson. 20th American edition. New York: Funk & Wagnalls, n.d.

Youngblood, Ronald F., ed. "Priests." In *Nelson's New Illustrated Bible Dictionary*, edited by Ronald F. Youngblood, 1029–30. London: Thomas Nelson, 1995.

Name Index

Subject Index

Scripture Index

Exodus (continued)

Leviticus

Numbers

Deuteronomy

Judges

1 Samuel

Psalms (continued)

Proverbs

Ecclesiastes

Isaiah

Jeremiah

Ezekiel

Matthew (continued)

Mark

John (continued)

Acts

Romans

1 Corinthians

2 Corinthians

Galatians

Ephesians

Revelation (continued)